The Judiciary and Democratic Decay in Latin America

The Judiciary and Democratic Decay in Latin America

Declining Confidence in the Rule of Law

WILLIAM C. PRILLAMAN

Westport, Connecticut
London

Library of Congress Cataloging-in-Publication Data

Prillaman, William C., 1967–
    The judiciary and democratic decay in Latin America : declining confidence
in the rule of law / William C. Prillaman.
        p. cm.
    Includes bibliographical references and index.
    ISBN 0-275-96849-9 (alk. paper)–ISBN 0-275-96850-2 (pbk. :
alk. paper)
    1. Justice, Administration of–Latin America.   2. Political questions
and judicial power–Latin America. 3. Law reform–Latin America.   I. Title.
KG495.P75   2000
340'.3'09821–dc21   99–046403

British Library Cataloguing in Publication Data is available.

Library of Congress Catalog Card Number: 99–046403
ISBN: 0-275-96849-9
      0-275-96850-2 (pbk.)

First published in 2000

Praeger Publishers, 88 Post Road West, Westport, CT 06881
An imprint of Greenwood Publishing Group, Inc.
www.praeger.com

Printed in the United States of America

The paper used in this book complies with the
Permanent Paper Standard issued by the National
Information Standards Organization (Z39.48–1984).

10 9 8 7 6 5 4 3 2 1

Contents

Acknowledgments

A number of individuals and institutions assisted me throughout the completion of this project. All of them contributed significantly to my understanding of judicial reform and democratic decay, although none of them are responsible for any errors of fact or analysis.

David O'Brien played an important role in helping me to understand the various forms of—and threats to—judicial independence, while Gerard Alexander offered invaluable advice on crafting a set of measurable indicators that applied across a series of case studies. John Norton Moore provided numerous insights into the role of the judiciary in fostering economic development, while Tim Power helped relate all of those components to the broader question of democratic consolidation. The guidance of David Jordan was crucial throughout the project; this book would not be possible without his patience, intellectual support, and deep commitment to assessing the fate of the modern democratic regime.

I am also grateful to Ambassador Lincoln Gordon of the Brookings Institution for reading the manuscript and offering his thoughtful comments. Paul Lewis, Brian Latell, and Riordan Roett also were kind enough to review the manuscript and offered helpful suggestions based on their own deep expertise in the region.

In South America, my analysis benefitted greatly from the cooperation I received from Brazil's Library of Congress, as well as from several provocative discussions with federal deputies from the Workers' Party and the Liberal Front Party. In Argentina, the staff of the Libra Foundation provided useful material, as did officials working with the access-to-justice program in the Chilean Ministry of Justice. In Washington, the InterAmerican Bar Foundation graciously opened up its archives on several occasions. I have also had the opportunity to hold several frank discussions with employees of the U.S. Agency for International Development and the U.S. Department of State, and their insights have helped me understand the opportunities and limits offered by various judicial reform programs.

The entire staff at the Greenwood Publishing Group has been a pleasure to work with, offering helpful comments and graciously accepting last-minute changes along the way. In particular, I would like to thank Rebecca Ardwin for her patience and diligence in managing this project to completion.

Finally, I would not have been able to complete this book without the patience and support of my family, particularly my parents and my wife Kristin.

Chapter One ―――――――――――――――――――

Toward a Theory of Judicial Reform in Latin America

Any effort to understand democratic consolidation in Latin America must pay particular attention to the process of institution-building, particularly those institutions that sustain accountable government and nurture a strong democratic culture among the public and political elites. The role of the judicial branch in this regard is critical. At the most basic level, a strong judiciary is essential for checking potential executive and legislative breaches of the constitutional order, laying the foundations for sustainable economic development, and building popular support for the democratic regime.

Observers have long noted the critical role of the judiciary in sustaining the democratic regime. The framers of the U.S. Constitution were among the earliest to express this view, explicitly acknowledging the fallen nature of man and arguing that structural checks on the exercise of power were necessary to enable one department of government to resist the encroachments of another—hence the classic maxim that "ambition must be made to counteract ambition."[1] Alexis de Tocqueville would later echo this notion in his classic work, *Democracy in America*, writing that an independent judiciary—particularly one empowered with judicial review—"is yet one of the most powerful barriers ever erected against the tyranny of political assembles."[2] In this framework, an independent judiciary serves as the ultimate guarantor of constitutionalism: sovereignty is derived from the people, but the courts ensure that no agency of government acting on behalf of the people violates the principles of the rule of law.[3]

Scholars also have stressed the judiciary's role in laying the foundations for sustainable long-term economic growth, ensuring predictability in the marketplace, and facilitating the formation of a civil society economically independent of the regime in power.[4] Critical preconditions for economic development are predictable laws governing the marketplace and a legal regime that protects capital formation and ensures property rights from one administration to the next.[5] Douglass North and Robert Paul Thomas found that the Industrial Revolution in Europe was made possible largely because of the ability of the state bureaucracy to enforce contracts and protect technological innovations, which gave civil society the incentive to invest, innovate, and develop. North also has shown that one of the most critical components in the efforts of developing countries to increase per capita income has been the commercialization of new technologies, a process that relies heavily on public sector legal institutions capable of ensuring the opportunity to earn a fair return on investments.[6] Recent research has shown that private sector leaders attach considerable importance to a stable legal order; in fact, the existence of a judiciary that bases rulings on predictable and transparent criteria may be more important than the content of specific government fiscal or monetary policies in determining investment patterns.[7] An independent, accessible, and efficient judiciary also is essential for ensuring that the entire citizenry—including small businesses and the average citizen—has the opportunity to enter and compete in the economic playing field to establish a system of truly competitive economic arrangements.[8]

Finally, a healthy judiciary is crucial to building popular support for the rule of law and ultimately the democratic regime. Former U.S. Supreme Court Justice William O. Douglas stressed that a transparent and accessible judiciary "breeds understanding" of the rule of law and that "any confidence based on understanding is more enduring than confidence based on awe."[9] More rigorous empirical research has borne out such assertions. For example, studies of low-income citizens have found that those who had gained access to the courts—regardless of the verdict they received—displayed more favorable attitudes toward the rule of law and were less cynical of democracy than those who never sought recourse through the formal legal system.[10]

Despite the crucial role of the judicial branch in sustaining the democratic regime, recent observers have become increasingly aware that in the current wave of democratization, some institutions have simply not fared very well, creating a deep and widening gap between the role that institutions theoretically serve in a democracy and that which they actually perform.[11] Scholars have pointed to an uneasy structural tension in Latin American democracies, in which progress in some social and political arenas coexists alongside stagnation, degeneration, and decay in other realms.[12] Felipe Agüero and Jeffrey Stark have employed the useful metaphor of democratic "fault lines": pressure points that call into question the depth, quality, and ultimately even the durability of many of the post-authoritarian regimes in Latin America.[13]

The implications are profound when the judiciary is one of those institutions experiencing extended periods of crisis. At the most basic level, a democracy with a weak judiciary probably will be unable to ensure a healthy arrangement of checks and balances on elected officials who may at times test the bounds of constitutionalism. In this case, the current wave of democracies may prove no better than their predecessors in curtailing the tendency of leaders to govern on the basis of an extreme majoritarianism that bases its claim to legitimacy on representing the general will.[14] In short, a democracy with a weak or politicized judiciary will have great difficulty ensuring a fair degree of horizontal accountability between the various branches of government.[15]

A democracy with a weak judiciary also will likely be unable to create the conditions for adequate levels of economic development.[16] Researchers are already beginning to quantify the full extent of the damage caused by a weak court system. For example, Beatrice Weder of the International Monetary Fund has found that investor perceptions of judicial corruption and inefficiency account for 14 percent of the variance in economic growth rates in Latin America—a weighting similar to variables such as literacy rates, fiscal policy, and consumption patterns.[17] Similarly, Robert Sherwood and associates at the World Bank speculate that—among Latin American countries pursuing economic liberalization policies—those countries "suffer at least a 15 percent penalty in their growth momentum if the judicial systems are weak. That is to say, if GDP growth were otherwise capable of reaching something like 3 percent, a weak judicial system would restrain growth to perhaps 2.6 percent."[18] Country-specific studies have borne out these general findings.[19]

A democratic regime with a persistently weak judicial system also will have trouble building popular support for the rule of law. James Holston and Teresa P. R. Caldeira have noted that the basic concept of citizenship so central to a democracy at a minimum entails a sense of fairness, legality, access, and universality.[20] In a country in which significant portions of the population view the legal system as inaccessible and unreliable, individuals may experience what Guillermo O'Donnell has referred to as "incomplete citizenship" or "low-intensity citizenship," an arrangement in which basic freedoms and liberties are perpetually insecure or even trampled, and popular commitment to the regime is half-hearted, at best.[21] At issue ultimately is the quality and depth of the regime. As Alberto Binder has bluntly stated, "If the people do not trust the administration of justice, the democratization process cannot be profound."[22]

Despite the obvious need for a strong judiciary in Latin America, our understanding of what constitutes a healthy judicial system is hampered by three factors: an absence of literature examining the subject, the lack of an agreed-upon framework for measuring what constitutes a successful judicial reform, and several core assumptions of reformers that, when examined in closer detail and measured against specific case studies, have consistently proven to be inadequate, insufficient, and in some cases counterproductive.

The lack of literature on the subject is in many respects surprising. Scholars have become increasingly aware of the importance of the courts in building a democratic regime in other parts of the world, but have consistently ignored trends in Latin America.[23] Recent years also have witnessed a resurgence of scholarship on Latin America focusing on institutions—particularly legislatures, the presidency, political parties, and even nongovernment organizations—and their role in the democratization process.[24] Other works have examined the changing missions and worldview of the armed forces, the ideological evolution of the once radical left, and even the role of local governments—but neglected the role of the judiciary.[25] Indeed, in its first nine years of publication, the National Endowment for Democracy's *Journal of Democracy* did not publish a single article on the role of the judiciary in Latin America, while *The Journal of Inter-American Studies and World Affairs*, the leading journal on Latin

American contemporary political developments, has published only one article on the subject in nearly two decades.

Moreover, the scarce literature that does exist has taken only a fragmented approach and has not approximated a coherent theory of judicial reform. Various monographs and articles have tended to be country-specific and have focused on only a particular aspect of the courts, such as whether they are able to issue rulings against the government on politically sensitive cases or whether they have legal aid programs for the indigent. One study on judicial politics in the region confined itself to a discussion of how civilian regimes treat human rights abuses committed under military rule, without drawing broader conclusions about the role of the courts in the consolidation process or whether other aspects of the judiciary are critical to gaining popular confidence.[26] Similarly, a recent in-depth study on judicial reform in Peru reached important conclusions on that country's efforts, but, like most studies, did not draw implications about whether and how a particular feature of the courts relates to other components of the judiciary, what larger intervening variables may facilitate or hamper reform efforts, and what role the reform process plays in democratic consolidation.[27] Adding to the inadequacy of the existing literature is that it has consistently shied away from developing a set of benchmarks to help determine whether or not a reform is successful, leaving, in effect, no indicators to measure whether or not reforms are producing the desired results. Instead, observers have preferred impressionistic conclusions—they know a successful judicial reform program when they see it—even though such an approach is largely anecdotal. In fact, the World Bank, which has established a comprehensive set of performance indicators for seventeen different types of reform projects—agriculture, education, environment, poverty reduction, oil and mining liberalization, wastewater management, and so on—inexplicably has avoided offering a set of criteria for assessing the success or failure of a judicial reform program, despite the fact that it devotes nearly $200 million annually to such efforts worldwide.[28]

Finally and most fundamentally, our understanding of what constitutes a successful judicial reform has been constrained by judicial reformers themselves. Lacking a theory of judicial reform, they have implicitly fallen back on a number of traditional assumptions that either have been accepted in other disciplines or that fit with conventional wisdom about Latin American politics and which, in and of themselves, seem sensible enough. Judicial reformers typically have focused on a narrow range of variables, seeking first to isolate and consolidate specific individual advances and then to move on to other variables in an orderly, sequential fashion.[29] The approach seems sensible enough and fits with the decades-old prevailing views of public policy experts, who argue that interest group politics in a separation-of-powers system is inherently prone to incremental change.[30] The assumption also fits with what we intuitively know about state capacity in Latin America and what numerous case studies have demonstrated in the past: most Latin American governments, lacking a critical mass of technical expertise and possessing limited bureaucratic capabilities, are encouraged to narrowly focus their efforts and to build on the progress in a piecemeal, incremental manner.[31] The biases are not explicit but are familiar nonetheless, roughly similar to the early modernization theory of the 1950s: one reform is thought to lead naturally to another in an orderly, unilinear fashion.[32]

The notion that one variable can be isolated from another is replicated in the reformers' approach to politics as a whole. Just as it is thought to be possible to isolate one reform variable from another, so too is it possible—and desirable—to isolate the judicial reform process as a whole from the broader political forces at play. In this framework, any public sector bureaucracy has been presumed to represent a unique subsystem that can be singled out in its "wholeness" from other forces with which it is normally interdependent.[33] By publicly stressing the degree to which judicial reform is a "collective good" that will bring a number of inherent benefits to society, reformers aim to relegate judicial reform to the technical, administrative realm where it ostensibly will not be corrupted by partisan politicking. Overhauling a judiciary is somehow thought to be much like restructuring any other institution or bureaucracy; the prescriptions are standard and formulaic, impervious to the larger political forces in a country and roughly akin to the modern principles of "total quality management" or other faddish notions of public administration.[34] In this framework, the checklist of measures to reform any bureaucracy is largely self-contained and self-implementing, involving routine, universally applicable steps such as "adopting technologies," "building partnerships," introducing "cross-cutting technologies," "recognizing diversity," and "developing multiple motivators."[35]

Implicit (and occasionally stated directly) in this approach is a clear bias as to whom should lead the reform process. Whether the reform is initiated by the executive or political parties or the courts themselves, the burden for implementing the reform is presumed to fall within the judicial branch, on the understandable assumption that judicial personnel are best qualified to determine and manage their institutional needs and that politicians in Latin America historically have not distinguished themselves in their handling of the judiciary. Presidents, parties, and congresses may enter the equation initially—through focus groups and foreign travels to observe judicial systems in developed countries—but are expected to withdraw rapidly so that the reforms can move ahead.[36] Political forces, to the extent that they are factored at all into the reform equation, enter the process initially and only briefly; their role is presumed to be something that can (and should) be overcome by rigorous planning or skilled implementation. Successful reforms, the assumption runs, are best left in the hands of the judiciary.

AN ALTERNATIVE THEORY OF JUDICIAL REFORM

In fact, all of these assumptions and the policies they produce are inadequate and usually counterproductive. At the most basic level, it is difficult if not impossible to determine whether a judicial reform program is having success without a clear sense of what one is measuring, what variables serve as indicators, and whether and how those factors affect other aspects of the judiciary. Second, the traditional approach is mistaken in the notion that it is possible to isolate a single variable and improve it without taking into consideration the other structural flaws in the judicial system; in fact, all aspects of the judiciary are closely related, and reforms in one area may have unintended consequences that stymie or undermine other aspects of the reform program. Third, and most fundamentally, judicial reform cannot be isolated from the broader political and economic forces at play in a polity. Judicial reform, for better or worse, is an inherently political rather than technical process entailing a series of political judgments at every stage.

First and most basically, some set of indicators is necessary to determine whether a judicial reform program is failing or succeeding. Previous studies have purported to monitor changes in a judicial system over time, but in actuality have confined themselves to lamenting the sorry state of their own judiciaries or reciting a laundry list of pledged reforms without examining whether they were actually implemented—and offering no insights into whether those judicial systems are improving or decaying and what indicators one would look at to make those judgments.[37] Chapter Two provides that framework, arguing that a successful judicial reform program includes three critical and interrelated variables: independence, efficiency, and access. These variables are not chosen randomly; to varying degrees, each is crucial to ensuring democratic governance, providing the foundation for sustainable, long-term economic development, and building popular respect for the rule of law. The framework developed here argues that the fate of a reform ultimately can be measured by a basket of qualitative and quantitative reform inputs—the number of judges hired, introduction of new case management methods, creation of small claims courts, passing of new laws—but also by whether they produce a certain set of observable outputs: whether courts are able to issue rulings against other powerful branches of government, whether trial delays are increasing or decreasing, and whether the public perceives the judicial system to be more efficient and accessible over time.

Second, reformers are mistaken in assuming that it is possible to isolate a single variable and improve it without taking into consideration other structural flaws in the judicial system.[38] One positive reform does not inevitably lead to another, and in fact the opposite appears closer to the truth: the unreformed aspects of the courts invariably overwhelm the reformed aspects of the judiciary, creating a negative synergy that undermines the reforms. In El Salvador (Chapter Three), laudable efforts to enhance individual independence of judges and improve court efficiency were undercut by the Duarte administration's simultaneous failure to secure the structural independence of the courts. Subsequent efforts to buttress structural independence, while achieving some successes, were barely recognized by the public, as reformers had never focused on expanding judicial access that would have brought the courts closer to the average citizen.[39] The same pattern prevailed in Brazil (Chapter Four) under very different circumstances and by pursuing a different combination of reform variables. Authors of the 1988 Constitution included extensive guarantees for individual and institutional independence of the courts and enhanced access, but failed to follow through on efforts to enhance efficiency. A decade later, opinion was unanimous that unfettered access for everyone had produced, not surprisingly, access for no one. Meanwhile, a judiciary increasingly acclimated to inefficient norms became sufficiently autonomous so that it was able to resist even those measures that would have enhanced judicial efficiency and introduced greater accountability.[40] This process of negative synergy also emerged under two civilian administrations in Argentina (Chapter Five). President Raúl Alfonsín (1983–89) set out to boost judicial independence by pursuing controversial human rights cases against members of the former military junta, on the logic that the ability of the courts to hold other branches of government accountable for their actions would enhance independence and boost public faith in the courts. Despite achieving some notable successes, Alfonsín left office with the credibility of the courts gradually declining: his modest successes were overshadowed by his simultaneous neglect of efficiency and access. Alfonsín's successor, Carlos Menem (1989–1999) reached similar results through the opposite approach. Despite impressive strides toward enhanced efficiency and access, public confidence in the courts dipped to the single digits by the late 1990s in the face of Menem's simultaneous politicization of the judiciary. Menem himself belatedly learned the dangers of negative synergy when he found that ill-qualified, partisan judges could not be relied on to implement many of his innovative, efficiency-maximizing reforms that would have reduced the discretionary power of senior judges.[41]

The Chilean judicial reform experience (Chapter Six) appears to offer an encouraging—if tentative—corrective to conventional wisdom. Reformers in Chile set out to do what international development agencies would advise against: they ignored a strategy of narrow, sequenced incrementalism and instead sought to reform all three variables simultaneously. Despite the risk of becoming overextended in their efforts—and reformers did, in fact, suffer repeated setbacks and legislative defeats along the way—Chile is the sole case in which simultaneous reform helped mitigate the perils of negative synergy. The *pace* of reforms may have been gradual, but their *scope* and *breadth* were comprehensive. Efforts to enhance independence were balanced with efforts to ensure accountability. Various efficiency-maximizing measures were successfully implemented because concomitant measures to boost accountability ensured that respected jurists rather than partisan hacks were responsible for implementing reforms, including those measures that reduced their own bureaucratic authority. More efficient courts were able to handle the increased work load generated by access-creating measures, and the public was willing to resort to the formal legal system in part because judges were slowly becoming viewed as more independent.[42] The process in Chile clearly has much further to go before the courts are viewed with widespread credibility, but the trend lines are favorable and the public is slowly gaining trust in the judiciary.

A third and more fundamental error in the conventional wisdom relates to the true nature of judicial reform. At bottom, judicial reform is not merely a sterile, apolitical administrative issue or a universally-desired collective good that can be managed through narrow and staggered institutional tinkering. Rather, it is, for better or worse, an inherently *political* undertaking. To be sure, reforms sometimes fail or succeed on their own technical merits, and technical considerations serve as indicators of whether a reform is producing its desired effects. But other times the explanation for success or failure lies beyond the program itself. More often than not, reforming a judiciary entails a series of judgments and policy decisions that are clearly political: whether a president or party should expend scarce political capital on an issue that probably will not yield immediate electoral dividends; what pace to press ahead and what priorities to stress; whether to force an entrenched bureaucracy to change its pattern of conduct; and how to sell reforms to a resistant bureaucracy and a cynical public often distracted by more immediate social and economic concerns. Even seemingly routine or minor questions—how to make the courts more accessible, how to properly calibrate the ideal caseload per judge—affect core institutional interests and are intensely political: whether to force a bureaucracy to change its operating patterns, whether to restructure institutional relationships between entrenched interest groups, and whether and how much to interfere in the most internal of the courts' institutional affairs. Judges and court personnel are not value-neutral automatons who respond immediately to policy dictates; they, too, are self-interested actors who have considerable leeway in deciding, how, whether, and when to support the judicial reform process.[43] Indeed, in all of the case studies, a striking point is the degree to which the judiciary consistently has opposed judicial reform—even those measures that objectively would have enabled the courts to do a better job of providing quality justice. Judicial reform is thus not at all a universally-desired collective good; it is a political goal that affects core political interests and may be resisted by a range of actors, even if the specific judicial reform design is sound. Judicial reform may not need politicization, but it clearly needs politics—or at least the political will to push for reforms in a persistent, coherent fashion.

With this understanding, it becomes easier to identify why certain reform programs meet a certain fate. In El Salvador, efforts at judicial reform were supposed to help end the civil war; instead, the civil war essentially helped end judicial reform. In Brazil, well-intentioned reforms were in fact never implemented in the face of cumulative inflation reaching 84 *million* percent between 1985 and 1994. Even judicial reforms that may have been sensible in and of themselves were never really given a fair chance: they were quickly undermined by the statist nature of the 1988 Constitution, a document so prescriptive and detailed that it constitutionalized a staggering range of minor issues and flooded the courts—even the Supreme Court—with the most trivial cases.[44] Alfonsín's efforts to use the courts to rein in the armed forces were dashed when the armed forces resisted and asserted its own authority; compromises on the scope and duration of the trials were intolerable in Argentina amidst the perception that the courts were once again bending to political pressures.[45] In short, judicial reform does not shape the nature of consolidation politics; politics shapes the nature of the judicial reform.

Where, then, are we left after more than a decade of judicial reforms? The case studies suggest that judicial reform requires the support of larger political forces, but those same forces are largely responsible for the lack of reform to date. How does meaningful democratic consolidation proceed until Latin American governments overcome this conundrum? The short answer is that they do not—or at least that they have not yet. The case studies examined here generally suggest that Latin American judiciaries have not come especially far or fared especially well since the end of military rule; a variety of public opinion data confirms that the public in three of the four case studies is more cynical and more distrustful of the courts than before the reform process began. The implications for democratic consolidation are serious. As Arthur Vanderbilt observed, "If they [citizens] have respect for the work of the courts, their respect for law will survive the shortcomings of every other branch of government; but if they lose their respect for the courts, their respect for law and order will vanish with it to the great detriment of society.[46] Based on the studies examined here, public dissatisfaction has fostered heightened mistrust of key institutions that has contributed significantly to democratic decay in civilian Latin America: an increasingly cynical public willing to tolerate police abuses and responsive to the calls of populist, law-and-order politicians; citizens willing to periodically trade civil liberties for a more intrusive and heavy-handed state because they no longer trust the courts to hand out justice; and voters with declining faith in democratic institutions and more willingness to tolerate politicians who pledge to rule without them or to sweep them away.[47] As Guillermo O'Donnell has noted, democracies perish not only by sudden events such as coups and civil wars, but also by a "slow death" that entails "the gradual erosion of freedoms, guarantees, and processes that are vital to democracies."[48] The danger, then, is not that Latin American governments will revert to military rule, but rather that they will face gradual deterioration, with civilian governments slipping into a nebulous "semidemocratic" status, with mounting concerns about the depth and quality of governance: executives unchecked by counterbalancing institutions, societies unable to contain rising violence and crime, and a public increasingly willing to rely on mob justice rather than the courts—in short, a far less civil civil society.

NOTES

1. James Madison, "Federalist #10," in *The Federalist Papers* (New York: NAL Penguin, 1961): 78–79. Alexander Hamilton was particularly convinced that the judiciary could restrain an overzealous legislature, noting that "the courts were designed to be an intermediate body between the people and the legislature, in order among other things, to keep the latter within the limits assigned to their authority." See "Federalist #78," p. 465. According to Gordon Wood, the framers agreed that "the judiciary must also defend the constitution against violations by the other departments, particularly the legislature." Gordon Wood, *The Creation of the American Republic, 1776–1787* (New York: W. W. Norton and Company, 1969): 454.

2. Alexis de Tocqueville, *Democracy in America*, ed. J. P. Mayer (New York: Harper and Row, 1966): 261.

3. Bruce Ackerman, *We the People: Foundations* (Cambridge, Mass.: Harvard University Press, 1991): 60. Alexander Hamilton cautioned that the power to declare a law unconstitutional did not "by any means suppose a superiority of the judicial to the legislative power." Cited in "Federalist #78," in *The Federalist Papers*, p. 465.

4. The dominant pattern in Latin America has been for the established regime to sustain itself by establishing exclusive relationships with a handful of economic cartels, claiming to defend capitalism while actually practicing some variant of mercantilism. As a result, aspiring entrepreneurs are unable to seek relief through the courts because economic decisionmaking is based on political concerns rather than the rational dictates of the rule of law. Even parties ostensibly espousing market principles have used state power to advance "cartel capitalism" rather than a system of competitive economic arrangements. See Douglas A. Chalmers, Maria do Carmo Campello de Souza, and Atilio A. Boron, eds., *The Right and Democracy in Latin America* (Westport, Conn.: Praeger, 1992).

5. A concise summary of this view can be found in Beatriz Bosa, "The Importance of Judicial Reform for Foreign Investment," *El Comercio* (Lima), 2 November 1993, in FBIS-LAT, 9 December 1993.

6. See Douglass North and Robert Paul Thomas, *The Rise of the Western World* (London: Cambridge University Press, 1973).

7. *Crime and Violence as Development Issues in Latin America and the Caribbean* (Washington, D.C./Rio de Janeiro: The World Bank, 1997): 2–8. See also Beatrice Weder, "Legal Systems and Economic Performance: The Empirical Evidence," in *Judicial Reform in Latin America and the Caribbean*, ed. Malcom Rowat, Waleed H. Malik, and Maria Dakolias (Washington, D.C.: The World Bank, 1995): 22. In Ecuador, a 1993 World Bank survey of the private sector leaders found that businessmen listed the poor performance of the judicial sector as one of the country's main constraints on private sector investment. See *Ecuador: Judicial Sector Assessment* (Washington, D.C.: The World Bank, 1994): 1. Other constraints listed were political instability, inflation and price instability, lack of skilled labor, lack of infrastructure, high level of taxation, access to credit, and lack of services.

8. According to Edgardo Buscaglia, "In the absence of an impartial and efficient judiciary, the performance of mutually beneficial transactions will be limited to those cases where a well-known reputation and/or repeated transactions exist among parties. This requirement excludes many potentially socially beneficial transactions involving previously unfamiliar parties or start-up businesses." See Edgardo Buscaglia and Pilar Domingo Villegas, "The Impediments to Judicial Reform in Latin America," Paper presented at the Latin American Studies Association, XIX International Congress, 28–30 September 1995, p. 2. Hernando de Soto has detailed how the lack of an efficient and accessible legal system discriminates against low-income citizens. His research found that the average start-up time for a business took a mere four hours if a foreign investor was willing to pay the bribes necessary to gain the requisite business licenses. By contrast, a Peruvian national willing to abide by the legal process and pay only the minimum number of bribes required to nudge forward the process faced an average start-up time of 289 days—more than 1,500 times longer than an investor willing to circumvent the legal system. See Hernando de Soto, *The Other Path* (New York: Harper and Row, 1987): 133.

9. Cited in Joseph Goldstein, "The Opinion-Writing Function of the Judiciary of Latin American Governments in Transition to Democracy: *Martinez v. Provincia de Mendoza*," in *Transition to Democracy in Latin America*, ed. Irwin P. Stotzky (Boulder, Colo.: Westview Press, 1993): 304.

10. Jorge Correa Sutil, ed., *Justicia y Marginalidad: Percepciones de los pobres* (Santiago, Chile: Corporación de Promoción Universitaria, 1993).

11. Guillermo O'Donnell, "Illusions About Consolidation," *Journal of Democracy* 7 (April 1996): 40–41.

12. Jonathan Fox, "The Difficult Transition from Clientelism to Citizenship," *World Politics* 46 (February 1994): 183.

13. Felipe Agüero, "Conflicting Assessments of Democratization: Exploring the Fault Lines," in *Fault Lines of Democracy in Post-Transition Latin America*, ed. Felipe Agüero and Jeffrey Stark (Miami, Fla.: North-South Center Press, 1998): 9.

14. These leaders typically have stressed that the will of the majority can never be mistaken and that any leader entrusted with representing the general will should be freed from bureaucratic constraints—such as a judiciary capable of striking down executive actions on constitutional grounds—that represent allegedly unnatural limits on popular sovereignty and that could undercut efforts to advance the interests of the masses. This mindset broadly re-

flects the European continental tradition of democracy that has been prone to radical lurches and power shifts, millennial solutions, and non-empirical, grandiose solutions for a nation's problems and that has explicitly rejected an inductive system of checks and balances typical in the Anglo-American version of democracy. It reflects the heavy influence of Jean-Jacques Rousseau in Latin America. For a discussion, see Jefferson Rea Spell, *Rousseau in the Spanish World Before 1833* (Austin: University of Texas Press, 1938), and Salvador de Madariaga, *The Fall of the Spanish American Empire* (New York: The Macmillan Company, 1948). Spell writes that "it is probably no exaggeration to say that Rousseau, for a century after his death, wielded more influence in shaping the thought of Spanish America than did any other single writer," (p. 255) while Madariaga states definitively that "the leader of Creole America was Rousseau" (p. 222).

15. Guillermo O'Donnell, "Delegative Democracy," *Journal of Democracy* 5 (January 1994): 55–69.

16. The absence of a legal system to enforce the rules of economic competition on a rapidly changing playing field impedes the process of development. As Edgardo Buscaglia has written, "Countries without developed legal systems lack the ability, as a society, to create or absorb applied knowledge. . . . A country's legal system has a powerful impact on its economic development and process of technological innovation." Edgardo Buscaglia, "Legal and Economic Development: The Missing Links," *Journal of Inter-American Studies and World Affairs* 35 (Winter 1993–94): 157, 161.

17. Beatrice Weder, "Legal Systems and Economic Performance: The Empirical Evidence," in *Judicial Reform in Latin America and the Caribbean*, p. 22. Weder's regression ran judicial corruption against a series of variables that included rate of investment, per capita GDP in the base year, illiteracy rates, inflation, school enrollment, and consumption patterns.

18. Robert Sherwood, Geoffrey Shepherd, and Celso Marcos de Souza, "Judicial Systems and Economic Performance," *Quarterly Review of Economics and Finance* 34 (Summer/Special Issue 1994): 101–16. Examining the inability of the courts to effectively manage soaring crime rates, some researchers have established a strong correlation between the efficacy of the criminal justice system and economic development in the region. In Colombia, for example, studies by the InterAmerican Development Bank found that gross capital formation would be approximately 38 percent higher today if murder rates had remained merely at their 1970 levels. See Maurio Rubio, "Crimen y crecimiento en Colombia," *Hacia un enfoque integrado del desarrollo: ética, violencia, y segúridad ciudadana, encuentro y reflexión* (Washington, D.C.: Banco Interamericano de Desarrollo, 1996): 15.

19. Research by one Brazilian scholar has found that judicial inefficiency slows domestic private sector investment by an amount equal to 10 to 15 percent of GDP. See Arnaldo Galvão, "Lentidão e burocracia comprometem a Justiça," *O Estado de São Paulo*, 11 April 1999, 6.

20. They write that "the democratic state exists only through the political participation of its citizens and citizenship only through the state's application of the principle of legality and its defense of equality, liberty, and dignity." See James Holston and Teresa P. R. Caldeira, "Democracy, Law, and Violence: Disjunctions of Brazilian Citizenship," in *Fault Lines of Democracy in Post-Transition Latin America*, p. 281.

21. He writes that "A state that is unable to enforce its legality supports a democracy of low-intensity citizenship." See Guillermo O'Donnell, *On the State, Democratization, and Some Conceptual Problems: A Latin American View with Glances at Some Post-Communist Countries* (Notre Dame, Ind.: Helen Kellogg Institute for International Studies, 1993): 11.

22. Alberto Binder, *Reform of the Penal System in Latin America* (Arlington, Va.: National Council of State Courts, 1991): 2.

23. See, for example, C. Neal Tate and Torbjorn Vallinder, eds., *The Global Expansion of Judicial Power* (New York: New York University Press, 1995), and Donald W. Jackson and C. Neal Tate, eds., *Comparative Judicial Review and Public Policy* (Westport, Conn.: Greenwood Press, 1992). These thoughtful studies assess the global rise of judicial power, although they do not include a treatment of Latin America.

24. Most of the scholarship on presidentialism has been published in the *Journal of Democracy* but has been gathered and expanded in Juan J. Linz and Arturo Valenzuela, eds., *Presidential Democracy* (Baltimore, Md.: Johns Hopkins Press, 1994), in which various authors speculate whether parliamentary systems would have prevented a breakdown in democratic rule in various case studies. An important response to those arguments—also from an institutionalist perspective—is found in Scott Mainwaring and Matthew Soberg Shugart, eds., *Presidentialism and Democracy in Latin America* (Cambridge: Cambridge University Press, 1997). An overview of the role of parties in democratic consolidation can be found in Scott Mainwaring and Timothy R. Scully, eds., *Building Democratic Institutions: Party Systems in Latin America* (Stanford, Calif.: Stanford University Press, 1997); and Scott Mainwaring, "Presidentialism, Multipartism, and Democracy," *Comparative Political Studies* 26 (1993): 196–228. The role of NGOs in contemporary democracies has been discussed in Margaret Keck and Kathryn Sikkink, *Activist Beyond Borders: Advocacy Networks in International Politics* (Ithaca, N.Y.: Cornell University Press, 1998); Kathryn Sikkink, "Nongovernment Organizations, Democracy, and Human Rights in Latin America," in *Beyond Sovereignty*, ed. Tom Farer (Baltimore, Md.: Johns Hopkins University Press, 1996): 150–68; and Hügo Fruhling, *Derechos humanos y democracia: la contribución de las organizaciones no gobermentales* (Santiago: Instituto Interamericano de Derechos Humanos, 1991).

25. Two of the most prominent works on the Left have been Jorge Castañeda, *Utopia Unarmed* (New York: Vintage Books, 1993), and Barry Carr and Steve Ellner, eds. *The Latin American Left* (Boulder, Colo.: Westview Press, 1993), while an early look at the willingness of regional militaries to withdraw from their traditional missions can be found in Paul W. Zagorski, *Democracy vs. National Security* (Boulder, Colo.: Lynne Reiner Publishers, 1992): 21–96. More recently, see J. Samuel Fitch, *The Armed Forces and Democracy in Latin America* (Baltimore, Md.: Johns Hopkins University Press, 1998); and Wendy Hunter, *Eroding Military Influence in Brazil: Politicians Against Soldiers* (Chapel Hill: University of North Carolina Press, 1997): Chapter 1. For a discussion of the role of local government, see Jonathan Fox, "Latin America's Emerging Local Politics," *Journal of Democracy* 5 (Fall 1994): 105–16.

26. Irwin P. Stotzky, ed., *Transition to Democracy in Latin America: The Role of the Judiciary* (Boulder, Colo.: Westview Press, 1993).

27. See Lin Hammergren, *The Politics of Justice and Justice Sector Reform in Latin America* (Boulder, Colo.: Westview Press, 1998).

28. Robert Mosse and Leigh Ellen Sontheimer, *Performance Monitoring Indicators Handbook* (Washington, D.C.: The World Bank, 1996).

29. The logic mirrors the approach of Latin American heterodox economists, who argue for first reforming a single aspect of the economy—usually price stability—with the goal of then moving on to correct other structural distortions such as interest rates, exchange rates, and current account deficits. See, for example, "Inflação e experiencias de estabilização no Brasil," in João Paulo do Reis Velloso, ed., *Combate a inflação e reforma fiscal* (Rio de Janeiro: Jose Olympio Editora, 1992): 105–30.

30. The classic statement in defense of incrementalism is found in Charles E. Lindblom, *The Intelligence of Democracy: Decision-making Through Mutual Adjustment* (New York: Free Press, 1965). Similar arguments are made in Charles E. Lindblom, *The Policy-making Process,*

2nd ed. (Englewood Cliffs, N.J.: Prentice-Hall, 1980) and Charles E. Lindblom, "The Science of Muddling Through," *Public Administration Review* 19 (Spring 1959): 79–88. For a more recent treatment from a similar perspective, see Michael T. Hayes, *Incrementalism and Public Policy* (New York: Longman Publishing Group, 1992).

31. Various case studies reflecting this bias can be found in Merilee S. Grindle, *Bureaucrats, Politicians, and Peasants in Mexico: A Case Study in Public Policy* (Berkeley: University of California Press, 1977); Steven W. Hughes and Kenneth J. Mijeski, *Politics and Public Policy in Latin America* (Boulder, Colo.: Westview Press, 1984); and Merilee Grindle, ed., *Politics and Policy Implementation in the Third World* (Princeton, N.J.: Princeton University Press, 1988).

32. Samuel P. Huntington, "The Goals of Development," in *Understanding Political Development*, ed. Samuel P. Huntington and Myron Weiner (Boston: Little, Brown, and Co., 1987): 7. For one such example of this approach, see Gary Hansen and others, *Weighing In on the Scales of Justice* (Washington, D.C.: Agency for International Development, 1993), which provides a detailed decisionmaking tree that traces the ostensibly "proper" sequence for a judicial reform.

33. This bias is rarely stated explicitly but resembles "systems analysis" of previous decades. See Saul M. Katz, "A System Approach to Development Administration," in *Frontiers of Development*, ed. Fred W. Kiggs (Durham, N.C.: Duke University Press, 1970): 109–38.

34. One recent study typifies this approach, explaining that institutional change in Latin America is actually a relatively simple process that can be resolved by following a scripted, basic format. Reforming any institution in Latin America, the authors explain, merely requires that policymakers engage in "building integrated frameworks based on cutting-edge concepts of measuring results, categorizing the scope of strategy choices, understanding institutional dynamics, making paradigms explicit, and understanding how and when paradigms become obsolete." See Michael Fairbanks and Stace Lindsay, *Ploughing the Sea* (Cambridge, Mass.: Harvard Business School Press, 1996).

35. Marc Holzer and Kathe Callah, *Government at Work* (Thousand Oaks, Calif.: Sage Publishers, 1998): 57, 65, 82, 88–89.

36. An example of this approach is *Strengthening Democratic Institutions in Uruguay and Argentina* (Washington, D.C.: US Agency for International Development, 1994): 5.

37. Examples include Raúl Israel Olivera and Manuel J. Israel Olivera, *Corrupción en el Poder Judicial y el Ministério Público* (Lima: Editorial San Marcos, 1985); *Derechos Humanos y Poder Judicial en Mexico* (Minneapolis, Minn.: Abogados pro Derechos Humanos de Minnesota, 1995); *Elusive Justice* (Washington, D.C.: Washington Office on Latin American Affairs, 1990); *Strengthening Democratic Institutions Project: Administration of Justice* (Arlington: Development Associates, 1990); and Arthur Mudge, Robert Ewigleben, and Robert Page, *Project Evaluation of the Administration of Justice Project in Peru* (Washington, D.C.: Checchi and Co./US Agency for International Development, 1990).

38. Douglas Somerset, "The Myths of Reducing Delay," *Judges' Journal* 26 (Fall 1987): 26–27.

39. "El Salvador Judicial Reform Program Update: Progress and Problems—1984 to the Present," U.S. Department of State unclassified telegram San Salvador 06365, 23 May 1991.

40. Eduardo Oinegue, "Exhaustos meritíssimos," *Veja*, 26 March 1997, 109.

41. See "Critican la duración de la feria judicial," *La Nación*, 14 July 1997, 1; and Adrián Ventura, "Atrasos en la Corte por las ausencias," *La Nación*, 3 October 1997, 2.

42. Juan Enrique Vargas Viancos and Jorge Correa Sutil, *Diagnóstico del sistema judicial chileno* (Santiago: Corporación de Promoción Universitaria, 1995): 36, 57.

43. The concept of state actors as autonomous agents is discussed in Barbara Geddes, *Politician's Dilemma* (Berkeley: University of California Press, 1994): Chapter One; and B. C. Smith, *Understanding Third World Politics* (Bloomington: Indiana University Press, 1996): 221–23.

44. Drausio Barreto, *Justiça para todos* (São Paulo: Editora Angelotti, 1994): 67.

45. Jaime Malamud-Goti, *Game Without End: State Terror and the Politics of Justice* (Norman: University of Oklahoma Press, 1996): 4.

46. Arthur T. Vanderbilt, *The Challenge of Law Reform* (Princeton, N.J.: Princeton University Press, 1955): 4–5.

47. Larry Diamond, "Democracy in Latin America," in *Beyond Sovereignty*, ed. Tom Farer (Baltimore, Md.: Johns Hopkins University Press, 1996): 75.

48. Guillermo O'Donnell, "Do Economists Know Best?" *Journal of Democracy* 6 (January 1995): 27.

Building a Healthy Judiciary: Independence, Access, and Efficiency

Before turning to specific case studies, it is necessary to first define the conceptual framework that will shape that analysis. This chapter briefly identifies the key variables of independence, efficiency, and access, explains how they relate to the development of a healthy judiciary, and provides an overview of how Latin American courts have traditionally fared on those variables. It concludes with a discussion of what indicators will be used to measure progress or backsliding in each of the case studies.

DEFINING THE VARIABLES

If students of democratic theory have historically agreed that the judiciary is an essential component for dividing political power through competing and overlapping institutions, there has been less consensus about identifying the criteria that enables the judiciary to provide an abstract definition of justice. The theoretical debates about what constitutes an ideal definition of "justice" date back to Aristotle and have never produced an agreed-upon consensus, although it is safe to argue in the contemporary era that a judiciary approaches an abstract definition of providing "quality justice" when it simultaneously demonstrates independence, efficiency, and access.

These variables are not chosen randomly; to varying degrees, each one is linked with the ability of the judiciary to ensure the democratic regime, foster economic development, and build popular faith in the rule of law. Efficiency coupled with independence lends an air of predictability and bolsters popular faith in the courts. If the judicial process is viewed as fair and transparent, litigants are typically satisfied with the process even if they are unsatisfied with the narrower ruling on the case.[1] Several studies have detailed empirically what is obvious intuitively: those judicial systems that reduce pretrial delays garner greater public confidence than do those systems that are viewed as inefficient or excessively slow.[2] Proponents of this view stress that the ability of the courts to administer their internal affairs in a timely, efficient fashion is closely linked with the quality of democratic governance—hence the popular maxim that "justice delayed is justice denied."[3] The success of these reforms, in turn, relies on the perception that the courts are accessible for the average citizen. Former Salvadoran Minister of Justice René Hernández Valiente has noted the success of broader judicial reforms anywhere is meaningless unless these changes are understood and internalized by the population at large; otherwise citizens will continue to perceive the courts, whatever the virtues of a particular reform, as unfriendly to the average citizen.[4]

If it can be established that independence, efficiency, and access are the three components that constitute a healthy judiciary, it is equally necessary to give greater definitional precision to those terms—particularly in a study that purports to measure changes in those variables over time. Judicial independence probably is the most complicated and misunderstood term. No agreed upon framework exists to categorize the various forms of (or threats to) judicial independence. Luis Salas and José Maria Rico have located and defined the threats to judicial independence with reference to the source of influence, and thus write of "internal" and "external" independence.[5] By contrast, Shimon Shetreet has de-emphasized the origins of the threats to independence and offered a framework based on the stage of the judicial process in which the offending act occurs, proposing categories such as "substantive" and "decisional" independence.[6] Owen Fiss presents yet another framework by stressing the alleged nature of the threat and whether it is "political" or "procedural."[7] Despite these various labels, all of the authors describe—albeit in different terms—two basic types of threats to judicial independence: those that challenge the broad institution of the judiciary, and those that affect individual judges in specific instances.

Both types of independence—for the institution of the judiciary and for judges on the bench—typically have been viewed as a well-defined position along an imaginary continuum that ranges from a completely autonomous judiciary to the opposite extreme of politicized subservience. In this framework, the degenerative form of an independent judiciary is a politicized court system in which judicial decisions are subject to heavy external pressures or even control—the most common structural defect in developing regions such as Latin America. This model, however, is not so much incorrect as it is incomplete. That is, it mistakes independence as an absolute rather than a relative term, and overlooks the fact that an independent judiciary can degenerate not only into a politicized bureaucracy but also into an insular, unaccountable one.[8] A healthy judiciary thus requires a balance between independence and accountability. Some explanation is in order.

First, no branch or agent of government in a separation of powers system is completely "independent" from the other branches. Courts rely on other branches of government for their budgets and enforcement of their rulings; the judicial nomination process often depends on executive nomination and legislative approval; and appointees may be subject to legislative impeachment. Thus, no judiciary is completely removed from the affairs of the more political departments of government. According to Jerome Cohen

> Judicial independence is not something that exists or does not exist. Each country's political-judicial accommodation must be located along a spectrum that only in theory ranges from a completely unfettered judiciary to one that is completely subservient. The actual situation in all countries lies somewhere in between.[9]

Historically, an important reason for this structural overlap has been a suspicion of making any branch of government too independent, for fear that such autonomy may degenerate into unaccountability; hence, the framers of the U.S. Constitution created a system of overlapping competencies with the dual aim of keeping any branch from exercising preponderant power over the others and blocking any branch from becoming too isolated from civil society.[10] Thomas Jefferson expressed some of these concerns when he wrote that unelected judges with life tenure may become part of a permanent and entrenched bureaucratic elite, motivated by parochial interests rather than by an unbiased reading of the law and who would become "effectively independent of the nation itself."[11] Putting these concerns in more modern terms, Peter Evans has warned of the dangers of excessive "embedded autonomy" in which any portion of government—whether a military or civilian bureaucracy—is given inordinate control over its own selection, recruitment, promotion, and disciplinary procedures and becomes indifferent to civil society and assumes predatory attributes.[12] Owen Fiss explains

> It is simply not true that the more insularity the better, for a judiciary that is insulated from the popularly controlled institutions of government—the legislative and the executive branches—has the power to interfere with the actions or decisions of those institutions, and thus has the power to frustrate the will of the people. . . . *We are thereby confronted with a dilemma. Independence is assumed to be one of the cardinal virtues of the judiciary, but it must be acknowledged that too much independence may be a bad thing.* We want to insulate the judiciary from the more popularly controlled institutions, but should recognize at the same time that some elements of political control should remain.[13]

Judicial efficiency also has been an elusive term in need of greater clarity.[14] Defining what constitutes a "modern" state or a "modern" judiciary is imprecise, although the framework offered by Max Weber at the turn of the century remains useful. According to Weber, a modern bureaucracy is identified by both structural and behavioral attributes. Structurally, the public sector becomes more complex and specialized, performing increasingly specific tasks and using more modern technology over time. Behaviorally, a modern bureaucracy conducts its administrative affairs in a routinized, impersonal manner, with increasingly less consideration given to political connections or partisan affiliation, and with agents of the state holding increasingly less discretionary and arbitrary power in their decisionmaking.[15] Turning specifically to the judiciary, no widely accepted definition exists that objectively out-lines what constitutes "judicial efficiency." Scholars who have examined the subject have stressed that there is no ideal judicial procedure or institutional structure and that it is thus impossible to craft a precise, neutral definition of "judicial efficiency." Initial research stressed that judicial efficiency could best be identified in broad terms by observing delays in times to disposition, whether those rates were increasing over time, and perceptions of whether those times were reasonable and manageable.[16] More recently, Edgardo Buscaglia and associates have refined this approach by ex-amining those factors that contribute to court delays.[17] According to Buscaglia, inef-ficiency is best understood by distinguishing between "random" and "controlled" variations in the life of a case. In any process—including judicial procedures—a re-former "can never eliminate all variation, even in the simplest process;" the key is that in an efficient system periodic delays are inherent in the process but can be min-imized and do not pose a challenge to the system's credibility. Inefficiency emerges, he writes, with the presence of "uncontrolled variations," those that arise from sys-temic distortions that are not inherent in the process itself and that can be identified and eliminated—but are not. Opportunities for uncontrolled variation are greatest when procedural norms allow for excessive discretionary or arbitrary behavior by ac-tors in the judicial process. Specifically, Buscaglia targets factors such as vague or out-dated laws, differences in skill levels of judicial personnel, the number of court officials working on a specific case, and the overall "quality of inputs" that determine the life cycle of a case.

The final reform variable in need of definition is judicial access. Comparative legal scholars such as Mauro Cappelletti have argued that "one essential—possibly *the* essential—feature of a really modern system of administration of justice must be its effective, and not merely theoretical, accessibility to all."[18] In their study of the administration of justice in more than sixty countries, Cappelletti and Bryant Garth concluded that access entails at least two components: the social and cul-tural perceptions of low-income citizens and whether they perceive barriers to the court system, and the more concrete factors linked to a judiciary's actual physical presence in a country. That is, inaccessibility may be shaped by a series of forces ranging from sociological aspects, such as excessive formalism, to more concrete factors, such as high court costs and mandatory filing fees.[19] Edgardo Buscaglia and Pilar Domingo reach similar conclusions in their recent study on Latin America, noting that inaccessibility to the courts is defined by tangible factors such as geo-graphic remoteness—particularly in poor and rural areas—as well as by persistent so-cial, ethnic, linguistic, and cultural cleavages that serve as barriers to the poor or socially marginal.[20]

HOW HAS LATIN AMERICA FARED ON INDEPENDENCE, EFFICIENCY, AND ACCESS?

Most Latin American governments have fared poorly in their efforts to achieve in-dependence, efficiency, and access. At the admitted risk of generalization, it is worth briefly examining the region's record, both to demonstrate how far Latin America has been from a well-functioning judiciary as well as to highlight the key types of challenges that reformers face when they set out to overhaul the judiciary. Each is reviewed briefly.

Independence and Accountability

Perhaps the most noted phenomenon in Latin American judiciaries has been the inability to achieve the delicate balance between judicial independence and judicial accountability, particularly because of the various measures that politicians have used to reduce institutional independence: limiting tenure, packing courts, purging court personnel, and creating special tribunals under the executive branch that bypass or replace the formal judicial hierarchy.

Limited Tenure. Various administrations have enacted legislation that sharply limits the tenure of judges and allows for regularized, sweeping overhauls of personnel through constitutional means. This practice follows naturally from the traditional Latin American expectation that an incoming president ought to have full authority to shape and staff the national bureaucracy in a way consistent with his agenda. Not surprisingly, this arrangement has made judges extremely susceptible to partisan pressures after they have assumed a seat on the bench and despite some of the formal guarantees ostensibly aimed at protecting independence. For example, Paul Lewis notes that even though Paraguayan judges formally enjoyed broad powers, including the right of judicial review, under the Constitution of 1954, a clause permitting the legislature to review all appointments every five years had the chilling effect of making all judges vulnerable to political influences.[21] Similarly, El Salvador's Constitution of 1950 gave the president the right to review all Supreme Court appointments every three years, while the Constitution of 1966 allowed the president to seek the removal of a judge by a simple majority in the unicameral legislature. Both features allowed civilian and military governments to easily remove renegade judges while simultaneously respecting the formal trappings of republican constitutionalism.[22] At various points during this century, constitutions in Honduras and Venezuela have limited judicial tenures to coincide with presidential inaugurations, so the new chief executive could replace sitting judges.

Court Packing. Civilian and military governments also have resorted frequently to court packing to shape more pliable courts.[23] Following the April 1964 military coup in Brazil, the governing junta forced a number of justices allegedly sympathetic to former presidents Getúlio Vargas and João Goulart to step down, and replaced them—on a court expanded from eleven members to sixteen—with justices more willing to uphold the government's extensive use of emergency decree powers. Several years later, the military lowered the number of justices back to eleven, removing additional judges ostensibly sympathetic to populist causes.[24] More recently, Argentine President Carlos Menem (1989–99) gained approval of a proposal that increased the number of Supreme Court justices from five to nine—on the specious grounds that an expanded court could handle more cases and thus act more efficiently.[25]

The Purge. A more blatant form of institutional control has been to purge the courts of judges, a practice frequently employed by military governments that are seeking to maintain the façade of judicial independence but are unwilling to be constrained by judges appointed by the previous government. The Argentine Supreme Court has been replaced *en masse* six times this century, and all but one justice has been replaced on two other occasions.[26] In Bolivia, the membership of the Supreme Court has been overhauled seventeen times since 1950; one expert has calculated that chief executives in Bolivia have so frequently replaced court officials that the average tenure of a Bolivian judge throughout the history of the Republic has been less than two years.[27] Another survey of Bolivian judges in 1991–92 found that only 40 percent of all judges interviewed had been in their position for more than four years, and only 10 percent of them had served on the bench for more than ten years.[28]

Creating New Courts. Another method of reducing the institutional autonomy of the courts has been simply to bypass the ordinary court system by creating more malleable institutions such as special tribunals that can be brought under the executive branch through the ministries of justice or interior.[29] A recent use of special tribunals came in Nicaragua under the Sandinista regime (1979-90), when the government created the special Antisomocista Popular Tribunal, the Sandinista Defense Committees, agrarian reform courts, and housing tribunals; the Sandinista National Directorate placed these tribunals under the control of the Ministry of the Interior—which answered, in turn, only to the President.[30] All of these organizations were dominated by party militants with scant legal expertise and were empowered to rule on issues such as land and housing confiscations or whether individuals should be jailed for "counterrevolutionary activities;" their decisions could not be appealed to the Supreme Court.[31] Even relatively sympathetic observers remarked that the end result was "the creation of a number of special courts motivated by political expediency, characterized by summary procedures and segregated from the traditional court system. In effect, they became a parallel system of justice."[32]

Independence on the Bench

Latin America also has not fared well in its efforts to protect individual independence on the bench. Often, a particular judge—rather than all sitting judges—has his decision-making compromised by a range of sources outside and—though less acknowledged—inside the government and specifically from within the judiciary itself.[33]

Internal Politicization. In many cases, the main threat to individual independence has come from within the courts, in which senior judges sympathetic to the current government or the past regime exercise their disciplinary powers to intimidate lower court judges.[34] This pattern has been especially pervasive in those countries employing a national or unitary system of governance in which control of the judiciary is exercised by the Supreme Court. During the Pinochet regime in Chile, Supreme Court justices sympathetic to the military government would exercise their disciplinary powers to rein in or remove lower court judges who pursued charges of human rights violations against the military government.[35] Similarly, when judges in El Salvador began investigating sensitive human rights cases that could have embarrassed the government in the 1980s, the Supreme Court president would rotate judges to unattractive posts located in the midst of war-torn regions.[36] After one judge sentenced several members of the National Guard to prison in 1985, the Supreme Court reversed his decision on alleged technical errors and transferred the lower court judge to a remote province controlled by insurgents, which required the judge to take a four-hour, round-trip commute each day.[37]

Violence Against the Bench. Perhaps the most extreme challenge to individual independence has been in the form of violence and terror to intimidate court officials. The use of violence is not exclusive to any particular regime type, civilian or military, rightist or leftist. It may be employed by government agents (such as the president), by private groups (such as local economic chieftains, criminal bosses, or narcotics syndicates) or by ostensibly private groups that nonetheless have links to the government (such as paramilitary organizations and some death squads) and may be motivated by political or economic concerns.[38] Colombia is the clearest example of this pattern.[39] The International Commission of Jurists reports that between 1979 and 1991, incidents of violence against Colombian judges and lawyers reached 515, and more than half of the incidents were murders or attempted murders. Of the approximately 4,500 judges in the country, roughly 1,600 of them had received death threats to themselves or their families.[40] According to the National Association of Judicial Employees, the judicial sector's public union, 50 percent of all public order judges—whose identity is supposed to be concealed to protect them from violence—have received death threats.[41]

Insularity: The Perils of Too Much Independence

Despite the recurring politicization, the region also has struggled with judicial accountability, reflecting the statist, corporatist nature of the state. Signs of a lack of accountability are evident in various countries, particularly in the tendency of many judges to ignore internal judicial regulations establishing criteria for professional conduct.[42] The World Bank has reported that judges in Ecuador routinely ignore deadlines to render verdicts, with no fear of internal sanction from their superiors.[43] Random surprise visits to courts in Lima have found that 70 percent of Peruvian judges in the capital city arrive for work late on a daily basis, apparently confident that they will not be disciplined for their behavior.[44] Former Bolivian Justice Minister René Blattman has complained that judges in his country ignore internal guidelines and fail to comply with statutory deadlines to render verdicts, creating the public perception that judges are accountable to no one.[45]

Such insularity often is reflected in—and perpetuated by—the judicial appointment process. Several countries, in an effort to avoid the historic problems of external politicization of the legal apparatus, have instituted strict tenure and seniority systems, and empowered the upper courts to make most judicial selections to lower courts—an approach that has allowed a handful of senior judges to dominate the court system.[46] This lack of accountability has created an environment in which nepotism has flourished. Colombia is an example—though clearly not the only one—of this trend.[47] Despite the frequent assaults on individual judges, the courts enjoy a high degree of institutional autonomy. Because senior judges rather than politicians appoint most lower-court judges, magistrates in Colombia typically have appointed personal cronies rather than skilled jurists to the bench, leaving the country with many judges that are ill-informed on even the most basic aspects of modern law. (A surprise minimum qualifications test administered by the Gaviria administration in 1990 found that 30 percent of all sitting judges were unable to pass a basic competence exam.)[48] Meanwhile, owing to the strong political clout enjoyed by ASONAL—a left-leaning union of court personnel—judicial employees have life tenure and cannot be removed for any reason, including poor performance.[49] The organization has blocked the government from transferring clerks and court staff to new jurisdictions—despite the recurring problem of overstaffing in some regions and severe personnel shortages in others.[50]

Administrative Inefficiency

Latin American courts have been notable for their chronic inefficiency. Using Weber's notion that a modern bureaucracy is identified by both structural and behavioral attributes, Philippe Schmitter applied this framework to Latin America in the 1970s and observed that most Latin American public sector institutions developed along distorted bureaucratic lines and emerged as "structurally overbureaucratized" but "behaviorally underbureaucratized."[51] Schmitter meant that bureaucracies had become increasingly larger and proliferated into a complex maze of ministries, secretariats, and autonomous agencies, many with no clear chain of accountability and often demonstrating complex and redundant organizational structures. At the same time, institutional behavior remained underdeveloped. Public posts served as personal bureaucratic fiefdoms, raffled off as a reward for political support; the frequent presence of civil service job requirements has been routinely ignored as top posts and assignments are distributed among those with scant technical expertise. The result is that the public sector's organizational structure grows more byzantine over time, while its reliability remains primitive, dependent on personal contacts and political favors.[52]

Most judiciaries in the region reflect a cumbersome, outdated bureaucratic structure that slows the administration of justice.[53] Latin America generally has lagged behind the global trend to establish a professional managerial class to tend to the affairs of the court, and responsibility for administering the judicial apparatus has fallen strictly within the purview of the courts, even though most judges have no formal training in management, finance, accounting, or organizational planning.[54] Buscaglia notes that "in most countries, there are no actual centralized administrative court procedures: this generates an immense duplication of efforts and prevents judges from concentrating their available time on adjudicative tasks."[55] Budgets are prepared without adequate forecasting of expected filings, dispositions, and pending cases, resulting in anomalous allocation of resources.[56] The results are ironic. Courts are underfunded and ill-equipped, yet so poorly organized that they sometimes are unable to spend the scarce resources they receive.[57] Citing Bolivia as an example, the World Bank has noted:

> Despite the autonomy the Court enjoyed in the management of personnel matters, it failed to develop a career system aimed at promoting professional excellence. . . . There were no established policies guiding personnel-related decisions. . . . The absence of sound practices for personnel management, combined with the low prestige of the judiciary, has resulted in low quality and effectiveness of staff. . . . The deficiencies in human resource management described above give rise to an incentive framework that thwarts professionalism and, at the very least, discourages efficient and principled performance of staff working in the judicial branch. . . . The judiciary in Bolivia is a highly rigid bureaucracy, lacking institutional capacity in planning and strategic management. The prevailing managerial culture is a reactive one, with no well-defined corporate strategy or objectives that would guide the allocation of institutional resources.[58]

Scholars also have attributed the perpetual inefficiency of the courts to the fact that many judges are distracted by having to devote a considerable portion of their time to routine administrative work rather than hearing cases. One recent survey of Latin American magistrates found that judges in Argentina spend up to 70 percent of their time on simple bureaucratic tasks such as filling out forms to order office supplies, while similar chores consume up to 65 percent of a judge's time in Brazil and 69 percent in Peru.[59] In Ecuador, Supreme Court justices charged with administering the court system devote more than four days a week to administrative matters, and the Supreme Court president personally dispenses funds to purchase gasoline for prosecutors visiting crime scenes and approves leave requests for judicial employees.[60]

Administrative efficiency also is slowed by severe resource constraints and the poorly-equipped nature of most courts.[61] Many countries lack a number of basics—such as computerized filing and records systems—meaning that no central records are available to study past rulings. Visitors have reported that the Colombian judiciary lacked basics ranging from computers to telephones, electric typewriters and photocopiers—sources of frequent delays because virtually all court documents are still recorded by hand.[62] The result is that cases linger indefinitely because of a lack of resources.[63]

A final source of inefficiency is that in many countries, laws have failed to keep pace with the needs of the courts and the changing patterns of cases that come before judges, which Alberto Binder has linked with the judiciary's "crisis of efficiency."[64] The point is not that Roman law systems are inherently "outdated," and there is little empirical research confirming that code modernizations alone, absent other reforms, significantly reduce delays.[65] Nonetheless, the World Bank posits that outdated codes likely are a strong contributing factor to case bottlenecks, noting that "the more changes in the political, social, or economic spheres a country goes through, the more pressing the need to reform the legal framework to reflect these [changes]."[66] Because most civil codes also have not changed with society, many routine commercial transactions that in the developed world require a notary public or approval by other public sector officials require a trial date and presence of a judge. In Ecuador, the physical presence of a judge is required before hospital authorities can pronounce a corpse as dead—a law that often requires judges to travel to remote rural areas simply to sign a death certificate in the presence of the corpse. Normal commercial transactions—purchasing a used car or buying livestock—require a court date and an appearance before the judge. Lawyers argue that updating these codes would reduce the congestion of court cases and accelerate the administration of justice.[67]

Limited Access

Finally, the judiciary is perceived as inaccessible to much of the population throughout the region. General frustration with the courts is shaped by real and specific grievances with particular aspects of the courts. Research by Buscaglia and Thomas Ulen found that those viewing their judiciaries as "inaccessible" for the average citizen reached a level of 47 percent in Ecuador and 67 percent in Venezuela.[68] A separate study conducted in the early 1980s in Peru found that 66 percent of all respondents said that they would not seek redress through the courts if they were victims of crime, with half of them saying that such a process simply would be a "waste of time."[69]

The lack of access to the courts can be measured by examining the judiciary's lack of a physical presence in many countries. A 1993 study conducted by the Federal Supreme Court in Brazil found that the country needed approximately 100,000 judges—more than ten times the current number—to meet current staffing demands and to allow judges to devote reasonable consideration to their cases; a separate study found that 81 percent of Brazilian judges believed the country did not have enough judges, while 73 percent blamed lengthy pretrial delays on the shortage of judges.[70] In neighboring Ecuador, judicial staffing requirements have failed to keep pace with changing demographics. The World Bank reports that the number of civil and commercial judges in Quito and Guayaquil remained constant from the late 1970s to the early 1990s, even though the population had increased nearly 15 percent during the same period.[71]

Not surprisingly, the shortage of judges is most acute in the poorer, more rural regions of most countries, where the public sector most often lacks an institutionalized presence. This demographic disparity further prejudices the administration of justice against the indigent by requiring the poor to miss several days of work to travel to a court in a neighboring city or town. In Bolivia, the ratio of population to judges is as much as four times higher in rural areas than in urban centers, despite the wider dispersion of clients in rural towns.[72] Other studies have shown that the typical peasant in rural Peru must travel an average of 73 miles to reach a courthouse in order to appear for a hearing, a process that requires the individual to miss several days of work.[73]

Court personnel such as public defenders also are in short supply throughout the region. Various countries have either marginal or nonexistent programs to provide legal assistance to the indigent, despite constitutional requirements obligating them to have such services.[74] In Ecuador, self-representation in court is not allowed—making the need for public defenders all the more essential—even though there are twenty-one public defenders serving a population of more than ten million.[75] And despite the pledges of former Guatemalan President Vinicio Cerezo to reform the administration of justice, his administration was able only to double the number of public prosecutors in Guatemala City—from one to two—to handle more than 3,000 cases annually in the capital city.[76] Even when low-income citizens eventually gain physical access to the courts, several features of the courts work against making the access meaningful for the average citizen. Some responsibility rests on the nature of the inquisitorial system, which comparative studies have found often fail to gain the trust of participants because the process is viewed as arbitrary and inaccessible.[77] An additional factor is an excessive formalism in Latin America that biases court proceedings against lower class citizens and fosters the perception that the courts serve only a limited portion of the population, creating what André Tunc refers to as an additional "psychological cost" for the poor.[78] This rigid formalism has made judicial proceedings unintelligible or indecipherable to the average citizen—particularly when the courts do not provide translators for those speaking an indigenous language other than Spanish—further eroding the courts' already low credibility.[79] Highlighting how court proceedings are barely understandable to most citizens, one noted Brazilian scholar recounted his experience during the 1992 Supreme Court announcement that it would uphold the congressional impeachment of former President Fernando Collor:

> I had a very interesting thing happen during Collor's trial. A few minutes after it started, I received a telephone call from a television station *complaining that no one was able to understand what the judges were saying—whether they supported Collor or were against him. I ended up going there to translate.* Many times even the attorney has difficulty [understanding]. The defect is not just the fault of judges. It is also the fault of the judicial system and the law schools, which are more interested in teaching procedure than in teaching law.[80]

A FINAL WORD ON JUDICIAL CORRUPTION

Before turning to a discussion of how judicial reform will be measured, a final issue that merits consideration is judicial corruption. Observers universally agree that judicial corruption is a significant challenge to the creation of a more effective judiciary in Latin America, although they disagree on whether it is primarily a problem of independence, efficiency, or access. Most scholars tend to identify judicial corruption as a threat to individual independence, as it establishes a relationship between the court and a litigant that results in a final decision based on considerations other than the reading of the law.[81] Others have viewed corruption primarily as a problem of efficiency. Beatrice Weder, for example, has found that perceptions of judicial corruption account for at least 15 percent of the total variance in economic growth in Latin America. Still others have viewed judicial corruption as a problem of access, as low-income citizens are those least able to afford financing the rent-seeking activities of corrupt court officials. Buscaglia has noted that judicial corruption—primarily through judicial personnel seeking payments to create delays by misplacing court documents—represents approximately 15 percent of total court costs.[82] In any event, this distinction is made because when countries tackle judicial corruption, they may do so by identifying it as a problem of independence, efficiency, or access, and the framing of the proposed reforms may have an important bearing on how they are received by members of the judiciary and the public at large.

MEASURING JUDICIAL REFORM

Before turning to the specific case studies, it is worth noting how success—and failure—are measured in various judicial reform efforts. A few words on the subject are necessary, as the mere intent to reform is not sufficient evidence of a successful venture.

No agreed-upon framework exists for measuring judicial reform, in large part because of the lack of literature on the subject. As noted in Chapter One, even the World Bank has been reluctant to establish a set of indicators to determine whether its judicial reform efforts are having success.[83] Other studies have focused almost exclusively on a single country and a single aspect of reform—usually "efficiency-maximizing" strategies—without reference to larger or comparative lessons and without suggesting which indicators one would look to to determine whether a program is having success.

In general, approaches to judicial reform implicitly have focused almost exclusively on one of two approaches. The first approach tracks and monitors the creation of so-called "inputs" in the reform process—adding a certain number of judges, updating certain laws or procedures, increasing budgets and resources—whose implementation are assumed in and of themselves to represent a step forward in the reform process in the 1980s.[84] Typical of this approach was the U.S. Agency for International Development/Harvard University Project to reform the judiciary in Guatemala. Project consultants decided from the outset that Guatemala's judiciary would be best served by adopting a hierarchy roughly similar to that of the United States; reformers thus gauged their success by their ability to replicate a system of local, national, and appeals courts that would only try certain types of cases and in which an attorney general and public prosecutor with expanded powers would perform certain distinct roles analogous to those performed in the United States.[85] Others have played down the importance of reform "inputs" and focused on whether these inputs produce certain "outputs." That is, whatever the reform taken, its value is measured by examining whether it leads to specific and observable improvements, either qualitatively or, more usually, quantitatively. This approach has been especially popular among those monitoring judicial efficiency, because some aspects of reform (such as times to disposition) are more easily measured.[86] Neither approach is entirely satisfactory, however. Critics of an input-based approach stress that good intentions are insufficient and that changes in one area may trigger unanticipated and undesired changes in other areas; this is the case in Brazil, for example. As detailed in Chapter Four, efforts to increase access for the public so glutted the courts that trial delays swelled, and the system became unable to provide timely justice for anyone. Critics of an output-based approach attack that method for being too reductionist; they stress that some issues such as judicial independence cannot be quantified, and that merely measuring efficiency by tracking times to disposition is misplaced, arguing that "faster justice is not necessarily *better* justice."[87]

Cutting across this basic distinction are several complicating factors. Most basic is the unavailability or unreliability of accurate court data, particularly in the smaller Latin American countries where reformers themselves are unable to determine with any certainty whether their measures are having the intended effect.[88] More fundamental is the definitional fuzziness that emerges when a proposed reform becomes the main goal in and of itself, so that the initial input becomes the only output to show for reform efforts. The point is important. A main criticism of many judicial reform programs in Latin America is that reformers lose sight of the desired output—independence, efficiency, access—and come to view the policy means, or input, to that goal as an end in and of itself. This blurring of ends and means is an important indicator of whether judicial reformers are losing sight of their goals and whether the project is drifting off course.

Against this backdrop, it is impossible to rely on a single gauge or indicator, and any effort to evaluate the successes of judicial reform must include some mix of reform "inputs" and "outputs" and some combination of both qualitative and quantitative indicators, with the understanding that no single indicator or approach will have the same weight in all case studies and all reform components. More specifically, several indicators will be used to measure each reform component, with different weight given to inputs and outputs depending on the reform aspect under consideration. Independence is measured primarily by tracking various reform "inputs" of structural change and only secondarily by the outputs, while efficiency and access are measured by a combination of factors weighted slightly more in favor of reform "outputs."

Independence

As Keith Rosenn notes, judicial independence is "extraordinarily difficult to ascertain or measure" and is perhaps the hardest of all reform components to assess; he notes that "all attempts to quantify judicial independence suffer from serious methodological infirmities."[89] Scholars who have tracked judicial independence in developing countries have usually adopted a framework that stresses reform inputs. The most common approach focuses on the creation of formal mechanisms to strengthen the separation of powers, laws guaranteeing the irreducibility of judicial salaries, budgetary autonomy, mechanisms to ensure more nonpartisan selections, and the creation of judicial career systems to reduce political influence and ensure more regularized promotions.[90] Because politicization and insularity share the common trait of a lack of professionalism, accountability can be tracked by following many of the same type of indicators—monitoring the creation of disciplinary and impeachment procedures, judicial councils, and evaluation systems to ensure transparency.[91]

Less weight is given to tracking outputs of judicial independence, although the notion has certain merits. Paulo Gonzalez Casanova has tried to measure judicial independence by tracking outputs, and, while less successful, offers possible avenues for assessing reforms. González Casanova examined nearly 4,000 decisions by the Mexican Supreme Court between 1917 and 1960 and found that in those cases involving the executive, the High Court ruled against the executive 34 percent of the time and in favor of the executive 34 percent of the time, concluding that the Court was relatively independent.[92] Yet as Rosenn explains, these statistics do not tell us anything about the political salience of the cases under review, such as whether the case in question is a trivial affair or a sensitive political case in which the executive has an overriding interest. Similarly, Rosenn cautions that the quantitative approach is misleading: in most Latin American countries, petitions against the government automatically name the president as the offending party because he signs the bill into law, not because he is interested in the case at hand. Thus, Rosenn concludes, a strictly quantitative, output-based approach has serious limitations.[93] That said, focusing on outputs has some merit as a starting point for consolidating democracies, at least if court behavior is considered in sensitive, high-profile human rights cases in which the civilian government or past military regime clearly has a vested interest in the outcome. Applying the maxim of John Hart Ely—"one of the surest ways to acquire power is to assert it"—judicial independence can be measured by broadly tracking the willingness of the courts to rule against the government in important human rights cases that invariably emerge in all Latin American transitions and in which the executive branch often has a strong interest. Buscaglia and Dakolias argue that this approach reflects the ability of the courts to serve as an autonomous branch of power checking the governmental power of the other branches.[94]

Efficiency

Determining whether judicial reforms are producing greater efficiency also can be measured by comparing reform inputs and outputs. It is especially important to make the distinction between reform measures and their results—particularly on efficiency-creating measures, generally the most common reform in Latin America—because several of the judicial reform efforts examined in the following chapters show a very low correlation between reform expectations and actual results.[95] An input-based approach focuses on what Buscaglia refers to as the "quality of inputs," those measures intended to reduce arbitrary or rent-seeking behavior of court officials. These steps typically include computerization of court records, the development and application of more streamlined court proceedings and case management techniques, and post-entry training for court officials and judges. An output-based approach focuses not on the intent of these measures but more specifically on their results. As suggested from the foregoing discussion of Buscaglia and Guerrero-Cosumano, in some respects it is easier to measure changes in judicial efficiency than to determine efficiency itself. That is, although no precise definition exists for "judicial efficiency," it is possible—in those countries that maintain detailed court statistics—to measure changes in times to disposition and pretrial detention rates.[96] Measuring these at least provides an indication of whether the reforms are leading more quickly to the administration of justice.

Access

Like independence and efficiency, access can be measured by both inputs and outputs. The most common reform inputs include tracking whether reformers create institutional or procedural mechanisms such as small claims courts, reduce onerous court fees, introduce forms of alternative dispute resolution, provide translators and low-cost legal aid, and increase the number of courts, judges, and public defenders, all measures that aim to pare the direct and indirect court costs.[97] Whether these measures are having their intended effects may be reflected by the following outputs: increases in the number of claims filed before a court; the total number of cases entering the system over time; and changes in the number of cases handled by justices of the peace, small claims courts, or resolved through alternative dispute resolution.

A final indicator cutting across all of these categories is the gauge of public opinion polling. Clearly polling is an imperfect indicator in Latin America. Public attitudes often are volatile: voters in many countries may express unduly optimistic expectations once a transition to civilian rule has occurred, and cynicism and disillusionment may increase because of unmet expectations even when the actual performance of the courts has not changed significantly. Moreover, in some cases growing public frustration is a catalyst for reform while in other instances it merely leads to increased cynicism.[98] On balance, however, comparisons of polling data over time provide a sense of whether the courts are gaining or losing confidence and whether average citizens believe that they may gain access to the courts in a timely manner; it tells us, as Frances Hagopian notes, a great deal about citizen perceptions of institutions, their linkages among citizens, and whether voters have faith in or are cynical about democratic institutions.[99] Because democratic consolidation rests so heavily on public confidence, polling also provides an indication of whether confidence in the rule of law is growing—an extremely useful indicator for tracking democratic consolidation and decay.

NOTES

1. Michael Lea and Laurens Walker, "Efficient Procedure," *North Carolina Law Review* 57 (March 1979): 361–79; John Thibaut and Laurens Walker, "A Theory of Procedure," *California Law Review* 66 (May 1978): 541–66; and Edgardo Buscaglia and Pilar Domingo Villegas, "The Impediments to Judicial Reform in Latin America," Paper presented at the Latin American Studies Association, XIX International Congress, 28–30 September 1995, p. 2.

2. See, for example, William A. Hamilton, "Computer-Induced Improvements in the Administration of Justice," *Computer Law/Journal* 4 (Summer 1983): 55–76; James R. Maher, "How to Integrate A Criminal Justice Computer System," *LAW/Technology* 23 (1990): 1–18; and Rafael A. Bielsa and Marcelo Perazolo, "Alrededor de la informática, al eficiencia y la reforma del servicio de justicia," *Jurismatica* 5/6 (1994): 43–67.

3. This is the main theme of *Justiça: Promessa e Realidade* (Rio de Janeiro: Editora Nova Fronteira, 1995), a recent collection of essays on various judicial reform efforts in South America.

4. Hernández Valiente, "Justice in Central America in the Nineties," pp. 64–66.

5. Luis Salas and José Maria Rico, *Independencia Judicial: Replantamiento de un tema tradicional* (San José: Centro para la Administración de Justicia, 1990).

6. Shimon Shetreet, "Judicial Independence: New Conceptual Dimensions and Contemporary Challenges," in *Judicial Independence: The Contemporary Debate*, ed. Shimon Shetreet (Boston, Mass.: Dorderecht, 1985): 598–600.

7. Owen Fiss, "The Right Degree of Independence," in *Transitions to Democracy in Latin America: The Role of Judiciary*, 56–60.

8. Maurice J. Sponzo, "Independence vs. Accountability," *Judges' Journal* 26 (Spring 1987): 13–16, 42–43.

9. Jerome Cohen, "The Chinese Communist Party and Judicial Independence," *Harvard Law Review* 82 (1969): 972.

10. Theorists ranging from Montesquieu to Kant have noted correctly the critical need to keep judicial decisionmaking functions divided from those of the legislature and the executive in order to maintain limits on government power; thus Montesquieu warned that "there can be no liberty where the judicial and executive powers are united in the same person." Yet that division of power is not absolute. As Madison writes in Federalist #47, judicial independence does "not mean that these departments [the executive and the legislature] ought to have no *partial agency* in, or no *control* over, the acts of each other"; indeed, Madison argued in Federalists #10 and #51 that an important way to limit government power and restrain its activism was to create a system of overlapping competencies between different branches of government. The real danger, Madison warned, is when "the *whole* power of one department is exercised by the same hands which possess the *whole* power of another department, [and] the fundamental principles of a free constitution are subverted." See Madison, "Federalist #47," pp. 302–3.

11. Jefferson wrote: "Our judges are as honest as other men, and not moreso. They have, with others, the same passions for party, for power, and the privilege of their corps. Their maxim is '*boni judicis est ampliare jurisdictionem*'–a good judge will enlarge his jurisdiction." Cited in Dumas Malone, *Writings of Jefferson: Jefferson the President, First Term, 1801–1805* (Boston: Little, Brown, and Company, 1970). The first quote is taken from his letter to Spencer Roane. Jefferson's concerns have been reiterated in modern times by a number of observers. Former U.S. Circuit Court Judge Learned Hand lamented the emergence of a "chamber unaccountable to anyone but itself," while scholar Robert Nagel has written of the perils of a court system that, in the pursuit of professionalism, acts "to isolate itself from the general culture, retaining ties of language and intellectual approach only to an academic elite." Learned Hand, *The Bill of Rights* (Cambridge, Mass.: Harvard University Press, 1958); and Robert Nagel, *Constitutional Cultures: The Mentality and Consequences of Judicial Review* (Berkeley: University of California Press, 1989): 3.

12. Peter Evans, *Embedded Autonomy* (Princeton, N.J.: Princeton University Press, 1995): 12.

13. Owen Fiss, "The Right Degree of Independence," in *Transitions to Democracy in Latin America: The Role of Judiciary*, ed. Irwin Stotzky (Boulder, Colo.: Westview Press, 1993): 56. Emphasis added.

14. Maria Dakolias has suggested that any institution—including the judiciary—gravitates toward inefficient norms when it has a monopoly on the supply of a particular good (in this case, "justice") and hence can act inefficiently without fear of retribution because the public lacks an alternative supplier. See Dakolias, *The Judicial Sector in Latin America and the Caribbean: Elements of Reform*, p. 23.

15. Max Weber, *The Theory of Economic and Social Organization*, trans. Talcott Parsons (London: William Hodge, 1947).

16. See, for example, James Kakalik, Molly Selvin, and Nicholas Pace, *Strategies for Reducing Civil Delay in the Los Angeles Superior Court* (Santa Monica, Calif.: Rand Corporation, 1990) and Patricia Ebener, *Court Efforts to Reduce Pretrial Delays in the Los Angeles Superior Court* (Santa Monica, Calif.: Rand Corporation/Institute for Civil Justice, 1981).

17. Edgardo Buscaglia and José Luis Guerrero-Cosumano, *Quality Control Approach to the Understanding of Court Delays* (Washington, D.C.: Georgetown University School of Business Administration, 1995): 2. Information from the rest of this paragraph, unless otherwise cited, comes from this study.

18. Mauro Cappelletti, *The Judicial Process in Comparative Perspective* (Oxford: Clarendon Press, 1989): 294.

19. Mauro Cappalletti, "Alternative Dispute Resolution Processes within the Framework of the World-wide Access-to-Justice Movement," *Modern Law Review* 56 (May 1993): 282–85.

20. Buscaglia and Domingo, "Impediments to Judicial Reform in Latin America," p. 6.

21. Paul H. Lewis, *Paraguay Under Stroessner* (Chapel Hill: University of North Carolina Press, 1980): 113. Because Congress functioned as a rubber stamp for the Colorado Party almost the entire century, judges generally served at the discretion of the ruling party. The Supreme Court did not have a non-Colorado justice this century until Christian Democrat Irala Burgos was appointed in 1990. See *Paraguay: An Encouraging Victory in the Search for Truth and Justice* (New York: Human Rights Watch/Americas Watch, 1992): 7.

22. Even when the tenure of judges has been constitutionally guaranteed, the notion of independence has been more illusory than real, as the Mexican experience demonstrates. Under the Constitution of 1917 and its subsequent amendments, judges are nominally protected from political considerations by the guarantees of life tenure and irreducibility of salaries. Yet those guarantees have been largely meaningless over time. Mexico has been governed by the same party since the early 1920s and judicial appointees have made the courts an arm of the ruling Institutional Revolutionary Party (PRI); federal judges are often transferred from one region of the country to another and the federal government may unilaterally transfer cases from the docket of one judge to another. Because judgeships are viewed as stepping stones to more financially lucrative political careers, judges are reluctant to rule against the ruling party on most issues, despite the independence ostensibly protected through life tenure. See Leonel Pereznieto Castro, "La reforma judicial," *Examen* (January 1995): 13–19.

23. While executives can be expected to appoint judges that share their basic philosophical outlook, Latin American governments—both civilian and military—appear exceptional in their willingness to manipulate the size of the courts to advance partisan agendas. For a discussion of court packing in western democracies, see Henry J. Abraham, *The Judicial Process*, 6th ed. (New York: Oxford University Press, 1973): 71–74.

24. James D. Rudolph, "Government and Politics," in *Brazil: A Country Study*, ed. Richard F. Nyrop (Washington, D.C: The American University, 1983 [4th ed.]): 244–46. Anastasio Somoza in Nicaragua and Jean-Claude Duvalier in Haiti employed similar tactics to shape a more agreeable court.

25. Owen Fiss, "The Right Degree of Independence," in *Transition to Democracy in Latin America: The Role of the Judiciary*, p. 52. According to some accounts, Menem tried to induce opposition party judges on the Court to retire by offering them lucrative ambassadorial posts overseas. See also Jaime Williams, "Reformas de la administración de justicia," in *Conferencia Iberoamericana sobre reforma de la justicia penal* (San Salvador: Ministério de Justicia, 1991): 17

26. Following the March 1976 coup in Argentina, the ruling military junta dismissed all of the Supreme Court judges in the provinces and suspended the tenure of all federal judges. The junta also required all judges to swear that they would uphold the institutional acts decreed by the military and that their allegiance would be to the goals of the junta rather than the Constitution, removing all judges that refused to comply. Robert E. Biles, "The Position of the Judiciary in the Political Systems of Argentina and Mexico," *Lawyer of the Americas* 8 (1976): 287–318.

27. This turnover has prompted most judges to avoid probing legal thought and to confine themselves to technical questions and narrow, administrative issues. See "Bolivian Supreme Court Crisis–Unclassified Wrap-up," U.S. Department of State, unclassified telegram La Paz 08969, 22 June 1991.

28. *Sondeo de Necesidades de Capacitación en Cortes Superiores de Distrito, Juzgados de Partido e Instrucción de la República de Bolivia* (San José: ILANUD, 1992).

29. Helen Clagett, *The Administration of Justice in Latin America* (New York: Oceana Publications, 1952): 57. Clagett notes, "The principal objection with respect to the creation of autonomous, extrajudicial tribunals or other organs is not so much that they are alien to judicial power, but rather that they are exempt from its control."

30. The Ministry of the Interior was led throughout the 1980s by Tomás Borge, one of the original founders of the FSLN and long considered one of the most doctrinaire Marxists-Leninists in the ruling junta.

31. See Roger Miranda and William Ratliff, *The Civil War in Nicaragua* (New Brunswick: Transaction Publisher, 1993): 199. Because the definitions of what constituted a crime against the state was so broad–having been a member of the National Guard under the Somoza dynasty was grounds for imprisonment, even if the courts had no evidence of criminal wrongdoing–the special court system quickly became an arm of the ruling junta. See John T. Philipsborn, "Nicaragua: a legal system developing in difficult times," *Judicature* 71 (December–January 1988): 46.

32. Luis G. Solis and Richard J. Wilson, *Political Transition and the Administration of Justice in Nicaragua* (Miami: Florida International University, 1991): 24.

33. The notion of internal threats to judicial independence is often overlooked. For example, Mark Ramseyer argues that politicization can come only from politicians, noting that an independent judiciary is one that is defined "as courts where politicians do not manipulate the careers of sitting judges" and in which "politicians do not try to intervene in the courts to reward or punish sitting judges for the politics of their decisions." Politicization from senior judges is never considered as a possibility. See J. Mark Ramseyer, "The Puzzling (In)dependence of Courts: A Comparative Approach," *Journal of Legal Studies* 23 (June 1994): 721–47.

34. This phenomenon is not unique to underdeveloped countries and has been observed in advanced democracies, as well. See, for example, David M. O'Brien and Yasuo Ohkoshi, "Stifling Judicial Independence from Within: The Japanese Judiciary," Paper Presented at the 1996 Interim Meeting of the Research Committee on Comparative Judicial Studies of the International Political Science Association, 1–4 July 1996.

35. In one well-known case from 1986, Appeals Court Judge Carlos Cerda Fernandez discovered that government-presented evidence had been falsified in a human rights case he was investigating. Coupled with other information gleaned from his investigation, Cerda indicted thirty-eight military personnel–including former junta member Air Force Gen. Gustavo Leigh Guzmán, a close ally of Pinochet. Less than two months later, the Supreme Court suspended Cerda and removed him from the case. When he returned to the bench in early 1991–a year

after the military had left power—he was again suspended and dismissed by senior judges, allowed to return only after pledging to drop the case and apologizing to the Supreme Court. See *Chile: A Time of Reckoning* (Geneva: International Commission of Jurists, 1992): 100-104.

36. Pedro Nikken, "Human Rights Accountability and Reform of the Police, Military, and Judiciary," in *El Salvador: Sustaining Peace, Nourishing Democracy*, ed. Gary Bland (Washington, D.C.: The Woodrow Wilson Center, 1993): 33.

37. See James LeMoyne, "The Case of a Salvadoran Judge: Does Valor Pay?" *The New York Times*, 3 May 1985, A2.

38. Ecuador's democratically-elected president León Febres Cordero deployed army tanks outside the Supreme Court in 1985 when the Court was deliberating on politically sensitive cases, only to withdraw the tanks when the courts bended to his political goals. In Sandinista Nicaragua, President Daniel Ortega would call Court members to warn that they were reaching the wrong conclusions. See U.S. Department of State, *Ecuador: Annual Human Rights Report* (Washington, D.C.: Department of State, 1985); and Mac Lafollette and John T. Philipsborn, "After the election, Nicaragua discusses reforms of its judicial system," *Judicature* 74 (August–September 1990): 102-4.

39. See, for example, Rachelle Marie Bin, "Drug Lords and the Colombian Judiciary: A Story of Threats, Bribes, and Bullets," *UCLA Pacific Law Journal* 5 (Spring–Fall 1986): 178-82.

40. See "Law is a dangerous job in Colombia," *International Commission of Jurist Newsletter* 51 (October 1992): 5. The ICJ report also stated that 98 percent of those crimes remained unpunished at the time of writing, and that investigations had never been opened in 80 percent of those cases. See also Michael Pahl, "Concealing Justices or Concealing Injustice?: Colombia's Secret Courts," *Denver Journal of International Law and Policy* 21 (Winter 1993): 432-33. Prominent judicial victims in Colombia since the early 1980s include former Minister of Justice Rodrigo Lara Bonilla, Bogotá Superior Court Judge Tulio Manuel Castro, Supreme Court Justice Hernando Buquero Borda, Attorney General Carlos Mauro Hoyo, and the entire Supreme Court in a 1984 insurgent attack on the Palace of Justice.

41. *Violencia en Colombia* (Lima: Comisión Internacional de Juristas/Comisión Andina de Juristas, 1990): 84-117. When ASONAL employees went on a nationwide strike in 1989, their demands were not for higher wages, but rather for the modest objectives of receiving 250 bulletproof vests, fifty armored cars, thirty private cars, eighty escort motorcycles, and five metal detectors for court entrances.

42. Maria Dakolias, *The Judicial Sector in Latin America and the Caribbean: Elements of Reform* (Washington, D.C.: The World Bank, 1996): 17.

43. *Ecuador: Judicial Sector Assessment* (Washington, D.C.: The World Bank, 1994): 17.

44. "Majority of Peruvian Judges Arrive Late for Work," Reuters news dispatch, 16 May 1997.

45. "Justice Minister Discusses Need for Reform," *Presencia* (La Paz) 22 July 1994, p. 2, in FBIS-LAT, 26 August 1994. Hugo Urquieta Morales, a former Undersecretary for Justice in Bolivia, has echoed this theme, expressing frustration with the government's inability to change the dilatory behavior of judges:

> Judges in Bolivia feel they are above the law, even though they are its direct representatives in society. They do not keep schedules, have no fixed working days, and have no time limits for solving judicial disagreements, even though the law penalizes the actions and stipulates a loss of jurisdiction. Judicial officials have found grounds and procedures to delay cases for periods of time that in many cases are ten times longer than stated in the law. No deadlines are applied. Simply put, judges ignore legal provisions and if they do comply with them, execute them in an informal manner.

46. Germán Hermosilla Arriagada has warned that such policies, while correctly aiming to improve the professionalism of the judicial sector, can nonetheless lead to a "stiffening of the joints" within the judiciary, cautioning that "incumbents who feel relatively secure in their positions and expectations, mainly on the basis of their seniority, may not feel motivated to improve themselves, to strive to perform better, or to seek out innovative or creative ideas with an eye to performing their functions better." See Germán Hermosilla Arriagada, "Training and Continuing Education for Judges," in *Justice and Development in Latin American and the Caribbean* (Washington, D.C.: Inter-American Development Bank, 1993): 103.

47. In Ecuador, the World Bank reports that the court system's Human Resource Division—established to monitor recruiting and selection criteria for judges—quickly found 450 cases of nepotism, many made with virtually no regard for or record of the professional criteria of the applicants and with no employee files to measure or record professional performance. In Brazil, the head of the country's labor court employed more than sixty relatives—at a total annual cost of more than $2 million—even though virtually none of them had formal legal or clerical training and had not taken the legally-mandated entrance exams. See *Ecuador: Judicial Sector Assessment*, p. 14; and "Brazil Labor Court Head Accused of Hiring Family," Reuters news dispatch, 10 November 1995. The problem of judicial nepotism in Brazil is discussed in detail in Chapter Four.

48. "Colombia's Judicial System: Crisis and Reform," See U.S. Department of State, unclassified telegram Bogotá 11656, 11 August 1989.

49. Information in this paragraph comes from "A Guide Through the Labyrinth: Justice in Colombia—The Existing Organizational Structure and the Prospects for Further Reform," U.S. Department of State, unclassified telegram Bogotá 08033, 22 May 1990; and "Weekend Violence Update: Seven Bombings, Two Assassination Attempts, Two Puzzling Massacres, and Some Guerrilla Activity," U.S. Department of State, unclassified telegram Bogotá 16900, 30 October 1989.

50. "Monthly Report of the U.S. Funded Narcotics Program—Colombia—October 1991," U.S. Department of State, unclassified telegram Bogotá 17603, 15 November 1991. During the administration of President Virgilio Barco (1986–90), members of the judiciary frequently mobilized to block the proposed creation of an Attorney General's office, arguing that the much-needed reorganization somehow might cost them their jobs or reduce the funding allotted to the judiciary in the annual budget process.

51. Philippe C. Schmitter, *Interest Conflict and Political Change in Brazil* (Stanford, Calif.: Stanford University Press, 1971): 34.

52. John Sloan summarizes the pattern of inefficiency: "Varying proportions of Latin American bureaucracies are characterized by *personalismo*, nepotism, job insecurity, high turnover rates, lack of expertise, inadequate use of existing expertise, failure to delegate authority, formalism, stultifying legalism, unsatisfactory information gathering and communication, use of the bureaucracy to relieve unemployment, and lack of coordination among agencies and departments." John W. Sloan, *Public Policy in Latin America* (Pittsburgh, Pa.: University of Pittsburgh Press, 1984): 136.

53. In some respects, it probably is more accurate to state that the source of inefficiency is not an archaic bureaucracy but rather the lack of a bureaucracy altogether, at least in the sense the term was employed by Weber. That is, there is a public sector and public sector employees, yet no structured, predictable bureaucracy—but rather what Evans calls "a collection of self-interested incumbents using their offices for purposes of individual maximization." Evans, *Embedded Autonomy*, p. 71.

54. "A Guide Through the Labyrinth: Justice in Colombia—The Existing Organizational Structure and the Prospects for Further Reform," U.S. Department of State, unclassified telegram Bogotá 08033, 22 May 1990.

55. Buscaglia and Domingo, "Impediments to Judicial Reform," p. 10. There is a similar redundancy between Colombia's Technical Judicial Police, the Federal Police, and the Civil Police—all with similar mandates yet no clear division of labor. Such lack of coordination in even the most basic functions appears to have had a considerable impact on the effectiveness of the administration of justice. Former Minister of Justice Fernando Carrillo Flores has remarked that "the greatest source of impunity here has been the lack of a coordinated effort at assembling evidence." Cited in Michael R. Pahl, "Wanted: Criminal Justice—Colombia's Adoption of a Prosecutorial System of Criminal Procedure," *Fordham International Law Journal* 16 (1992–93): 618.

56. In Bolivia, the World Bank reports that resources are inexplicably allocated in inverse proportion to the population in each region. See *Bolivia: Judicial Reform Project*, p. 5.

57. In the early 1990s, civilian governments in Ecuador and Peru increased the budgets of the judiciary, although at year-end the courts returned a portion of their funds to the Executive because they were unable to spend it all. See Dakolias, *The Judicial Sector in Latin America and the Caribbean: Elements of Reform*, p. 32.

58. *Bolivia: Judicial Reform Project*, pp. 5–7. Ecuador is another example. The Supreme Court assigns court personnel for the entire judicial hierarchy without reference to caseload and changing demographics. As a result, every first instance judge in the country has five support staff, and every superior court judge has exactly six. The result is that some courts are perpetually overstaffed while others are understaffed. See Edgardo Buscaglia, Maria Dakolias, and William Ratliff, *Judicial Reform in Latin America: A Framework for National Development* (Stanford, Calif.: Hoover Institution, 1995): 14. In Colombia, the organization of the justice system is so byzantine that former President Barco's *Carrera Judicial*—established in 1988 to oversee and streamline the operations of the judiciary—was unable to determine how many judicial sector employees were in the country after more than three years of efforts. See "A Guide Through the Labyrinth: Justice in Colombia—The Existing Organizational Structure and the Prospects for Further Reform," U.S. Department of State, unclassified telegram Bogota 08033, 22 May 1990; and Steven Flanders, "Court administration in Colombia: an American visitor's perspective," *Judicature* 71 (June–July 1987): 36–39.

59. Edgardo Buscaglia, "Stark picture of justice," *Financial Times*, 21 March 1995, 12.

60. Dakolias, *The Judicial Sector in Latin America and the Caribbean: Elements of Reform*, p. 23. The sparse court administration that does exist is heavily centralized, with extensive powers vested in the hands of the Supreme Court and its staff. As a result, lower courts often must request Supreme Court approval for even the most mundane items—such as ordering staplers and paper clips—resulting in costly delays.

61. In most countries, at least 60 percent of the judiciary's budget goes to meet payroll costs. Citing Ecuador as an example, the World Bank reports that nearly 90 percent of the judiciary's budget goes to salaries for judges. Cited in *Ecuador: Judicial Sector Assessment*, p. 13.

62. One U.S. legal scholar visiting Colombia in 1989 noted that "telephones are at a premium, with several secretaries and midlevel office managers sharing not only the same line, but the same phone." See Richard L. Fricker, "A Judiciary Under Fire," *ABA Journal* (February 1990): 56.

63. Citing how resource constraints undercut the courts' efforts, U.S. officials note that in Bolivia "honest, energetic prosecutors who wish to carry out investigations often have no vehicles available for transportation. Even when there is a vehicle there is no money for gasoline.

Prosecutors and court officials often have no office supplies." See "Bolivia International Narcotics Control Strategy Report–1987," U.S. Department of State, unclassified telegram La Paz 00816, 28 January 1987.

64. Binder, *Perspectives of the Penal Reform Process in Latin America*, p. 4.

65. As Alberto Binder writes: "Latin America does have codified laws, but it must be understood that continental Europe abandoned that system two centuries ago. Even Spain, which implemented the system in Latin America, abandoned it about a century ago. Therefore, the Latin American system resembles the one used in continental Europe in the Middle Ages, not the one currently in use." See Binder, *Perspectives of the Penal Reform Process in Latin America*, p. 1.

66. *The World Bank and Legal Technical Assistance* (Washington, D.C.: The World Bank, 1995): 32. To take only a few examples, Brazil's criminal code has not been significantly updated since the early 1940s, when it was drafted by the authoritarian Vargas regime, while Mexico's criminal code dates from 1931, Paraguay's from 1910, Venezuela's from 1926, and Chile's from 1874. See Fernando Henrique Cardoso, *Mãos A Obra, Brasil: Proposta de Governo* (Brasília: [no publisher given], 1994): 161; and Luis Salas and José Maria Rico, *The Administration of Justice in Latin America* (Miami: Florida International University, 1993): 20. A 1995 study conducted by the Brazilian Magistrates Association found that over 80 percent of judges expressed the view that Brazil's outdated laws were responsible for lengthy court delays; a separate 1995 survey by a respected São Paulo-based think tank reported nearly identical results. Compare "Juizes culpam leis pelos errores que cometem," *Jornal do Brasil*, 11 May 1995, 4; and Maria Tereza Sadek, "A Crise do judiciário vista pelos juízes: resultados da pesquisa quantitativa," in *Uma Introdução ao Estudo da Justiça*, ed. Maria Tereza Sadek (São Paulo: Editora Sumare/IDESP, 1995): 17–23.

67. Laura Chinchilla and David Stodt, *The Administration of Justice in Ecuador* (Miami: Florida International University, 1993): 45.

68. Edgardo Buscaglia and Thomas Ulen, "A Quantitative Analysis of the Judicial Sectors in Latin America," Paper presented at the Annual Meeting of the American Law and Economics Association, 12–13 May 1995, pp. 18–21. Meanwhile, a Gallup International poll found that 88 percent of the Argentine public said that the courts do little or nothing for low-income citizens. See *Estudio de Opinión Acerca de la Justicia en Argentina* (Buenos Aires: Instituto Gallup de la Argentina, 1994): 1.

69. Luis Pasara, *Jueces, justicia, y poder en Peru*, pp. 26, 28.

70. See "Ideal é 100 mil juízes mas so há 7,8 mil," *Jornal do Brasil*, 1 January 1994, 3, and "Magistrados avaliam o propio trabalho," *Jornal do Brasil*, 9 January 1994, 3. By way of comparison, Germany has 30,000 judges and a population roughly half the size of Brazil. Meanwhile, in Peru, the Supreme Court estimates that there is a 25 to 30 percent shortage of judges in the country, while a 1993 study conducted by the Catholic University in Lima reported that most judges in Peru estimated that a manageable caseload would be approximately 250 per month, although the shortage of judges meant that each magistrate had an average monthly caseload of 550. See Victor Andres Ponce, "Judicial Reform," in *Expreso* (Lima), 12 March 1994, A6, in FBIS-LAT, 23 March 1994.

71. *Ecuador: Judicial Sector Assessment*, p. 6.

72. A World Bank study on Bolivia notes that the discrepancy "confirms the inaccessibility of the judicial branch to the low-income rural community." See *Bolivia: Judicial Reform Project*, p. 7.

73. Buscaglia and Domingo, "Impediments to Judicial Reform in Latin America," p. 13.

74. In Nicaragua, for instance, publicly-funded defenders and court-ordered lawyers to represent the poor are virtually non-existent—despite a constitutional requirement that the courts provide such services—and their professional qualifications are questionable. See Solis and Wilson, *Political Transition and the Administration of Justice in Nicaragua*, p. 25.

75. *Ecuador: Judicial Sector Assessment*, p. 25.

76. *The Administration of Injustice: Military Accountability in Guatemala* (Washington, D.C.: Washington Office on Latin America, 1989): 23-27.

77. Laurens Walker, E. Allen Lind, and John Thibaut, "The Relations Between Procedural Justice and Distributive Justice," *Virginia Law Review* 65 (December 1979): 1401-420. Walker found a statistical correlation supporting his argument that participants were more likely to view an adversarial system as producing a more legitimate decision, even if litigants were unsatisfied with the actual ruling.

78. André Tunc, "The Quest for Justice," in *Access to Justice and the Welfare State*, ed. Mauro Cappelletti (LeMonnier: Firenze, 1981): 327. Dakolias refers to this as an "informational barrier" to justice. See *The Judicial Sector in Latin America: Elements of Reform*, p. xiii.

79. Salas and Rico note that one factor accounting for the inaccessibility of the Honduran judicial system is the lack of clarity of the country's laws. More than 70 percent of the population—and 87 percent of lawyers and 90 percent of prosecutors—say the country's laws are unclear. See Salas and Rico, *La Justicia Penal en Honduras*, p. 170.

80. Jorgemar Felix, "Crise da Justiça é da cúpula," *Jornal do Brasil*, 14 May 1995, 12. Emphasis added.

81. See, for example, Carlos J. Sarmiento Sosa, "Judicial Corruption and the Administration of Justice: A Comparative International View," Paper Presented to the XXXIII Conference of the InterAmerican Bar Association, Caracas, Venezuela, 9 August 1995.

82. Buscaglia and Domingo, "Impediments to Judicial Reform, p. 12. A World Bank study on Peru found that 39 percent of all users of the courts blamed the extensive judicial corruption on court clerks, who would expedite or delay cases based on bribes. See *Peru: Judicial Sector Assessment* (Washington, D.C.: The World Bank, 1994): 44. Weder's study can be found in Beatrice Weder, "Legal Systems and Economic Performance: The Empirical Evidence," in *Judicial Reform in Latin America and the Caribbean*, p. 22.

83. See Robert Mosse and Leigh Ellen Sontheimer, *Performance Monitoring Indicators Handbook* (Washington, D.C.: The World Bank, 1996).

84. An example of this approach can be found in "Update on Administration of Justice Efforts, June 1991-December 1991," U.S. Department of State, unclassified telegram San Salvador 00448, 1992. In that report, reform consultants outline their reform components which amount to quantifying inputs—such as the number of judicial reform articles placed in the local media, the number of laws passed, and the number of judges hired.

85. *Final Report: Evaluation of Harvard Law School Program: Guatemala* (Washington, D.C.: Checchi and Co., 1989).

86. This is the implicit approach in Buscaglia and Ulen, "A Quantitative Approach," pp. 3-5.

87. See *Strengthening Democratic Institutions in Uruguay and Argentina* (Washington, D.C.: U.S. Agency for International Development, 1994): 5. Emphasis in the original.

88. *Diagnóstico sobre el órgano judicial en El Salvador* (San Salvador: ILANUD, 1987): anexo 4.

89. Rosenn, "The Protection of Judicial Independence in Latin America," p. 9.

90. José Maria Rico, *Independencia Judicial en América Latina: Replantamiento de un tema tradicional* (San José: Centro para la Administración de Justicia, 1990).

91. Mauro Cappelletti, "Who Watches the Watchmen? A Comparative Study on Judicial Responsibility," *American Journal of Comparative Law* 31 (Winter 1983): 17–19.

92. This is the only study of which I am aware that has taken this approach. See Pablo González Casanova, *La democracia en Mexico*, 6a. Ed. (Mexico: Ediciones Era, 1974): 33–37. This study was later criticized on methodological grounds, as the Mexican Supreme Court would generally honor habeas corpus requests in trivial cases but consistently failed to accept petitions in more politically sensitive cases—a fact that was concealed by Gonzalez Casanova's strictly quantitative approach.

93. Rosenn writes that "judicial independence is both too complex and too subtle a concept to be measured by such crude and misleading techniques as calculating the percentage of habeas corpus or *amparo* cases decided against the government." See Rosenn, "The Protection of Judicial Independence in Latin America," p. 12.

94. See John Hart Ely, *Democracy and Distrust: A Theory of Judicial Review* (Cambridge, Mass.: Harvard University Press, 1980): 48; and Buscaglia and Dakolias, *Judicial Reform in Latin America: Economic Efficiency vs. Institutional Inertia*, p. 43.

95. Rogelio Pérez Perdomo, "Justice in Times of Globalization: Challenges and Perspectives for Change in the Administration of Justice in Latin America," in *Justice and Development in Latin America and the Caribbean* (Washington, D.C.: InterAmerican Development Bank, 1993): 135. For example, he notes that Colombia is the most technologically advanced judiciary in Latin America—and also faces the largest backlog of cases.

96. One problem in Latin America—particularly in the smaller Central American countries—is that most courts do not maintain detailed judicial statistics that enable reformers to determine whether their measures are having success. This problem is discussed in chapter four with specific reference to El Salvador.

97. Earl Johnson, "Talking About Access: A Preliminary Typology of Possible Strategies," in *Access to Justice: A Worldwide Survey*, p. 363.

98. An indication of the volatility of public opinion polling comes, ironically enough, from polling data itself. Throughout the region, large percentages of the population demonstrate only minimal knowledge of what constitutes a democracy, what the rights of a citizen are in a democracy, and what role the courts ought to play. The lack of so-called "civic knowledge" is highlighted in *Latin Americans See Need for Civic Education* (Washington, D.C.: United States Information Agency, 1996): 1–3.

99. Frances Hagopian, "Democracy and Political Representation in Latin America in the 1990s: Pause, Reorganization, or Decline?" in *Fault Lines of Democracy in Post-Transition Latin America*, ed. Felipe Agüero and Jeffrey Stark (Miami: North-South Center Press, 1998): 101, 126.

El Salvador and the Dangers of Thinking Small

El Salvador is perhaps the clearest test case of the merits of a narrow approach to judicial reform. Amidst the context of an ongoing civil war, judicial reformers in the early 1980s began with what would have seemed like an ideal approach: a clear set of goals, coherent plans for how to achieve them, and an abundance of international financial and technical support for their efforts. Reformers sought two well-defined objectives: to increase the individual independence of judges hearing sensitive human rights cases and to overcome the chronic inefficiency of the courts. Similarly, their reform inputs to achieve these ends were explicitly laid out from the beginning: judicial protection units would ensure the physical safety of judges, a special investigative unit would be trained in state-of-the-art techniques that would strengthen the hands of judges investigating sensitive cases, a legal revisory panel led by an elite group of judicial officials would update and modernize El Salvador's antiquated legal codes, and a training program for judicial personnel would improve professionalism and efficiency. The logic was thought to be mutually reinforcing and would lead to clear outputs: judges protected from threats of violence and empowered with modern, scientific investigative techniques could end the impunity of the security forces and establish the courts as an independent branch of government, while the application of modern criminal codes would give increased prominence to legal rather than political considerations, gradually leading to greater independence for the judiciary as a whole. Reformers were not oblivious to the larger political context of an ongoing civil war—hence the explicit recognition of the need to protect judges from political violence—but believed that a successful judicial reform could actually overcome those constraints and help create the conditions that would lead to an end to the war itself, advancing the democratic process.

The case study of El Salvador raises several interesting practical and theoretical questions about a narrowly defined approach to judicial reform. At the most basic level, did the reforms result in more judicial independence and efficiency? Is it possible to enhance individual independence while sidestepping larger questions of structural independence? Can judicial personnel be relied on to take the lead in increasing judicial independence and efficiency? Is it possible to improve the image of the courts by isolating the variables of independence and efficiency and relegating to the back burner questions of access creation? When politically-defined reform goals are placed in the hands of recognized, apolitical experts, does it improve chances for success by giving the measures a stamp of neutrality in the eyes of politicians? Does widespread frustration with the courts logically lead the public to prioritize judicial reform as a primary concern? And finally, can a judicial branch reformed in this manner play a leading role in aiding the process of democratic consolidation?

Based on the results of El Salvador's judicial reform program, the answer to all of these questions is a fairly compelling "no." Despite more than $30 million in external assistance and foreign training from a host of foreign governments, the courts emerged neither more independent—violence against judges continued unabated—nor more efficient. The most well-intended reforms and the most academically rigorous debates were implemented awkwardly and ineffectively; others were unsound on their own merits or clearly insufficient in the context of a civil war. Some measures consistently encountered insurmountable political constraints—ranging from mild indifference in Congress to outright hostility from within the highest levels of the judiciary; the fact that access creation strategies were given almost no attention virtually assured public indifference even if the reforms had been successful. One candid (if belated) assessment from sponsors of this approach highlighted the degree to which the ultimate success of judicial reform hinged on larger political forces unrelated to narrow changes in the judiciary:

> The assumption from the beginning seemed to be that we were focusing on a discrete system, albeit one burdened with serious weakness. In fact, the judicial system in El Salvador, as anywhere else, does not operate in isolation; it is a reflection of the social and political structures and the values of the society in general, and of the distribution of power. What we were really seeking in El Salvador with a relatively modest judicial reform effort was a complete overhaul of Salvadoran social structures—reform of the military, redistribution of power, greater respect for the individual, a reduction in authoritarianism—which had lying behind them centuries of tradition.[1]

More meaningful judicial reform did not occur until the early 1990s when Salvadorans began addressing the larger question of structural independence, and then under very different—and more favorable—domestic conditions. The civil war had ended, and previously obstructionist political forces—the Marxist insurgents and the rightist National Republican Alliance (ARENA)—took an overriding interest in the reform process. For the first time, Salvadorans themselves were addressing judicial reform and focusing on structural flaws in the system. Political will preceded judicial reform and politics defined the parameters of it—not vice versa.

Despite the encouraging steps after 1991, the costs of negative synergy were abundantly clear. Public confidence in the courts had fallen so low that a real question became whether reformers had produced too little, too late. In a country where access creation strategies were never given top billing, it is not surprising that the public felt itself increasingly distant from the courts; public contempt for the discredited judiciary curiously coexisted alongside an apparent disinterest in reforming the courts at all—particularly in the face of more immediate political and economic concerns. Indeed, sometimes it mattered little what measures reformers put forward because the public had grown so disinterested in the reform process, so distant from the courts, and so willing to settle disputes through violent, extralegal means. Despite the harrowing experience of a civil war that claimed the lives of more than 70,000, polls in the late 1990s consistently revealed a growing tendency for Salvadorans to give up on the formal justice system, take law enforcement into their own hands, and tolerate—even encourage—vigilante justice. The failure to reform the legal system and to incorporate the average citizen's needs into the reform design had done what the worst effects of the civil war could not: it had made an increasing number of Salvadorans inured to violence, skeptical of the benefits of protecting civil liberties, and cynical about the merits of relying on the rule of law.

A JUDICIAL SYSTEM IN CRISIS AND DECAY

When junior military officers staged a coup against the high command in October 1979, observers were cautiously optimistic that El Salvador would begin making progress on a range of social and economic concerns that had come under increasing domestic and international criticism in recent years.[2] The new junta quickly announced plans to lay the conditions for a return to democracy, protect human rights, and dissolve political movements that had been linked with death squad activity.[3] They pledged to conduct an extensive land reform program that would address grossly uneven land tenure patterns and create a nation of independent farmers who, upon owning their own plot of land, would no longer seek deliverance through leftist ideologies, a process that would begin healing the deep social cleavages that had characterized politics for more than a century.[4]

The cautious optimism faded quickly. The agrarian reform program triggered the strong opposition of landowners and conservatives, and junior officers were unable to wrestle control of the government's security forces from senior hardliners within the armed forces. The entrance of internationally-respected Christian Democrat José Napoleón Duarte into the government in 1980 did little to improve the image of the junta; Duarte was essentially powerless as he watched the growth of an armed insurgency and mounting abuses by the security forces.[5] To the extent that Duarte or his caretaker successor had any agenda at all, their focus was almost exclusively on containing the rise of violence and invigorating the economy.[6]

In this climate, not surprisingly, El Salvador's judiciary was notable for its politicization and inefficiency. Foremost among the impediments to an independent judiciary was the March 1980 declaration of a state of emergency and the ensuing Decree Law 507 of December 1980, which destroyed any façade of judicial independence by suspending all guarantees of civil liberties and due process.[7] Military judges were empowered to conduct all investigations in secret and to base their rulings entirely on uncorroborated oral confessions, a practice that contributed to the rise of coerced confessions and reduced reliance on the presentation of physical evidence. Even when Duarte returned to the presidency in June 1984 as a democratically elected civilian, the legislature, controlled by opposition parties whose commitment to democracy was questionable at best, routinely extended the decrees over the President's objections, preventing the courts from serving as an independent arbiter of legal disputes.

Internal and external politicization of the courts was firmly institutionalized. The Constitution of 1950 gave judges a brief, three-year tenure subject to presidential renewal. Its successor, the Constitution of 1966, introduced five-year terms that coincided with presidential elections and in which appointments were subject to a simple congressional majority—a pro forma process for a Congress that served as a rubber stamp of the executive. This selection process was retained under the Constitution of 1983.[8] The Supreme Court, in turn, appointed all lower court judges and all 300 justices of the peace throughout the country and was empowered to remove any lower court judge or judicial branch worker for any reason.[9] The Supreme Court licensed all practicing attorneys and could bar them from practice at any time, an arrangement that made El Salvador's bar associations reluctant to speak out against the courts.[10]

Other forms of politicization were far more extreme. With the rise of unparalleled levels of violence in the early 1980s, which included frequent acts of violence against court officials that were intended to shock and warn the public, judicial officials faced constant threats to their individual independence. To cite only some prominent examples:

- In February 1980, Attorney General Mario Zamora was assassinated three days after Roberto D'Aubuisson, leader of the ultraconservative National Republican Alliance (ARENA) party, publicly charged that Zamora was a member of an unspecified but dangerous clandestine leftist group.[11]

- On 27 March 1980, the judge responsible for investigating the assassination of Archbishop Oscar Romero received death threats and left the country. Upon returning to the country several months later, the judge dropped the case, citing undisclosed personal reasons.[12]

- In October 1981, the Supreme Court building was bombed—presumably by Marxist insurgents—and the president of the Court was seriously injured.[13] Meanwhile, five family members of a judge investigating abuses by the security forces in 1981 were assassinated, with the victims' heads placed at his doorstep.[14]

Such violence created a chilling effect on virtually any case involving members of the security forces, as judges frequently resigned from sensitive cases and the government had difficulty finding replacements.[15] When judges began investigating the murder of four U.S. churchwomen killed by members of the security forces, the first two judges assigned to the case resigned—one of whom left the country—for unexplained reasons.[16] Violence against juries and prosecutors became commonplace, contributing to conviction rates as low as 10 percent in parts of the country.[17] Salvadoran court statistics in 1984 indicated that more than 230 cases failed to come to trial because of a lack of Salvadorans willing to serve as jurors.[18]

Under these circumstances, it is not surprising that the courts were chronically inefficient. The judiciary did not attract qualified applicants and did not receive the funds necessary to improve its own performance.[19] Meanwhile, the legal system was characterized by considerable bureaucratic overlap and inefficiency: record-keeping was non-existent in most rural courts, and the absence of reliable court statistics prevented rational, long-term planning.[20] Judges and support staff were in short supply, resulting in what former Minister of Justice René Hernández Valiente called the "paradoxical state of affairs in which judges are wasting time on strictly administrative tasks while mere employees are taking over their judicial functions."[21] The criminal code dated from military rule in the 1940s, while the civil code had been updated only once since it was drafted in the late 1870s.[22] In a concise summary, one foreign observer noted that the judiciary

> represented the quintessential Latin American justice system—politicized, corrupt, underfinanced, poorly organized, governed by archaic procedural and substantive laws and outdated managerial and administrative practices, and staffed by underpaid and undertrained personnel. Appointments at all levels of the system (particularly the Supreme Court and justices of the peace) were highly politicized but also ruled by the practice of using them, like the rest of the public sector, as a kind of public employment bureau.[23]

As a result of these combined factors, observers across the spectrum shared a view that the judiciary was in profound crisis.[24] A team of researchers from one U.S. NGO returned from San Salvador to describe the judicial system as "close to paralysis" and "dangerously close to collapse."[25] Another group reported a "complete breakdown of the rule of law in El Salvador," while yet another organization remarked that "the criminal justice system in El Salvador is in a state of collapse":

> The collapse of El Salvador's criminal justice system is general and pervasive. Indeed, as best as we can tell, the system has never functioned effectively in the criminal justice field. The civil war in which the nation has been engulfed since 1980 has exacerbated and revealed the inadequacy of El Salvador's legal system, but even if the war were to end tomorrow, major changes would be required in Salvadoran society to create a modern criminal justice system and to permit the system to function fairly and effectively.[26]

DEFINING THE REFORM INPUTS: A NARROW APPROACH TO INDEPENDENCE AND EFFICIENCY

When Duarte assumed office on 1 June 1984, he faced a series of daunting challenges: ending a war that had taken over 20,000 lives, staving off repeated encroachments into civilian authority by the military high command, and reinvigorating an economy in which nearly 50 percent of the national budget went to finance war efforts and whose GDP has declined 23 percent in real terms since 1979.[27] Coupled with the fact that Duarte's PDC had a legislative minority and intransigent adversaries on the left and right, judicial reform was not a top priority, neither for the public nor the president.[28] In fact, most of Duarte's policy pronouncements during 1984–85 were deliberately vague; a frequent criticism was not that Duarte had bad priorities but rather no priorities at all.[29] When Duarte periodically would turn to judicial matters, his record was decidedly mixed. Faced with the opportunity to name a new Supreme Court president in 1984, Duarte bypassed respected jurists and tapped defeated 1984 presidential candidate José Francisco Guerrero, a career politician with few legal credentials, in an effort to curry favor with moderate rightist parties.[30]

The Duarte administration reluctantly took several steps toward judicial reform less than six weeks in office.[31] Most available evidence indicates that Duarte initiated these measures not because they were a high priority for him—he gives no mention to judicial reform in his autobiography, for example—but because he was under considerable pressure from the international community, which conditioned urgently-needed international assistance on progress on human rights.[32] The U.S. government was especially insistent on judicial reforms for at least two reasons. First and most broadly, senior U.S. officials believed that the conditions for a viable democracy capable of resisting Cuban aggression could not be met entirely by military assistance and required a series of structural economic and political changes—including reforms in the administration of justice.[33] Second and more immediately, administration officials needed to justify to the U.S. Congress the extensive foreign assistance programs to El Salvador—more than $300 million annually in the early 1980s—by being able to point to progress in El Salvador's performance on high-profile cases involving the murders of U.S. citizens.[34] Because the Salvadoran Congress was controlled by opposition parties, most reform efforts were confined to measures that Duarte could enact by executive decree—a politically convenient strategy in the early 1980s, but one that would become a liability by the 1990s.

El Salvador's reforms were narrowly focused from the outset. The judicial reform program had two main goals: enhancing the individual independence of specific judges who were trying high-profile human rights cases, and increasing the technical and investigative capabilities of the criminal court system.[35] More sweeping measures that would tackle the structural independence of the courts or increase access of ordinary citizens were relegated to the back burner, with an implicit assumption that more independent-minded judges would somehow emerge from the process and serve as a catalyst to undertake broader reforms across other aspects of the judiciary.[36]

The means to achieve the desired outputs also were clearly defined. They included (1) a judicial protection unit (JPU) that would provide physical protection to judges hearing controversial cases, (2) a special investigative unit (SIU) to aid judges in directing investigations and a forensic unit (FU) that would enhance the government's ability to pursue sensitive cases with a greater degree of professionalism and efficiency, (3) a legal revisory panel that would update the country's civil and criminal codes, and (4) an administrative and training program that would modernize the institutional capabilities of the judiciary. The logic was mutually reinforcing. Judicial protection units would help foster independence on the bench so that judges—empowered with state-of-the-art investigative techniques, modern training, and up-to-date codes—could hold both government and civil society accountable for their abuses. Similarly, a greater emphasis on rules of evidence and modern criminal codes would give increased prominence to technical and legal considerations rather than political concerns, strengthening efforts to boost independence. Each aspect involved considerable planning.

Judicial Protection Units

JPUs were the government's most direct attempt to address the politicization that had compromised the independence of judges. They were envisioned as eventually forming a professional cadre that would include a witness protection program, witness relocation, and protection for jurors deliberating on sensitive cases.[37] The administration formed a sixty-man force and first deployed it in the 1985 trial involving the 1981 murder of four U.S. church workers and again in February 1986 in a case involving the assassination of two U.S. land reform consultants.[38]

Special Investigative Units and the Forensic Laboratory

The Duarte administration created the Commission on Investigations (COI) to professionalize the evidence-gathering and investigative capabilities of the criminal justice system.[39] The need for reform was apparent enough. Under Salvadoran law, physical evidence could be submitted only if it met two onerous conditions: its collection must have been ordered by a judge, and it must have been gathered and presented by an "auxiliary agent," defined by the criminal code to include only the armed forces, the Treasury Police, the National Guard, and the National Police.[40] The flaws in the system were clear. A judge investigating criminal activity involving members of the security forces relied entirely on evidence gathered by members of the same forces he was investigating, an arrangement that contributed to the general impunity of the armed forces. The SIU and the FU were created to address these needs. The SIU and FU initially included twenty-four investigators and four civilian attorneys; an additional twenty-four technicians and eight scientists were later detailed to the forensic lab.

The Legal Advisory Committee (CORELESAL)

The decision to form CORELESAL reflected a widespread recognition that the country's outdated criminal and civil codes caused lengthy pretrial delays.[41] The governing body of CORELESAL included a ten-member body with representatives distributed among members of the Ministry of Justice, Ministry of Defense, Public Ministry, law faculties, and the major bar associations.[42] Drafts of CORELESAL studies were to be vetted internally and distributed among academics and legal experts to solicit substantive recommendations—a government effort to broaden participation in what was otherwise viewed as a U.S.-directed project.[43]

The Administrative and Training Program

The final project component focused on improving the professional quality of court personnel by offering training and disseminating literature to improve case management. El Salvador did not have a career judicial system, and most courts were staffed by judges who served on a part-time basis and devoted half their day to private law practices. Meanwhile, courts had only the most rudimentary physical infrastructures, often lacking roofs, electricity, and safes to store court documents. Even in San Salvador there was no formal system of record keeping or case tracking.[44] A more technically proficient judiciary was thought to be more impartial; project auditors explicitly noted that "a better-educated judiciary will hopefully result in rulings that more closely adhere to the law."[45]

THE LIMITS OF A NARROW APPROACH TO JUDICIAL REFORM

By the early 1990s when the first phase of El Salvador's judicial reform efforts was drawing to a close, it was difficult to make the case that any project components had achieved significant success. Despite occasional pockets of progress, no project component met the reformers' goals: judges were not more independent, and the courts were not more efficient. Reformers failed to address the larger question of structural independence and did not tackle the political forces that pressured the institution of the judiciary, conditions that made individual independence meaningless and efficiency-creating measures extremely difficult.

The Judicial Protection Unit

The JPU, the government's main vehicle for bolstering individual independence, may have been one of the least successful components and eventually was phased out by late 1987 amidst acknowledgments that the program had failed. To be sure, the program met its most immediate, narrowly-defined objective—protecting the physical safety of two judges investigating murders of U.S. citizens—but never fulfilled its goal of providing greater security or enhancing independence for judicial personnel throughout the country.[46] The problems were both technical and political.

The initial problem for the JPU, which reformers had not anticipated, was determining who would compose the new unit. There was widespread recognition that the mission of protecting judges could not be entrusted to members of the security forces, and in an environment in which Duarte was in an uphill battle trying to convince extremists on the left and the right to lay down their arms, there was a general uneasiness about creating a new, armed force with no clear chain of command and a nebulously defined mandate.[47] The compromise solution was to staff the JPU with prison guards, an approach that satisfied no one. Prison guards in El Salvador were poorly trained and poorly educated; many had received dishonorable discharges from the armed forces or had criminal records because of past human rights abuses.[48] Duarte was caught in a dilemma. He could not rely on poorly trained prison guards, but any effort to establish a more professional force would require the luxury of time, which the administration did not have.[49] Meanwhile, it was becoming increasingly obvious that the JPUs could not be expanded rapidly enough to halt the climate of violence against juries or public prosecutors because of broader economic constraints. Attorney General Roberto García Alvarado dismissed the idea as impractical for El Salvador, noting simply, "That takes money—and this country is bankrupt."[50]

More broadly, these efforts—even if they had been effectively implemented—were virtually doomed to failure because reformers did not address the broader forms of politicization that compromised judicial independence. Throughout this period, internal politicization—which reformers did not address—remained a constant threat; the Supreme Court was hostile to human rights investigations against the security forces and served as a brake on any judge handling sensitive cases. In several instances, the Supreme Court president personally intervened in the investigations conducted by lower courts to steer police away from evidence pointing to the involvement of the military high command. In one case, when a judge indicted a member of the National Guard in 1985—an historic first initially lauded by the international community—the Supreme Court reversed the decision, citing alleged technical errors. The Supreme Court President then transferred the lower court judge to Chalatenango Province, a remote area controlled by leftist insurgents that required the judge to take a four-hour, round-trip commute each day.[51]

The lack of faith in the rule of law by both the Right and Left also highlighted the degree to which reforms that tinkered with particular aspects of the judiciary were simply irrelevant. Despite the creation of the JPUs, intimidation of judges and court officials persisted, particularly once the insurgents began targeting the courts. The number of reported threats made against judges and lawyers during the period from 1985–89 was generally similar to levels under military rule between 1979 and 1984, according to available estimates.[52] Among the prominent examples:

- Seven justices of the peace resigned under death threats from the FMLN in 1987 and another seven resigned in 1989 under similar circumstances. Twelve other justices resigned in 1987–88, citing threats made against them.[53]

- Judge Miriam Arteaga was the victim of two assassination attempts during her 1986–87 investigation of a kidnapping-for-profit ring that involved members of prominent families and elements in the security forces; she resigned from the bench in 1987. Judge Jorge Alberto Serrano, who assumed a portion of the case, was killed in 1988 while investigating the allegations.[54] Another judge declared that he would resign if the Supreme Court handed him Serrano's case.[55]

- In July 1987, Judge Antonio Romero Barrios summoned two witnesses to hear testimony involving alleged crimes committed by the Arce Battalion. Within days, the Arce Battalion moved into the area, and a lawyer representing the Battalion visited the judge to convince him of the need to drop the investigation—while members of the security forces tampered with court evidence at the scene of the murders.[56]

- In April 1989, FMLN insurgents murdered Attorney General José Roberto García Alvarado because of his membership in the conservative ARENA party. In November of that year, FMLN rebels also assassinated Francisco José Guerrero, a former president of the Supreme Court, for similar reasons.[57]

The SIU and the FU

None of the efficiency-creating measures appear to have had a significant effect. Again, the causes were twofold: inadequacies in the project design itself, and the larger structural politicization that ensured the security forces retained a vested interest in blocking the courts from becoming more efficient.

To be sure, the SIU and the FU acquired considerable expertise during phase one of the program. Members were trained in areas ranging from fingerprinting to firearm identification, polygraphy, photography, and toxicology, and outside visitors noted that some officials were relatively professional.[58] By the late 1980s, independent observers reported that the SIU and FU enjoyed relatively professional images and were training other Salvadorans in their newly acquired skills.[59] One measure of their success, according to program designers, was whether there was an increased willingness of other judges and prosecutors to call on the SIU and FU for evidence gathering and analysis, on the logic that an increase in requests would reflect growing confidence in the technical capabilities of the SIU and FU. The SIU started slowly but took more cases over time.[60]

Despite the gradual increase in their caseloads, the SIU and FU were far from efficient, first-rate criminal investigating units.[61] The SIU established a poor record on the most significant high-profile human rights cases it was charged with investigating. Its work did not lead to a conviction in any of the six human rights cases on which Duarte had pledged action upon taking office in 1984, for example, and by the end of his administration less than one third of the SIU's caseload was classified as human rights cases; the overwhelming majority were common crimes that could have been handled by the national police.[62] Observers also speculated that several of the political reforms passed during civil war inadvertently discouraged SIU and FU officials from more thorough performances. A case in point was a bill passed in 1987 that granted an amnesty to all "political crimes" but which allowed each judge to determine whether the specific case constituted a "political" crime. The result was a disincentive to rigorously pursue sensitive investigations given the possibility that a judge would dismiss the case as constituting a political rather than a criminal act.[63]

More serious were the daunting political constraints that shaped the new institutions. Many of the failures of the SIU and the FU can be traced back to Article 11 of the criminal code, which allowed evidence to be presented in court only if it had been collected by an "auxiliary agent" such as the security forces. Neither the SIU nor the FU enjoyed "auxiliary agent" status. Rather than risking political capital by pushing bills that would change the legal status of those organizations, reformers inexplicably decided to staff the SIU and the FU with active duty members of the armed forces, a move that ostensibly had two benefits. It ensured that any investigative work ordered by a judge could be introduced in court, and it provided senior officials in the SIU and FU with a cadre of workers who had at least some prior experience in anticrime efforts. As a result, both institutions were managed by an executive director and deputy director who were active duty colonels, with most of the investigators and technicians coming from the enlisted ranks and remaining responsible to the military chain of command.

The reliance on members of the security forces caused both narrow, tactical problems as well as broader, more fundamental problems for the SIU. First, investigators assigned to the SIU and FU were placed there on rotation; they remained on active duty and could be recalled to active service at any time, and hence did not even approach a career track job path.[64] Second, the revolving door of military personnel entering the SIU and FU and returning to active duty undercut its ability to be seen as an independent investigative arm for judges.[65] The logic was circuitous and the result was ironic. The SIU and the FU had been formed because judges could not rely on the security forces, and yet both institutions rapidly emerged as extensions of those same institutions the reformers had sought to circumvent. Despite pockets of individual competence, the SIU and the FU were as structurally politicized as the organizations that preceded them, a view confirmed in 1993 when the United Nations released a report detailing routine political interference in internal SIU affairs.[66] Again, political considerations—such as Duarte's reliance on the military—stymied what officials had anticipated to be a relatively easy reform.

CORELESAL

By all accounts, the logic behind CORELESAL was sound. El Salvador clearly needed criminal and civil codes that were consistent with a democratic regime, and much of the 1983 Constitution did not have the ordinary legislation needed to implement it. The manner in which CORELESAL moved forward with its proposals won initial praise. Its proposals were vetted by a group of 216 lawyers from the private sector and distributed for public debate among universities and think tanks. CORELESAL even began a serial publication intended to solicit reactions and to prevent charges that the organization was "made in the USA"; it held public forums to increase awareness of its efforts, and CORELESAL members traveled to rural villages to avoid concentrating excessively on the capital city.[67] External consultants reported that the organization initially had "gained institutional respect" within the legal community and that it had attracted a "high quality of commission members."[68]

Despite these positive first steps, three factors intervened to upset the plans of reformers: the lack of headway on structural independence measures that undercut CORELESAL's efficiency efforts, the lack of congressional support for CORELESAL's efforts, and poor project implementation. Reformers were caught in a vicious cycle that highlighted the interplay between political and technical considerations: the lack of political support to tackle larger reforms left it no option other than to focus on frankly marginal reforms—while the persistent focus on mundane issues assured that the body would never develop greater institutional credibility among political circles.

First, the failure to create a more independent and accountable High Court ultimately undermined efficiency-creating measures, because CORELESAL never emerged as an organization independent of the politicized Supreme Court. Half of the members of CORELESAL were justices on the Supreme Court, and the other half were lawyers licensed by the High Court. This arrangement, according to Argentine jurist Marcello Sancinetti, produced a chilling effect on the willingness of CORELESAL to criticize the behavior of the High Court, as the Supreme Court "seemed to be exercising excessive influence over the work of CORELESAL and distorting the outcome of the work to support its own political purposes."[69] Other foreign observers concurred.[70]

Second, CORELESAL failed to take steps to cultivate support in Congress, which virtually doomed its proposals to inaction. Duarte created CORELESAL by executive decree to keep the body aloof from political forces, but many recommendations of CORELESAL required congressional approval. Implementing the judicial reforms immediately became harder than conceptualizing them. One proposal, based on a two-volume, 819-page study that took nearly two years to draft, called for a major revamping of decree laws, restoring a range of functions to the civilian courts, and strengthening provisions for legal counsel for the detained. The bill, drafted without consulting the leading parties and apparently indifferent to the predictable opposition of the security forces, was gutted by rightist parties in Congress.[71] Another proposal defined the conditions for a National Judicial Council called for in the 1983 Constitution; the bill languished for five years in a Congress anxious to deny Duarte even the smallest legislative victory, and because of outspoken opposition from the Supreme Court, which announced that it would invalidate the law if passed by the legislature.[72] Despite periodic (but not especially energetic) lobbying by CORELESAL's director, the organization never made a sustained effort to help forge a political consensus on judicial reform among the political class.[73]

Third, with no real support from Congress and outright opposition from the High Court, CORELESAL was left to focus on issues that it could affect, and invariably they tended to be minor. During its first five years, CORELESAL conducted various theoretical studies—such as philosophical inquiries into the meaning of justice—and did not focus on more pressing legal reforms.[74] From 1985 to 1989, CORELESAL proposed eleven specific pieces of legislation, only three of which were implemented by 1990.[75] The criticisms of all of these reform proposals was identical: they failed to address the fundamental mandate with which CORELESAL had been charged. One CORELESAL proposal defined the criteria for a "small farmer" so that the government could move ahead with its agrarian reform program—an important social and economic issue, but one that could have been handled by other ministries and that was not critical to the efficient operation of the judiciary. Another proposal sought to modify the use of surnames to allow divorced women to use their maiden names, while another proposal called for the creation of a new adoption code and a national registry of infant names.[76] Assessing the achievements of CORELESAL, a study by the U.S. Government Accounting Office modestly noted that CORELESAL "has been criticized by some groups for its selection of laws to review."[77]

During this period, CORELESAL lost its reformist zeal and became yet another unaccountable bureaucracy. The rigorous internal debate, which had been a strong point in CORELESAL's early years, became stifled by pressures from above and gave way to a more inward-looking mindset that scaled back public debates; critics charged that CORELESAL members "became isolated and not open to outside suggestions."[78] Members were increasingly criticized for arriving late for work, producing fewer and fewer studies, and no longer soliciting outside or divergent views. Argentine jurist Marcello Sancinetti, upon examining the achievements of CORELESAL, remarked that CORELESAL seemed to lose "ownership" of its own proposals and came to view politics as beneath it, appearing "aloof and uninterested in the fate or the future of its efforts once they had been produced."[79] Distance from politics was thought to be a virtue in 1983. By 1990, it was recognized as a serious liability. In 1991, the United States—faced with CORELESAL's unimpressive track record—stopped funding the organization.[80]

Administration and Training Program

The judicial reform project included extensive efforts to increase the administrative efficiency of the courts, although the lack of reliable court statistics—itself a reflection of the success of the reform efforts—makes it difficult to determine the success of the programs. Relying on more than $4 million of U.S. assistance to supplement matching domestic funds, the Duarte administration and AID provided training for some 653 judicial personnel from 1984 to 1989. All 300 justices of the peace received a three-day training course in case resolution and court procedures, and fifty of them traveled to the United States for training on the roles of justices of the peace in civil law systems.[81] AID distributed copies of the criminal code (which many judges lacked) and compilations of major decisions of the Supreme Court to lower court judges, and established various law libraries, considered important first steps in the effort to introduce more predictable jurisprudence.[82] Finally, court officials created an administrative unit that assumed routine functions—such as budget preparations and preparation of time and attendance sheets—from judges, allowing them an extra hour each day to devote to their cases.[83]

These reforms appear to have had little effect, however.[84] The inability to achieve greater progress is the result of two factors: unanticipated external forces unrelated to the program, and the specific attributes of the reform program itself. First, a major earthquake in 1986 destroyed the Supreme Court and its Judicial Center in San Salvador. Because most of the incipient case management and case tracking experiments were conducted in those buildings, numerous records compiled over the previous eighteen months were lost in the damage. It is thus not possible to assess the initial progress (or lack thereof) in the first year or so, although the quake is a harsh reminder of the degree to which the judicial system cannot be isolated from unanticipated external forces.

More fundamentally, the courts made only token efforts to develop a statistical survey of the judiciary that would provide a better gauge of whether the reforms were successful. Reports from visiting international delegations indicated neither tangible improvements in efficiency nor the foundations for future progress; they consistently noted the persistence of a bewildering and redundant bureaucracy, coupled with the continued application of outdated technologies, throughout the legal system.[85] A comprehensive study by the General Accounting Office of the U.S. government in 1990 was also harsh, noting that the judiciary had failed to make significant headway in the past five years:

> [T]he judicial system in El Salvador is politicized, inefficient, corrupt, antiquated, and underfinanced, and does not deliver impartial justice to anyone—the poor, the wealthy, the political left or right, or the military. Even in times of relative peace, systematic and political problems impede it from dealing with the most routine civil or criminal matters such as family fights or thefts. . . . There is no evidence that El Salvador's judicial system has been functioning effectively. Political interference, a legacy of military control, overemphasis on paperwork and bureaucratic procedures, inadequate forensic and investigative capabilities, widespread corruption and intimidation of judges, and insufficient staff and resources have contributed to its inadequacy.[86]

Precise statistical information that would validate (or contradict) such broad conclusions was scarce. Because there was no record of how long cases had been pending, it was not possible to compare times to disposition and whether trial delays were increasing over time. By 1989, the most detailed information compiled by the Supreme Court offered only such basic figures as the total number of cases entering the system and the total number of prison detainees awaiting sentencing. Although both of these statistics allow for indirect inferences about trial delays, there is no record of how long cases had been in the system and whether the courts were conducting their affairs in a more timely fashion.[87] Indeed, the only effort to develop a comprehensive assessment of the courts' work load was conducted in 1987 by Florida International University, and the single data point does not allow for long-term comparisons. Even when court statistics were collected, there remained some question about their reliability. According to one study

> [S]taff in the courts and members of the Supreme Court comment that the statistical information from the courts is not reliable. The explanation given for the poor quality of the judicial statistics is that it is a manual system compiled from various sources. In fact, these statistics are ineffective because there are no manuals or other instructions to guide the gathering and reporting of the statistics. Furthermore, the task of keeping and preparing the statistical forms is relegated to the lowest and least capable employee. There is also a tendency to alter the statistical reporting to make it appear as though it has a greater volume of work than it actually has, and often, the task of preparing the

statistical form is left as a very low priority chore. This and foregoing conditions make the statistics definitely very unreliable.[88]

As a result, progress is difficult to measure, although available statistics—themselves of questionable reliability—point to only the most modest advances. Several pilot courts in El Salvador showed an increased ability to dispose of cases.[89] The successes of these pilot courts failed to have a significant impact on the broader judicial system, however, and by 1990 the courts were not more efficient than in 1984. In 1984, 82 percent of all prison detainees were awaiting a trial date; in 1989, that figure was at 80 percent but by 1993 had risen to 89 percent, an indirect gauge of pretrial delays. During that time, the total number of detainees awaiting sentencing rose approximately 20 percent, and nearly half of all detainees had served more time than they would have if convicted for the accused crime.[90] Similarly, only 8 percent of all cases that entered the judicial system in 1984 were resolved in their first year; by the early 1990s that figure remained fairly constant at 10 percent.[91] In 1986, judges were unable to complete the investigative phase within the legally required 90–120 day period in 53 percent of all cases; by 1991 that figure was 55 percent. In 1986, the criminal justice system faced a backlog of 37,500 cases; by 1990 that number had grown to nearly 80,000, with more cases entering the system annually than the courts were able to dispose of.[92] Various reform measures clearly had failed to produce greater efficiency.

PHASE TWO: A SECOND LOOK AT INDEPENDENCE

June 1989 was critical both for El Salvador and, ultimately, for its judicial reform efforts. Two days after taking office, President Alfredo Cristiani offered to begin peace talks with the FMLN rebels. Cristiani's overtures were not the result of successful administration of justice reforms that had brought the Left and Right under the rule of law. Rather, they reflected his own pragmatic recognition that the Right did not have the overwhelming domestic support necessary to end the civil war;[93] his advisers apparently understood that, in the rapidly changing international environment, the days of generous foreign assistance were over.[94] This logic also applied to the FMLN, which saw its prime external benefactors sink deeper into political and economic crises in the late 1980s.[95] Thus began an arduous, three-year process characterized by repeated negotiations, breakthroughs, and stalemates that frequently verged on collapse; talks limped along only with prodding from Colombia, Costa Rica, Mexico, the United Nations, the United States, and Venezuela.[96] On 16 January 1992, the FMLN and the government signed the historic Chapultepec Accords in Mexico, which declared a formal end to the twelve-year civil war. The contrast with the 1980s was dramatic: for the first time, groups previously hostile to discussing judicial reform were willing to tackle it—and under the broader context of peace talks to end the war.

Although the main focus of the Peace Accords was understandably on reforming the armed forces and security apparatus and demobilizing the guerrillas, judicial reform garnered considerable attention. FMLN negotiators and ARENA moderates focused on ensuring a larger degree of structural, institutional independence, particularly in altering how the courts selected judges; one of the key demands in the Spring 1991 talks was that the government would commit to devising new methods of appointing Supreme Court justices.[97] Judicial reformers—this time debating proposals openly and in the political realm—settled on a handful of measures: (1) creating a National Judicial Council, (2) revamping the selection process, (3) curtailing the disciplinary powers of the Supreme Court, (4) enhancing budgetary independence, and (5) depoliticizing the SIU and the FU.[98] Even though the results of the more recent Phase Two reforms are more difficult to measure, the process that produced the reforms are far more encouraging than the experiences of the 1980s. It is worth looking at how each goal survived the back-and-forth of legislative maneuvering, a process in which neither party gained all of its objectives but which nonetheless forced them to assume some ownership of the reforms.

The National Judicial Council (CNJ)

The CNJ, created in 1991, had been intended to foster the development of a more professional judiciary by establishing rigorous entrance requirements and offering post-entry training, but was accused of being an appendage of the Supreme Court: half of its membership was comprised of Supreme Court justices and the other members were practicing attorneys selected and licensed by the same Supreme Court.[99]

In 1992, Congress considered another measure aimed at creating a more independent CNJ. The constitutional changes passed in December 1992 fell short of their goal but—reflecting the overlap of politics with judicial reform—represented "what was politically possible" at the time, given the deep splits within Congress, according to Margaret Popkin.[100] Under the proposals, CNJ slots would be distributed among two lawyers nominated by the Supreme Court, lower court judges selected based on seniority, three lawyers chosen by bar associations, three law professors, and a member of the public ministry. The Supreme Court retained the right to discipline most members of the Council, could recommend any judge for removal at any time for unspecified "just cause," maintained the right to develop and administer the budget of the CNJ, and could unilaterally submit amendments to the CNJ budget directly to Congress.[101] Reform proponents were encouraged by the fact that CNJ appointees would be subject to legislative approval and removal by a two-thirds majority (rather than a simple majority), and expressed optimism that the balanced composition of the CNJ would ensure that the body exercised its powers with more professionalism.[102]

A Revamped Selection Process

One of the critical constitutional reforms that emerged during the peace negotiations focused on altering the structural independence of the courts—an issue that had received virtually no attention during the 1980s. Chief among those was a radically different method for selecting Supreme Court judges. Constitutional reforms passed in April 1991 abolished the practice of selecting Supreme Court justices by a simple legislative majority every five years. Under the new arrangement, all Supreme Court justices henceforth would be appointed to nine-year terms—an extended mandate intended to insulate the judges from partisan pressures but limiting the tenure enough to allow for some degree of accountability. Selections were staggered on three-year intervals to ensure that no president could appoint an entire court. In addition, congressional approval was made subject to a two-thirds majority; officials noted that henceforth it would be harder for any single party to dominate the selection process and that, in El Salvador's multiparty assembly, some bargaining and compromise would be both inevitable and healthy—and would obligate parties to present more qualified jurists rather than partisan hacks.[103] Cristiani and FMLN negotiators also took steps to blend technical and political considerations in the selection process. Under previous constitutions, the unicameral legislature approved a presidential nominee by a simple majority. Under the new constitutional reforms, the revamped National Judicial Council would prepare lists of candidates for nomination for half the seats on the Supreme Court and to appellate courts. The Federation of the Association of Lawyers, which represented eight separate bar associations, would propose the other half of the list.[104]

Internal Independence

Reformers failed to radically scale back the influence and powers of the High Court. Despite a tentative agreement between the government and the FMLN to remove from the High Court the power to select lower court judges, the legislative assembly failed to follow through, arguing—with the strong support of Supreme Court President Gutierrez Castro—that government-rebel peace talks were political rather than legal acts and hence not binding on the Congress. As a result, the Supreme Court retained the right to appoint justices of the peace and to administer the lower courts' budgetary and administrative affairs.[105] The Peace Accords produced the creation of a judicial training school—part of an effort to develop a judicial career that would eventually include post-entry training—although the school is administered by the Supreme Court.[106] Responding to intense lobbying from the judiciary, the legislature allowed the High Court to retain disciplinary control over judges and justices of the peace, and to license all attorneys.

Budgetary Independence

El Salvador had only mixed success in its efforts to guarantee institutional independence by securing a fixed budgetary allotment, showing clear signs of progress but stopping short of the reformers' goals. The legislative assembly passed an amendment setting aside 6 percent of the annual budget for the judicial branch, a measure that even critics of the judicial reform process praised.[107] By 1997, neither Cristiani nor his successor, President Armando Calderón Sol, had come close to fulfilling this constitutional obligation, although progress was apparent. The Cristiani administration slowly increased funding for the judicial branch from 1.6 percent of the annual budget in 1989 to 2.8 percent in 1993, while Calderón Sol increased the judiciary's budget to 4.7 percent in 1997—the highest percentage at any point since the republic began keeping statistics on annual budget allotments by ministry.[108]

Depoliticizing the SIU and FU

Reformers also sought to find a new home for the politicized SIU and the FU. Indeed, the Truth Commission even called for dismantling the SIU on the grounds that the politicization had made it an unsalvageable institution and that it had "been perceived in some quarters as one of the causes, by reasons of its lack of results at least, of the impunity with which violations of human rights have been committed."[109] The Truth Commission gave ample and shocking evidence to support those accusations.[110]

Cristiani took a number of steps aimed at salvaging the organizations. In October 1992, the administration moved the SIU and the FU away from the Ministry of Defense and placed it under the civilian oversight of the Office of the Attorney General. The solution was short-lived: constitutional amendments passed in 1991–92 had specified that the Civilian National Police (PNC) would be the only civilian investigatory force in the country, leaving the SIU in a legally dubious status. The administration was reluctantly forced to transfer the SIU to the PNC to ensure full civilian oversight.[111] To enhance the independence of the SIU and the FU and to distance them from the armed forces the administration relocated the physical offices of the SIU and the FU off military compounds and into a civilian, residential middle-class neighborhood.[112]

The result of the post-1989 reforms have produced some clear outputs that signify the beginnings of a more independent and accountable judiciary. On balance, the reforms of the 1990s have shown signs of progress. El Salvador's experience with the less politicized judicial selection process was at least more transparent and participatory than in the past.[113] Despite initial rough spots, the final results were encouraging. The first Supreme Court selected under these methods included several respected jurists, a human rights attorney and a dean of the University of Central America's law faculty, two women (a first for El Salvador), a labor lawyer, and a Supreme Court president with a record of defending human rights and with no party identification.[114] Even critics noted that the new Supreme Court was "more professional, politically independent and pluralistic than its predecessor."[115] Jack Spence, an initial skeptic of the process, conceded that "by all accounts the make-up of the court is far more professional than its predecessor."[116]

Because reformers had failed to scale back the powers of the Supreme Court, the more reform-minded High Court was able to take several steps intended to convince the public that it intended to conduct its affairs in an accountable manner. New Supreme Court President José Domingo Mendez announced that he would begin efforts to eliminate judicial corruption—an acknowledgment that would have been unthinkable under the Supreme Court of Gutierrez Castro—and within 90 days began removing judges that the Truth Commission had singled out for corrupt activities. By August 1995 the Supreme Court had followed through on the Truth Commission's recommendation to remove a dozen corrupt judges, launched investigations of 250 more, and strengthened an internal investigative unit of the Supreme Court to look into charges of malfeasance on the bench—measures that were applauded by legislators ranging from ARENA to the FMLN. The Court also began releasing to the public the reasons for the dismissals and disciplinary steps, another historic first for the country.[117]

During this period, the courts issued several rulings that have shown an emerging—if halting—ability of the courts to hold accountable other government branches. To cite several examples, in late 1990 a Salvadoran judge ruled that enough evidence existed to bring to trial ten members of the armed forces for their role in the 1989 murder of Jesuits at the University of Central America; in 1991 a criminal court convicted two active duty officers, the highest ranking military officials ever sentenced in El Salvador. The appearance of momentum was halted a year later, however, when a criminal appeals court judge amnestied the two officers, citing the Truth Commission's recommendation that it made little sense to jail junior-level officers if they were merely scapegoats for more senior officials.[118] Meanwhile, civil and criminal courts since 1990 also have issued verdicts against influential political actors such as business groups and suspected paramilitary organizations, achievements that, however modest, would have been unthinkable during the 1980s.[119]

FINAL THOUGHTS ON THE SALVADORAN EXPERIENCE

Several conclusions stand out about the Salvadoran judicial reform experience, both for the reform program itself and the broader implications for democratic consolidation. At the most basic level, the reforms of the 1980s, judged by their own technical criteria, failed to produce greater individual independence and efficiency. At every step of the reform process, most measures either ran up against insurmountable political resistance or were undermined by negative synergy. It is clear with the advantage of hindsight what should have been obvious at the time: reformers were tinkering at the margins when more fundamental reforms were needed, and a handful of individual judges could hardly have been expected to serve as a catalyst for bridging deep societal fissures when the survival of the state was in doubt. The broader external conditions were so fundamentally unfavorable that reforms were impossible, and staving off complete collapse of the judiciary was a more realistic objective. Former U.S. Ambassador Edwin Corr noted that in the context of a civil war, even holding the line against further deterioration was a dramatic success. Asked to assess the judicial reform program's successes, Corr replied, "On a scale of 10, even if it's a two, it's worthwhile."[120]

In such circumstances, any reform program conceptualized on such narrow grounds—even if generously funded by foreign capitals and designed by knowledgeable experts—was virtually doomed to failure. The collapse of the courts was not the cause of social breakdown; it was a result. One especially frank assessment is worth quoting at length because it reflects the degree to which initial judicial reforms, however modest, misdiagnosed the fundamental nature of judicial breakdown in El Salvador:

> The assumption from the beginning seemed to be that we were focusing on a discrete system, albeit one burdened with serious weakness. In fact, the judicial system in El Salvador, as anywhere else, does not operate in isolation; it is a reflection of the social and political structures and the values of the society in general, and of the distribution of power. What we were really seeking in El Salvador with a relatively modest judicial reform effort was a complete overhaul of Salvadoran social structures—reform of the military, redistribution of power, greater respect for the individual, a reduction in authoritarianism—which had lying behind them centuries of tradition. Nowhere was this more obvious than in the human rights cases which were considered by most to be the measure of success or failure of the judicial reform program. Successful prosecution of human rights abuses could be supported by reforms to the judicial system, but ultimately they depended on reforms in other camps as well.[121]

Reformers were thus asking the wrong questions about the wrong variables and ultimately saw their efforts undermined in part by negative synergy. The emphasis on individual independence—particularly at the expense of completely ignoring structural independence—is confounding. Even assuming that the ill-fated JPUs had been able to protect the safety of individual judges hearing sensitive cases, judges still would have confronted larger, structural challenges to their independence—such as a hostile Supreme Court that reserved the right to transfer judges or their caseload—that almost certainly would have hamstrung their efforts. To ask what more could have been done to buttress the JPUs is to ask the wrong question. The real question is whether those measures would have mattered in any event. To that end, the reforms of the 1991–92 time period are the most encouraging signal in El Salvador's entire judicial reform process, for at least two reasons. First, reformers finally began focusing on the broader issue of structural independence and seeking to ensure that the courts were no longer an appendage of the Supreme Court or the executive. Second, the reformers were Salvadorans themselves—and important Salvadoran political parties at that—not foreign consultants and anonymous technocrats. The political will to build a democratic regime proceeded judicial reform—not vice versa.

If reformers focused on variables they should have downplayed, the opposite also is true: they ignored variables that should have been given more weight. It is curious the degree to which access-creation strategies were never given more prominence in El Salvador's reform efforts—a striking omission because, as René Hernández Valiente explains, the success of broader reforms were destined to be meaningless unless they were understood and internalized by the population at large.[122] Reformers in Washington and San Salvador correctly sought to broaden the support for democratic rule and cut into the support base for the Marxist insurgents by giving increasingly more Salvadorans a stake in the democratic regime; hence the repeated efforts to jumpstart the land reform process, increase credits for small businesses, and so on. Yet at no time did reformers give due weight to the goal of bringing the courts closer to the public. Duarte virtually ignored the issue altogether. His administration's short-lived program to increase the number of public defenders—designed and funded entirely by the U.S. government—lapsed in the late 1980s because the Salvadoran government refused to provide matching funds for the efforts.[123] Similarly, the total number of justices of the peace remained constant throughout the 1980s, despite an 8 percent increase in population over the same period.[124]

Because reformers never addressed the question of access, it is not surprising that even the encouraging reforms of the 1990s failed to generate more public confidence in the rule of law. Indeed, the Salvadoran experience is an example of the negative synergy that develops when some reform variables are completely ignored at the expense of others. Insofar as democratic consolidation relies on incorporating a greater number of citizens into the political system and building confidence in the efficacy of civilian institutions, the record in El Salvador is, on balance, not encouraging. Polling attitudes give some amplification. In 1987, after Duarte's judicial reform efforts had been given several years to take root, polls conducted by the University of Central America's Public Opinion Institute found that only 20 percent of the public expressed "some" or "much" confidence in the judiciary; fully 66 percent expressed "little" or "no" confidence in the courts. The results are striking because even the armed forces—responsible for as many as 10,000 extralegal disappearances annually—enjoyed more trust than the courts.[125] By the mid- to late-1990s, opinions were nearly identical. One 1994 survey found that 60 percent of the public viewed the judiciary in a "negative" light, and by 1995 over 70 percent reported having little or no confidence in the courts; only 21 percent claimed to have "some" or "much" confidence—nearly the same level of satisfaction as during the 1980s.[126] A separate 1996 poll conducted by the InterAmerican Development Bank echoed these sentiments: only 25 percent of the public expressed "some" or "much" confidence in the courts.[127] Nor was the reformed Supreme Court any more credible with the public. To some degree, this development should be expected simply because Supreme Court reform was the most recent measure to be enacted and had the least amount of time to take root in the public's minds and expectations.[128] Yet even with that caveat, a 1994 USIA poll conducted before the new Supreme Court was seated found that 49 percent had "little or no confidence" in the Supreme Court; a 1995 survey conducted after the new court was seated found that 51 percent of the public had "little or no confidence" in the High Court, and a 1996 survey found that 45 percent believed that the Supreme Court did not reach its decisions in a fair manner.[129] Nor was the Supreme Court viewed as likely to have a fundamental effect on ending impunity. Asked in early 1995 if the Supreme Court was concerned with protecting the human rights of El Salvadoran citizens, 52 percent responded "no"; asked if the public would be affected "if the country could not rely on the Supreme Court," 87 percent responded negatively. The new Supreme Court may have been more committed than its predecessors to administering justice in a fair and transparent manner—and opinions of leading observers suggested that it clearly was—but the High Court clearly had not convinced the broader public.[130]

These results offer several additional insights, none of which augur well for democratic consolidation. The public clearly was frustrated with the courts and recognized the flaws in the judicial system. Yet frustration was not a sufficient catalyst to jumpstart the reform process. At some point, frustration degenerates into a cynicism that gives up on the idea of reform altogether. Thus, polls in El Salvador reveal an overwhelming disdain for the courts alongside public disinterest in judicial reform. Even as polls found 70 to 80 percent disapproval ratings for the courts, at no time since 1984 did the public identify judicial reform as a top priority.[131] It ought not to have been surprising to judicial reformers—as it apparently was—that the public placed immediate concerns, such as ending the civil war, ahead of more long-term structural reforms (like judicial reform), but the polling highlights a lesson: judicial reform was only one of a series of policy undertakings, requiring political capital to undertake it and political support to sustain it—and both were lacking throughout the 1980s.

Finally, the failure of judicial reform has contributed significantly to democratic decay in El Salvador, undermining the reformers' ability to broaden the notions of citizenship so critical to constructing a more democratic regime. Many of the top concerns of Salvadorans—reducing crime, ending impunity, attracting investment—all require a healthy judiciary, but the public clearly does not expect the courts to play a role in these processes.[132] The point is especially important given El Salvador's deeply conflictual political culture. With the end of the civil war and a consensus on the need to build more viable democratic institutions, a real question is whether citizens even consider the judiciary worth reforming. In short, El Salvador's judicial reforms may have produced too little, too late, a disturbing development for democratic consolidation. In contemporary El Salvador, the courts are not only inefficient; they also are irrelevant. Asked in 1995 "Who or what institution best defends human rights in your community?," only 3 percent volunteered the answer of "judges"—nearly identical to the 2 percent expressing that attitude when asked the same question in 1986.[133] By 1996, 75 percent thought that judges were "subject to political control," 59 percent did not believe that judges were independent, and those describing the judicial system as "corrupt" outnumbered those describing it as "honest" by a ratio of four to one.[134] Worse yet, the dramatic rise of crime since the demobilization of forces following the civil war seems to have undercut any positive momentum in judicial reform generated by the Peace Accords. With the size of the armed forces cut from 60,000 to just over 20,000, and another 10,000 FMLN rebels demobilized (but not necessarily disarmed), the mix has been explosive, leading to soaring crime rates and overwhelming the ability of state institutions to respond.[135] In a country in which 34 percent of respondents claim that they or an immediate family member have been a victim of crime in the past year, the willingness to tolerate the vagaries of the formal judicial system was in doubt and the return of vigilante justice was on the rise—often with public support.[136] Asked in 1996 if it was acceptable to "ignore laws and resolve problems without waiting for legal solutions," 49 percent somewhat or very much agreed; 45 percent said it was acceptable "to look for justice on one's own," and 46 percent agreed that "if the government cannot provide people with justice and security, they have the right to take the law into their own hands."[137] Perhaps most surprisingly, after a decade-long civil war, shocking and repeated abuses by the security forces, and persistent calls for enhanced human rights protections, 91 percent of respondents agreed that "it is better to live in an ordered society than to live in one that permits too many liberties."[138] A decade of failed judicial reforms had helped achieve what death squads and Marxist insurgents could not: they had helped shatter the faith of Salvadorans in the rule of law.

NOTES

1. "El Salvador Judicial Reform Program Update: Progress and Problems–1984 to the Present," U.S. Department of State, unclassified telegram San Salvador 06365, 23 May 1991.

2. While the levels of domestic repression were increasing by the late 1970s, there is some question as to whether the country's social inequalities were getting worse over time. See Joseph P. Mooney, "Was It a WORSENING of Economic and Social Conditions that Brought Violence and Civil War to El Salvador?" *Inter-American Economic Affairs* 38 (Autumn 1984): 61–69.

3. Enrique Baloyra, *Confronting Revolution* (Chapel Hill: University of North Carolina, 1982): 86.

4. The architect of the land reform program was Roy Prosterman, a U.S. consultant who had long argued that the subdivision of large estates would improve income inequality and thus reduce the appeal of Marxist movements. Prosterman lays out his case in "Land Reform in Latin America: How to Have a Revolution Without a Revolution," *Washington Law Review* 42 (Fall 1966): 189–211. He applies his framework specifically to El Salvador in Roy L. Prosterman, Jeffrey M. Riedinger, and Mary N. Temple, "Land Reform in El Salvador: The Democratic Alternative," *World Affairs* 144 (Summer 1981): 36–54; and Roy L. Prosterman, "The Unmaking of Land Reform," *The New Republic*, 9 August 1982, 21–25.

5. Duarte's inability to rein in his own security forces prompted Robert Armstrong and Janet Shenk to label him a "fig-leaf president." Speculating on why the previously respected politician would accept the job under such unfavorable conditions, they cited a colleague of the president, who remarked, "He is President at last, which he has wanted to be all his life. And he must want it obsessively to take it now." See Robert Armstrong and Janet Shenk, *El Salvador: The Face of Revolution* (Boston: South End Press, 1982): 178–79. The weakness of Duarte in controlling the abuses committed by the armed forces is traced in Martin Diskin and Kenneth Sharpe, "El Salvador," in *Confronting Revolution*, ed. Morris J. Blachman, William M. Leogrande, and Kenneth Sharpe (New York: Pantheon Books, 1986): 51–87.

6. Tommie Sue Montgomery, *Revolution in El Salvador* (Boulder, Colo.: Westview Press, 1995 [2nd ed.]): 163.

7. Similar to the pattern in various Southern Cone military regimes, the decrees allowed security forces to bypass the ordinary court system and to move all national security crimes—broadly defined to include any violent or criminal activity that undermined "national unity"—to the military courts; authorities could hold individuals incommunicado for up to 195 days without notifying civilian courts and military judges unilaterally determined whether there were sufficient grounds to extend the detention. See *El Salvador's Decade of Terror* (New Haven, Conn.: Yale University Press/Americas Watch, 1991): 71–73.

8. Public defenders and attorneys general also were subject to approval by a simple majority of the unicameral legislature. This process obviously is by no means antidemocratic, but, in a society in which the legislature is overwhelmingly responsive to the executive, is more subject to politicization and manipulation than a system that requires, for example, a two-thirds or three-fifths majority. Russell H. Fitzgibbon and Julio Fernandez summarize the historic politicization of the judiciary by noting that during the period since World War II, the courts in El Salvador had never ruled against the government on any significant policy issue. See Russell H. Fitzgibbon and Julio Fernandez, *Latin America: Political Culture and Development* (Englewood Cliffs, N.J.: Prentice-Hall, 1981): 113.

9. Reasons included such specious charges as "slandering the High Court." For an overview of these practices in the early 1980s, see "Report to Congress on El Salvador," U.S. Department of State, unclassified telegram State 100230, 1 April 1986.

10. Pedro Nikken explains: "The Supreme Court is not only the highest court in the land, it also appoints all other judicial officials, from judges to administrative level court clerks. The Supreme Court appoints forensic doctors, selects all officials related to the administration of justice, and issues license for practicing law. There is thus excessive pressure on the independence of the judges; their rulings, responsibilities, employees, and financial stability all depend on the Supreme Court. The independence of lawyers who practice law also is compromised, as the Supreme Court could suddenly deny them the ability to practice their profession." See his "Human Rights Accountability and Reform of the Police, Military, and Judiciary," in *El Salvador: Sustaining Peace, Nourishing Democracy*, ed. Gary Bland (Washington, D.C.: The Woodrow Wilson Center, 1993): 33.

The Truth Commission, in which Nikken participated, makes the same point: "One of the most notorious deficiencies of the Salvadoran judicial system . . . is the great concentration of powers in the hands of the Supreme Court. . . . This seriously diminishes the independence of lawyers and lower court judges." See *De la Locura a la Esperanza: La Guerra de 12 Años en El Salvador* (San Salvador: Naciones Unidas, 1992–93): 192.

11. *El Salvador: A Decade of Terror*, p. 73.

12. This incident is detailed in Robert Weiner, *A Decade of Failed Promises: The Investigation of Archbishop Romero's Murder* (New York: The Lawyers Committee for Human Rights, 1990). Weiner also details the repeated difficulties experienced by judges directing the criminal investigation, which included "lost" evidence, misplaced documents in custody of the security forces, false witnesses, and sharing of state's information with those suspected of having orchestrated the assassination.

13. *El Salvador: A Decade of Terror*, Chapter Six.

14. "Case Reports: El Salvador," *Center for the Independence for Judges and Lawyers Bulletin* 7 (1988): 26.

15. Loren Jenkins, "Salvadoran Courts Cowed by Violence," *Washington Post*, 2 May 1981, A1, A14. One diplomat claimed, "Ask anyone here how many people have been tried and convicted for any political crime—murder, kidnapping, arson, bank robbery. You will find the number is zero because no judge here has the courage to try anyone, be he left, right, or center. They know that if they do, they will be killed."

16. "Salvadorans Arraigned in Nun's Deaths," *Washington Post*, 11 February 1982, A1.

17. Adrian W. DeWind and Stephen L. Kass, "Justice In El Salvador: A Report of a Mission of Inquiry of the Association of the Bar of The City of New York," *The Record of the Association of the Bar of the City of New York* 38 (March 1983): 116, 119.

18. "Salvadoran courts: a fight for convictions," *The Dallas Morning News*, 23 December 1984, 1.

19. The Constitution of 1983 required only that an appointee to a justice of the peace have "some notion of the law," be at least 21 years of age, and "not be blind or deaf," clauses sufficiently elastic to ensure that those posts could be raffled off as favors to ill-qualified local political bosses. There were few signs that a more competent or reform-minded generation of judges were on the way. Writing in 1991, U.S. officials outlined the dismal state of the Salvadoran legal community:

> Only one of the law faculties attached to private schools has existed more than ten years. Not one has full-time professors; in fact, only one has a full-time dean. None have the resources, the research capability, or the independence to serve as the intellectual spearhead for judicial reform efforts, as is true in other countries. In fact, the decline of legal education is considered to be a serious problem in itself. This lack of academic leadership in the legal field puts El Salvador at a great disadvantage in its judicial reform efforts.

See "El Salvador Judicial Reform Update: Progress and Problems—1984 to the Present," U.S. Department of State, unclassified telegram San Salvador 06365, 23 May 1991.

20. *The Administration of Justice in El Salvador* (Washington, D.C.: Department of State/AID/DOJ, 1992): 17–20.

21. René Hernández Valiente, "Justice in Central America," in *Justice and Development in Latin America and the Caribbean* (Washington, D.C.: InterAmerican Development Bank, 1993): 65.

22. See *El Salvador: Revision of Laws Governing International Trade and Investment* (Washington, D.C.: Agency for International Development/Nathan Associates, 1993). The codes also included no provisions for a range of issues—treaty enforcement, international contract law, intellectual property rights, trademark enforcement, and financial crimes—needed to help attract private investment and reinvigorate the economy.

23. "Proposed Conference on Legal Services and Advocacy to Increase Access for the Poor," U.S. Department of State, unclassified telegram San Salvador 02870, 24 April 1995.

24. For opinions from a range of foreign visitors, see "Visiting Lawyers Find Collapse of Justice in El Salvador," *New York Law Journal*, 17 February 1983, A1.

25. *Underwriting Injustice* (New York: Lawyers Committee for Human Rights, 1989): 3.

26. The first quote comes from Michael Posner and R. Scott Bankhead, "Justice in El Salvador: A Report by the Lawyers Committee for International Human Rights on the Investigation into the Killing of Four U.S. Churchwomen," *Columbia Human Rights Law Review* 14 (Fall/Winter 1982–83): 193. The second passage comes from Adrian W. DeWind and Stephen L. Kass, "Justice In El Salvador: A Report of a Mission of Inquiry of the Association of the Bar of The City of New York," p. 119.

27. Montgomery, *Revolution in El Salvador*, p. 190.

28. To the extent that the public focused on human rights issues, the problem was seen primarily as a civil-military issue, not as a judicial problem. See "Seis tareas urgentes para 1985," *Revista de Estudios Centroamericanos* 40 (January–February 1985): 1–17.

29. "¿Hacia dónde vamos?" *Proceso*, no. 155 (3 September 1984): 1. So concerned were administration officials that Duarte would be perceived as a lameduck that they publicly stressed that Duarte would not be "an Alfonsín"—referring to Argentine President Raúl Alfonsín (1983–89), who repeatedly challenged the military and was forced to backtrack on various occasions. Alfonsín prematurely ended his tenure subservient to the military he pledged to rein in. See Montgomery, *Revolution in El Salvador*, p. 186.

30. Montgomery, *Revolution in El Salvador*, pp. 186–87.

31. Duarte took office 1 June 1984 and by early July had signed a $765,000 judicial reform project grant with the United States Government.

32. In his 284-page autobiography detailing his political career and focusing on his tenure as president, Duarte's comments on the judiciary amount to two innocuous sentences: "Since 1982, the rightist parties had controlled the legislative power, and through it the judicial branch as well. As long as they retained this control, they could block much of our Christian Democratic program for economic reforms and an effective judicial system." See José Napoleón Duarte, *My Story* (New York: Putnam's Sons, 1986): 231.

33. This position is advanced in *The Report of the President's National Bipartisan Commission on Central America* (New York: Macmillan Press, 1984). Constantine Menges, a Senior Director for InterAmerican Affairs at the National Security Council during the Reagan administration, later wrote that the most immediate concern in El Salvador—both for the outgoing Carter administration and the incoming Reagan team—was to "prevent a communist victory." See Constantine C. Menges, *Inside the National Security Council* (New York: Touchstone/Simon and Schuster, 1988): 133. For his part, Alexander Haig commented that El Salvador was the place to "draw the line" against Soviet and Cuban aggression in the hemisphere. See Alexander M. Haig, Jr., *Caveat: Realism, Reagan, and Foreign Policy* (New York: Macmillan 1984): 129.

34. The foreign aid figures come from Margaret Shapiro and T. R. Reid, "Reagan Wins Narrowly on Aid to El Salvador," *Washington Post*, 11 May 1984, 1.

35. U.S. Ambassador to El Salvador William Walker wrote in 1991 that the judicial reform project "could have begun with any number of proposed solutions," but that "the design of the project activities was largely defined by the congressional appropriation which earmarked funds." See "El Salvador Judicial Reform Update: Progress and Problems—1984 to the Present," U.S. Department of State, unclassified telegram San Salvador 06365, 23 May 1991.

36. Raúl Angel Calderón, "La realidad del órgano judicial," *Presencia* 1 (April–June 1988): 161–62.

37. "Report on El Salvador Judicial Reform Project," U.S. Department of State, unclassified telegram San Salvador 10538, 30 July 1986. The program also had the benefit of being more democratic than the "faceless judges" employed in Colombia, which were criticized as lacking transparency.

38. Both cases are detailed in *Justice Denied* (New York: Lawyers Committee for International Human Rights, 1985): 29, 69–77.

39. The COI was placed under the executive branch and led by a three-member team that included the Justice Minister, the Vice Minister of the Interior, and a presidential appointee, a slot that Duarte would later fill with a former Economy Minister.

40. Salvadoran judges and prosecutors agreed that the low conviction rates were due largely to the difficulties in assembling and presenting evidence. One trial judge in San Salvador expressed a frequently heard view when he complained that "We are still using 19th-century methods of criminal investigation in El Salvador." See Joseph Charney, "Most murder cases end in acquittals; trial procedures, juror alienation blamed," *Chicago Daily Law Bulletin*, 20 March 1984, 3.

41. CORELESAL's mandate was "to conduct critical studies and analyses of the judicial system and civil and penal laws, regulations, and procedures" and "elaborate laws and regulations which incorporate the proposed reforms . . . to improve the justice system." See *Underwriting Injustice*, p. 56.

42. It included a full-time staff of forty-nine assistants and researchers, and was divided among working groups on penal law, civil law, and administrative law, with separate units to conduct research, financial management, and administrative affairs. See "Report on El Sal-

vador Judicial Reform Project," U.S. Department of State, unclassified telegram San Salvador 10538, 30 July 1986.

43. *Efforts to Improve the Judicial System in El Salvador* (Washington, D.C.: Government Accounting Office, 1990): 23.

44. U.S. officials reported that "the scarcity of basic materials and equipment would have crippled a system that was otherwise problem-free." See "El Salvador Judicial Reform Update: Progress and Problems—1984 to the Present," U.S. Department of State, unclassified telegram San Salvador 06365, 23 May 1991. One AID consultant reported that "the typical court building consists of a few overcrowded rooms with handwritten files piled on bookcases, desks, windowsills, and floors. These files are critical in securing convictions in criminal cases, yet no copies are maintained. The risk of this information being misplaced, stolen, or destroyed is substantial." See *Underwriting Injustice*, p. 56.

45. *Efforts to Improve the Judicial System in El Salvador*, pp. 25, 27.

46. "Report on the Administration of Justice Program in El Salvador," U.S. Department of State, unclassified telegram San Salvador 01426, 3 February 1987.

47. Observers noted that reformers had not anticipated the Salvadoran "reluctance to create another armed force, of whatever potential good, in a country where official armed groups have a history of abuse." See "El Salvador Judicial Reform Update: Progress and Problems—1984 to the Present," U.S. Department of State, unclassified telegram San Salvador 06365, 23 May 1991.

48. *From the Ashes: A Report on Justice in El Salvador* (New York: Lawyers Committee for Human Rights, 1987): 38.

49. The training offered to JPU members was criticized for its excessive focus on weaponry. The Mudge team noted this heavy focus on firearms, concluding that the JPUs amounted to "purely a display of armed guards for the occasion, with little consideration given to long range planning for future contingencies." See Arthur Mudge, Steve Flanders, Miguel Sanchez, Adolfo Saenz, and Gilberto Trujillo, *Evaluation of the Judicial Reform Project* (Washington, D.C.: U.S. Agency for International Development, 1988): 20.

50. *Underwriting Injustice*, p. 69.

51. See James LeMoyne, "The Case of a Salvadoran Judge: Does Valor Pay?" *The New York Times*, 3 May 1985, A2.

52. Estimates vary, but the U.S. government reported during this period that threats "continued to mount" against judges. Loose comparisons from data compiled by the Center for the Independence of Judges and Lawyers also reflect no appreciable decline in acts of violence committed against judicial officials. See "Judicial System Troubled by Murders, Threats," U.S. Department of State, unclassified telegram San Salvador 07816, 11 June 1988.

53. *Underwriting Injustice*, p. 6, and *El Salvador: A Decade of Terror*, p. 79.

54. "Case Reports: El Salvador," *Center for the Independence of Judges and Lawyers Bulletin* 22 (October 1988): 3-4.

55. "Report on the Administration of Justice Program in El Salvador," U.S. Department of State, unclassified telegram San Salvador 01426, 3 February 1987.

56. *Underwriting Injustice*, p. 109.

57. *El Salvador: A Decade of Terror*, p. 79.

58. "Report on El Salvador Judicial Reform Project," U.S. Department of State, unclassified telegram San Salvador 10538, 3 July 1986. All SIU and FU officials received extensive foreign training from 1984–89; they participated in forty-eight separate training courses on a series of issues ranging from information gathering to weapons tracing, hair and fiber analysis, ballistics testing, photography, and polygraphy.

59. *Efforts to Improve the Judicial System in El Salvador*, pp. 5, 37.

60. From 1985 to early 1987 judges requested that the SIU take on an average of less than two cases per month. The average number of monthly requests increased from ten in the final months of 1987 to forty by 1991. See "El Salvador Judicial Reform Update: Progress and Problems—1984 to the Present," U.S. Department of State, unclassified telegram San Salvador 06365, 23 May 1991.

61. Audits of both agencies found that they did not spend all of their allotted funds between 1984 and 1989 because they were unable to absorb that amount of aid given their rudimentary institutional capabilities. The COI received start-up funding of $5.1 million from the U.S. government between 1984 and 1989, with additional matching funds from the government of El Salvador.

62. Margaret Popkin, *El Salvador's Negotiated Revolution: Prospects for Legal Reform* (New York: Lawyers Committee for Human Rights, 1993): 25. Efficiency measures were not conducted especially efficiently. Even on those human rights cases it did investigate, the SIU and FU were no more coordinated than their predecessors. Even though they were designed to avoid the overlap that had characterized the simultaneous investigative efforts of the National Police and the Treasury Police, auditors found that the SIU and FU shared the redundancy of the old institutions, in some cases causing critical delays that allowed the contamination of physical evidence. See *Underwriting Injustice*, p. 10.

63. Arthur Mudge explained, "Assuming the SIU leadership had the integrity to risk military disfavor, they should hardly have been expected to do so pointlessly." See Mudge et al., *Evaluation of the Judicial Reform Project*, p. 17.

64. A team of U.S. consultants observed that because they "are not committed to careers in police work, and may be subject to transfer back to military duty at any time, it is difficult to justify substantial investment in the training necessary for optimal performance." See Mudge et al., *Evaluation of the Judicial Reform Project*, p. 12.

65. U.S. consultants noted that the inflow of military personnel "substantially affects the image of the SIU and FU in the eyes of many," and that "although the commission provides civilian direction to the investigative units, the effect is significantly reduced by the use of military officers to direct the units." See Mudge et al., *Evaluation of the Judicial Reform Project*, p. 12; and *Effort to Improve the Judicial System in El Salvador*, p. 37.

66. In one case, civilian officials working with the SIU and FU stepped down in the late 1980s claiming that their military superiors ordered that sensitive investigations of human rights abuses be stopped. In another instance, officials reported that Duarte, under pressure from the high command when investigators began pointing to military involvement in a 1988 peasant massacre, privately pledged that no SIU investigation of the armed forces would be conducted without the prior consent of the president, apparently so that Duarte could derail any potentially embarrassing investigations. See *Efforts to Improve the Judicial System in El Salvador*, p. 29. The GAO team considered—but curiously dismissed—the possibility that investigations conducted by the SIU could be politically motivated: "We specifically asked if any such attempts had occurred and were informed by the SIU executive director that none had." The SIU executive director at the time was a colonel in the armed forces and hardly could have been expected to answer otherwise. See *Efforts to Improve the Judicial System in El Salvador*, p. 30. Potential witnesses in criminal cases also were discouraged from coming forward. The SIU and FU facilities were lodged at the compound housing the headquarters of the Ministry of Defense, so that any witnesses or outside experts had to pass through a military checkpoint to sign in. See Mudge et al., *Evaluation of the Judicial Reform Project*, p. 16.

67. "Report on El Salvador Judicial Reform Project," U.S. Department of State, unclassified telegram San Salvador 10538, 3 July 1986.

68. Mudge et al., *Evaluation of the Judicial Reform Project*, p. 3.

69. Marcelo Sancinetti, *Assessment of Performance of CORELESAL* (Washington, D.C.: Agency for International Development/Checchi and Company, 1990): 8.

70. U.S. Judge Ralph Smith noted: "Since much of CORELESAL's work goes through the hands of the Supreme Court before it is considered by the Assembly, and because of the presence of two Supreme Court justices as members of CORELESAL, the politicization of the court is perceived to be a real threat to the independence of actions by CORELESAL." See Ralph G. Smith, *Washington and El Salvador's Views on CORELESAL Priorities* (Washington, D.C.: Checchi and Company, 1990): 4.

71. *Underwriting Injustice*, p. 61.

72. *Efforts to Improve the Judicial System in El Salvador*, pp. 23–24.

73. Explaining why CORELESAL's proposals went nowhere in Congress, an official with AID explained, "If a proposal didn't have a godfather in the assembly, it didn't move." Cited in *Underwriting Injustice*, p. 64.

74. *Underwriting Injustice*, p. 8.

75. By 1991, CORELESAL had proposed fifteen laws, ten of which were enacted. See "El Salvador Judicial Reform Update: Progress and Problems—1984 to the Present," U.S. Department of State, unclassified telegram San Salvador 06365, 23 May 1991.

76. Despite the apparent marginality of such a proposal, CORELESAL members highlighted the so-called "use of names" bill as one of their primary accomplishments. See "Report on the Administration of Justice Program in El Salvador," U.S. Department of State, unclassified telegram San Salvador 01426, 11 February 1987.

77. *Efforts to Improve the Judicial System in El Salvador*, p. 13. The U.S. Embassy in San Salvador, which had administered the funding for most of CORELESAL's efforts, was even more direct: "These laws have not had a serious impact on the criminal justice system." See "El Salvador Judicial Reform Update: Progress and Problems—1984 to the Present," U.S. Department of State, unclassified telegram San Salvador 06365, 23 May 1991.

78. Smith, *Washington and El Salvador's Views on CORELESAL*, p. 4.

79. Sancinetti, *Assessment of the Performance of CORELESAL*, p. 15.

80. Rachel Sieder and Patrick Costello, "Judicial Reform in Central America: Prospects for the Rule of Law," in *Central America: Fragile Transition*, ed. Rachel Sieder (New York: St. Martin's Press, Inc./University of London, 1996): 185.

81. A complete list of the courses offered to Salvadoran judicial officials can be found in *Final Report: Judicial Reform Project I* (Washington, D.C.: Checchi and Company/U.S. Agency for International Development, 1994).

82. Like most Latin American countries, El Salvador did not apply the use of precedent in judicial decisions. See "Experience with Democratic Initiatives," U.S. Department of State, unclassified telegram San Salvador 12111, 10 September 1990; *Efforts to Improve the Judicial System in El Salvador*, p. 26; and *Underwriting Injustice*, p. 73.

83. The Supreme Court did not commission any studies to determine if this change resulted in a greater number of cases being adjudicated or shorter times to disposition in those courts where the administrative reforms were introduced. See "Report on the Administration of Justice Program in El Salvador," U.S. Department of State, unclassified telegram San Salvador 01426, 3 February 1987.

84. GAO officials who examined the project write that the effects can only be ascertained over the long-term, arguing that efforts to train and professionalize court personnel will take

at least a generation to have any measurable effect. Others suggest that the reform efforts that focused on technical and administrative aspects were misguided altogether. The Lawyers Committee for Human Rights cites an AID official involved with the project, who claimed:

> Just buying filing cabinets, what good does it really do? You can't get too far ahead of a government. If you can threaten a judge by telling him, "I'm going to kill you," what difference does it make what the penal code says? What difference does it make what the code on penal procedure says if the police don't follow it?

See *Underwriting Injustice*, pp. 75–76.

85. A decade after the reforms, observers remarked: "The offices of the Attorney General, the Public Defender, and the Human Rights Ombudsman do not efficiently divide their responsibilities. In fact, each office is involved in numerous, duplicative efforts: for example, each subdivision of the Public Ministry maintains separate offices for abused women and human rights. A study of the internal organization of these offices is badly needed to develop a rationalization plan that will make the most of scarce resources. . . . Recommended changes range from using clips in place of the antiquated process of hand-sewing court documents to introducing computer systems to keep records of court business." See "USG Support for Judicial Reform in El Salvador," U.S. Department of State, unclassified telegram San Salvador 05716, 13 June 1994.

86. *Efforts to Improve the Judicial System in El Salvador* (Washington, D.C.: Government Accounting Office, 1990): 1, 12.

87. *The Administration of Justice in El Salvador* (Washington, D.C.: Department of State, 1992): 8. The study is co-authored by the Agency for International Development, the U.S. Information Service, the Department of Justice, and the U.S. Drug Enforcement Administration. It notes, in part:

> Impeding a resolution of these institutional weaknesses is the absence of reliable court statistics on justice system performance. Although the court collects and periodically publishes statistics on judicial cases and the prison population, the data are not disaggregated so as to be useful for planning or performance monitoring. For example, of the over 75,000 criminal cases now in the court system, the statistics do not disclose the age of the cases, status, or other pertinent data that would enable managers to identify over- or under-burdened courts, how many cases are nearing the statue of limitations, etc. The Ministry of Justice and Attorney General also maintain some statistics, but again the data is not collected in such a way as to be correlated with court statistics, nor to be useful in sector planning.

88. *Analyses and Recommendations for Components One and Two For USAID Judicial Reform II in El Salvador* (Washington, D.C.: Checchi and Company, 1992): 71. The report noted the difficulty in determining the percentage of cases that had exceeded the legal time limits to come to trial. The Supreme Court reported that 61.37 percent of the cases had exceeded their legal limits; the Ministry of Justice reported that 80 percent had done so. No mechanism existed for reconciling the discrepancy.

89. In 1986, 1,045 new cases entered the courts of first instance in San Salvador, although judges disposed of only forty-five of them. By 1987, 2,323 new cases entered the courts while 508 were disposed of, and by 1989—when 3,591 cases entered the system—the courts disposed of approximately 1,500, a dramatic increase over just four years earlier. See *Diagnóstico sobre el órgano judicial en El Salvador* (San Salvador: ILANUD, 1987): anexo 4. The initial study was published in 1987, while the subsequent annexes were added in following years.

90. "The Salvadoran Penitentiary System: Abandon Hope All Ye Who Enter Here," U.S. Department of State, unclassified telegram San Salvador 05610, 4 June 1997. Conditions within these prisons worsened considerably during this period. The report notes that in 1980 El Salvador had thirty prison facilities housing 3,000 inmates. By 1992, destruction brought on by the civil war had reduced the number of facilities to fourteen—even though the number of prisoners had nearly doubled, to 5,500.

91. See Bernard Cohen, "The Salvadoran Criminal Justice System," *International Journal of Comparative and Applied Criminal Justice* 14 (Winter 1990); and *The Administration of Justice in El Salvador*, pp. l, 17.

92. *Diagnóstico sobre el órgano judicial en El Salvador*, p. 40, and *Analyses and Recommendations for Components One and Two For USAID Judicial Reform II in El Salvador*, p. l. The Checchi and Company study notes that the Salvadoran government did not even maintain statistics for the number of cases heard by justices of the peace or courts of first instance.

93. Robert Kurz explained the logic that became clear to both sides of the civil war: "There's no question that the guerrillas cannot defeat the army. There's also plenty of evidence that the army cannot defeat the guerrillas, so what you have is a stalemate of violence." See Susanne Sternthal, "Moderation Caught in a Cross Fire," *Insight*, 11 December 1989, 30.

94. See Douglas Farah, "Quayle's Salvadoran Visit Prompts Mixed Reaction," *The Washington Post*, 5 February 1989, A1.

95. For the Left, a key event causing a strategic reassessment of its prospects was its failed November 1989 offensive on San Salvador. See Mario Rosenthal, "Guerrillas Lose Hearts and Minds in Salvadoran Offensive," *The Wall Street Journal*, 15 December 1989, A15; and Tim Golden, "The Salvadorans Make Peace in a 'Negotiated Revolution,'" *The New York Times*, 5 January 1992, E3. An assessment of the FMLN's views on the changing international milieu can be found in Terry Lynn Karl, "Negotiations or Total War?" *World Policy Journal* 6 (Spring 1989): 333.

96. Tommie Sue Montgomery, "The United Nations and Peacemaking in El Salvador," *North-South Issues* 4 (1995): 1–5.

97. The focus on judicial reform increased dramatically with the March 1993 release of the UN's Truth Commission report, an effort to develop an "official accounting" of the most significant human rights abuses that occurred during the civil war. The Truth Commission emphasized the judiciary's alleged role in fostering a climate of impunity during the civil war, finding that Supreme Court President Mauricio Gutierrez Castro had conspired with the military high command to help cover up the armed forces' massacre of more than 500 peasants in 1981. It called for a number of controversial reforms ranging from the resignation of the entire Supreme Court to the creation of a more nonpartisan method for selecting judges. See Jack Spence and George Vickers, *A Negotiated Revolution?* (Cambridge, Mass.: Hemisphere Initiatives, 1994): 7. Judicial reform had broad support from civic action groups, particularly those on the center-left. A 1988 poll of leaders of sixty prominent NGOs meeting to discuss the country's problems found that fully 96 percent listed judicial independence as an "essential element" for democratic consolidation. 98 percent felt that the Supreme Court should be more assertive in challenging illegal acts committed by the government. See *Debate Nacional: Documento Final* (San Salvador: [no pub. given], 1990): 17.

98. The efforts of the Truth Commission are detailed in "El Salvador moves toward reconciliation: joint declaration signed," *U.N. Chronicle* 31 (December 1994): 24.

99. Popkin, *El Salvador's Negotiated Revolution: Prospects for Legal Reform*, p. 9.

100. Popkin, *El Salvador's Negotiated Revolution: Prospects for Legal Reform*, p. 15.

101. Michael Blackmore, "Justice in El Salvador: The Countdown for Reforms," *El Salvador Information Project,* 14 April 1994, 2. In addition, because the Supreme Court retained the right to license and discipline lawyers, many attorneys on the CNJ were said to be unwilling to challenge the Supreme Court, reflecting the same chilling effect that characterized the initial CNJ. In spite of these powers over the CNJ, Gutierrez Castro still objected to the CNJ and complained that it was "frankly politicized." See Mauricio Gutierrez Castro, *La Independencia Judicial* (San Salvador: Talleres Gráficos, 1992): 66–67.

102. U.S. officials noted that the two-thirds requirement was at least more rigorous than the simple majority requirement that had characterized the CNJ under the 1983 Constitution. See "Update on Implementation of Truth Commission Recommendations," U.S. Department of State, unclassified telegram San Salvador 02899, 24 April 1995.

103. "Corte Suprema no debe ser electa por 'grupos hegemónicos,'" *La Prensa Gráfica,* 11 January 1994, 3. Even Cristiani, initially skeptical of the measure, conceded that it would ensure that the assembly selected a diverse group of jurists.

104. The CNJ and the Lawyers Association each prepared lists of forty-two candidates. Congress was obligated to select fourteen candidates from the cumulative list of eighty-four. During the selection process, over 85 percent of all attorneys in the country participated in the selection of candidates for the list that was forwarded to Congress. See Michael Blackmore, "Summary of Concerns: The Peace Process," *El Salvador Information Project,* 14 March 1994.

105. Margaret Popkin, "Judicial Reform in El Salvador: Missed Opportunities," Paper Presented at the XXIV Latin American Studies Association, 28–30 September 1995.

106. Salvadoran officials trumpeted the judicial school as the first step toward eventual development of a judicial career that will include rigorous promotion standards. An early look at the goals and course curriculum for the judicial school can be found in *Democratic Strengthening Program* (San Salvador: Ministry of Planning and Coordination for Social and Economic Development, 1992).

107. Spence and Vickers, *A Negotiated Revolution,* p. 7.

108. *Informe sobre el sistema judicial de El Salvador* (San Salvador: Corte Suprema, 1993). Figures from 1994 come from the Planning Ministry. The amount included four percent for the courts and the other two percent for the Attorney General's Office, the State Counsel's Office, and the newly-created Human Rights Ombudsman. Previously, the judiciary had received less than two percent and even those funds were viewed as coming with political strings attached. See Popkin, Spence, and Vickers, *Justice Delayed: The Slow Pace of Judicial Reform in El Salvador,* p. 8.

When the Salvadoran Association of Judicial Organ Workers went on strike in 1996 over the government's failure to comply with its pledges to devote additional resources for the judiciary, the Supreme Court, which has budgetary control over the distribution of the judiciary's funds, acknowledged that it was sympathetic to their cause and would press the Assembly to increase resources for the courts, but that the funds simply were not available. See "Iglesia salvadoreña pide fin de huelga en poder judicial," Agence France Press release, 8 December 1996.

Some observers have been eager to dismiss the results of even these limited achievements. Pedro Nikken, for example, complained in 1993—only two years after the amendment was approved—"This increased budget allocation to the judicial system has not improved its operation; it has meant only that some judges have cars. If judicial power is to remain weak, at least it is a little wealthier." See Nikken, "Human Rights Accountability and Reform of the Police, Military, and Judiciary," p. 34.

109. Allegations of politicization in the SIU were increasingly common in the early 1990s after release of the Truth Commission report. See Nathaniel Sheppard Jr., "Peace in El Salvador

Founders on Two Issues," *Chicago Tribune*, 6 January 1994, 6. See also *A Negotiated Revolution*, p. 6; and Popkin, *El Salvador's Negotiated Revolution: Prospects for Legal Reform*, pp. 24–25.

110. It revealed that in the 1989 murder of six Jesuits at the University of Central America, the executive director of the SIU had participated in a coverup of army involvement, even going so far as instructing Colonel Guillermo Alfredo Benavides, the intellectual author of the crime, on how to destroy the weapons used in the crime and how to falsify evidence that the SIU would later examine. The Lawyers Committee for Human Rights noted that the SIU frequently botched politically-sensitive cases. In the investigation of the murder of the Jesuit priests, for example, the SIU was said to have "lacked competence, zeal, and good faith," and exhibited unusually sloppy habits in securing the crime scene and handling state's evidence. See *The Jesuit Case A Year Later: An Interim Report* (New York: Lawyers Committee for Human Rights, 1990): 25–27; and *El Salvador's Negotiated Revolution: Prospects for Legal Reform*, p. 26.

111. "Update on Administration of Justice Efforts—June 1991–December 1991," U.S. Department of State, unclassified telegram San Salvador 00440, 1992. See also Stanley, *Risking Failure*, p. 15; and Poplin, *El Salvador's Negotiated Revolution: Prospects for Legal Reform*, p. 22.

112. Popkin, *El Salvador's Negotiated Revolution: Prospects for Legal Reform*, p. 29.

113. Efforts to muster a two-thirds majority for candidates proved more difficult than most politicians originally anticipated, as legislators repeatedly complained about having to choose from externally proposed lists of candidates, and the selection process was so protracted that the country went for more than a month in 1994 without a Supreme Court, as the outgoing Court had stepped down and the Assembly was unable to agree on a successor. See "Negociación para elegir Corte es legítima pero no conveniente: Angulo," *La Prensa Gráfica*, 13 January 1994, p. 5.

114. Margaret Popkin, Jack Spence, and George Vickers, *Justice Delayed: The Slow Pace of Judicial Reform in El Salvador* (Washington, D.C.: Washington Office on Latin America, 1994): 3–5.

115. Spence and Vickers, *A Negotiated Revolution?*, p. 11.

116. Jack Spence, "Strong Language Versus Political Realities: Implementing the Peace Accords in El Salvador," Paper Presented at the XXIV Latin American Studies Association, 28 September 1995, 3. See also "Blind, at last," *The Economist*, 13 August 1994, 42.

117. For a review of steps taken by Mendez and his successor, Eduardo Tenorio, see "Judicial Notes: Judges and Lawyers Fired; GOES Appeals Drug Ruling; Judges Attacked and Threatened," U.S. Department of State, unclassified telegram San Salvador 08877, 4 November 1994; "New Supreme Court Cleans House; Judicial Council Evaluates Judges," U.S. Department of State, unclassified telegram San Salvador 07531, 14 September 1991; "El Salvador Democracy Report: Advances in Judicial Reform," U.S. Department of State, unclassified telegram San Salvador 05752, 23 August 1995; Robin Lubbock, "El Salvador's Judiciary Pressed to Reform," *Christian Science Monitor*, 11 March 1992, 1; and "Suspenden a 19 jueces por faltas cometidas en impartición de justicia," Notimex press service, 5 January 1997.

118. See *El Salvador: Un juicio por el asesinato de las Jesuitas: Una brecha a la impunidad aunque no un triunfo de la justicia* (Ginebra: Comisión Internacional de Juristas, 1991); and Martha Doggett, *Death Foretold: The Jesuit Murders in El Salvador* (Washington, D.C.: Georgetown University Press/Lawyers Committee for Human Rights, 1993): 276, 329.

119. See, for example, Lee Hockstader, "Indictments of 21 Startle Salvadorans," *The Washington Post*, 8 July 1991, A13; and Douglas Farah, "Courts Hold 9 in El Salvador," *The Washington Post*, 20 January 1990, A15.

120. Cited in *From the Ashes: A Report on Justice in El Salvador* (New York: Lawyers Committee for Human Rights, 1987): 38.

121. "El Salvador Judicial Reform Program Update: Progress and Problems—1984 to the Present," U.S. Department of State, unclassified telegram San Salvador 06365, 23 May 1991.

122. Hernández Valiente, "Justice in Central America in the Nineties," pp. 64-66.

123. In 1991, the government made a belated attempt to improve access, increasing the number of public defenders from 32 to 104 and increasing the frequency of their visits to local prisons. See "USG Support for Judicial Reform in El Salvador," U.S. Department of State, unclassified telegram San Salvador 05716, 13 June 1994.

124. *Una administración de Justicia honesta, pronta, y eficaz* (San Salvador: Corte Suprema de Justicia, 1993): 44-47. In 1983 there were 300 justices of the peace and 301 in June 1989. The number rose to 305 in 1992.

125. Ignacio Martín-Baró y Arely Hernández, *La opinión pública Salvadoreña, 1987-88* (San Salvador: UCA Editores, 1989): 138-40.

126. The 1995 polls are taken from Spence, Vickers, and Dye, *The Salvadoran Peace Accords and Democratization*, p. 25.

127. "Slow judicial reform," *Latin America Weekly Report*, 22 April 1997.

128. Similarly, in a predominantly rural country with 30 percent illiteracy rates, the average citizen can hardly be expected to follow the intricate daily debates of constitutional reform. To take an example, 40 percent of the public was unaware that the country had operated without a Supreme Court during the contentious 1994 debates over selecting a High Court. See "Sistema de justicia, delicuencia, y corrupción: la opinión de los salvadoreños," *Revista de Estudios Centroamericanos* 49 (October 1994): 1067.

129. "Los salvadoreños opinan sobre el sistema de justicia y los derechos humanos," *Boletín de Prensa*, 11 August 1996, 3; and Donald W. Jackson and J. Michael Dodson, "Protegiendo los derechos humanos: la legitimidad de las reformas del Sistema Judicial en El Salvador," *Revista de Estudios Centroamericanos* 54 (April 1999): 326.

130. See "Sistema de justicia, delicuencia, y corrupción: la opinión de los salvadoreños," p. 1068, and "Los derechos humanos en la opinión pública salvadoreña," *Revista de Estudios Centroamericanos* 50 (April 1995): 355. Asked if "impunity" had increased or decreased in the past year, 33 percent said it had increased while only 16 percent said it had decreased.

131. In 1984 the public cited as the nation's top priorities the end of the civil war, economic recovery, reducing human rights violations, and greater attention to the needs of those displaced by the war; by 1987, the main concerns were (again, in order) the economic crisis affecting the nation, domestic violence, unemployment, corruption, hunger, and the communist threat. In 1989 the results were nearly identical (economic crisis, war, unemployment, hunger, and health care), and by 1997 the top national concerns were crime, economic recovery, poverty, unemployment and inflation. These results are taken from the following surveys: "Tres años de política gubernamental y el incremento de las movilizaciónes populares de protesta," *Revista de Estudios Centroamericanos* 48 (May–June 1987); "Los salvadoreños ante la elección presidencial de 1989," *Revista de Estudios Centroamericanos* 43 (November–December 1988); "Los salvadoreños evaluan la situación del país a finales de 1996," *Revista de Estudios Centramericanos* 53 (January–February 1997): 58.

132. Asked to identify a government institution or a political group that most tried to resolve human rights issues in 1989, less than 2 percent of respondents cited the judiciary. See Martín-Baró y Arely Hernández, *La opinión pública Salvadoreña, 1987-88*, 23.

133. "Los salvadoreños evaluan a la Procuraduría para la Defensa de los Derechos Humanos," *Revista de Estudios Centroamericanos* 50 (October 1995): 982.

134. Jackson and Dodson, "Protegiendo los derechos humanos: la legitimidad de las reformas del Sistema Judicial en El Salvador," pp. 329, 331-32.

135. Douglas Farah describes the dynamic as "leaving about 40,000 people with military training and easy access to weapons to reintegrate into a civilian society where unemployment hovers around 35 percent." See his article "Salvadorans Complain Postwar Crime Defeating Rebuilt Police Force," *The Washington Post*, 15 March 1995, A2. By 1994–95, the United Nations reported that violent crime had risen 300 percent since the end of the civil war, and polls consistently revealed that the overwhelming number of respondents cited crime as their number one social concern. One 1993 study found that 73 percent cited crime as the "main problem" facing the country, with 34 percent saying that they or an immediate member of the family had been robbed in the past four months. See "La delicuencia urbana," *Revista de Estudios Centroamericanos*, no. 534–35 (April/May 1993): 471–79.

136. See, for example, Douglas Farah, "Death Squads Flex Muscle Again," *The Washington Post*, 13 October 1996, A42; Luis Armando Gonzalez, "Cruzada contra la delicuencia: democracia versus autoritarianismo?" *Revista de Estudios Centroamericanos*, no. 576 (October 1996); "Death squads reemerge in El Salvador," *NACLA Report on the Americas* 29 (November–December 1995): 2; and Larry Rohter, "El Salvador, 3 Years Later: A Country Remade by Peace," *New York Times*, 30 April 1995, A1.

137. "Las actitudes de los salvadoreños en torno a las leyes," *Revista de Estudios Centroamericanos* 51 (October 1996): 914; and Maria T. Perez, "Poll Shows People Trust Rights Ombudsman, Distrust Justice," in *San Salvador Latino*, 21 August 1996, 3, in FBIS-LAT, 26 August 1996.

138. "Las actitudes de los salvadoreños en torno a las leyes," p. 914.

Chapter Four ⸻

Brazil: A Shotgun Approach to Judicial Reform

> There is no power that can remove them, and they cannot be controuled by the laws of
> the legislature. In short, they are independent of the people, of the legislature, and of
> every power under heaven. Men placed in this situation will generally soon feel them-
> selves independent of heaven itself.
> —Robert Yates, on the judiciary[1]

If reformers in El Salvador defined judicial reform in excessively narrow terms, then the Brazilian efforts offer a stark contrast and raise the obvious question of whether merely taking a radically different approach is more likely to guarantee success. That is, are reforms more likely to succeed when reformers make sweeping pledges to simultaneously boost individual and institutional independence and enhance access for various social groups and the average citizen? In a country that has suffered decades of politicization of the judiciary, is it desirable to insulate the judiciary entirely from the more political branches of government? Are reforms more likely to generate a sense of political ownership when they are proposed by the judiciary and bar associations, debated among the major parties in Congress, vetted with leading intellectuals, and televised before the public? Can a judiciary that actively resisted military rule be counted on to take the lead in promoting and implementing reforms—and to use its newfound authority in a responsible and accountable manner?

After more than a decade of judicial reforms, a clear lesson from the Brazilian experience is that while there may be no clear maps for success, there are many roads to failure. Apparently sensible judicial reform inputs failed to produce the desired outputs. The backlog of cases clogging the court system increased by a factor of ten in just over a decade, and trial delays increased so dramatically—more than doubling—that access for everyone resulted, paradoxically, in access for no one. The goal of promoting individual and structural judicial independence clearly was successful; senior jurists proudly trumpeted their independence, and the courts frequently ruled against other branches of government on sensitive political and economic questions after 1988. An increasingly important question in post-reform Brazil, however, was whether reformers had gone too far and created a judiciary so autonomous that it was devoid of all accountability. The post-reform judiciary was rife with nepotism and corruption, indifferent to public and congressional calls for transparency, and capable of resisting any measures that would improve its efficiency or scale back the generous and unjustifiable perquisites the courts had granted themselves. It was, in the words of one legislator, "a power above the law."[2]

Why did the reforms meet such an unfortunate fate? The failure of the reforms reflected a combination of several factors. From the outset, the profound, sweeping nature of the planned reforms ensured that all of the new measures were not implemented; the final inputs were much less than promised. Comprehensive reform, in fact, was not comprehensive at all; many measures were never even implemented. Meanwhile, a number of broader structural problems—many of which were generated in the same constitutional review that produced the judicial reforms—overwhelmed the judiciary. Foremost among these impediments were egregious flaws in the Constitution, arguably the world's most statist constitution outside the Soviet bloc. The document included so many social and economic guarantees that virtually any type of social or economic interaction—ranging from divorce cases to bank loan defaults—quickly became a legal issue of constitutional importance; by 1997, the Supreme Court president complained that the highest court in the land, burdened with a backlog of more than 30,000 cases, had been reduced to a small claims court overwhelmed with the most trivial of issues.[3] Meanwhile, other aspects of the 1988 judicial reform—despite being amply debated, widely publicized, and codified as core elements of the Constitution—suffered from inattention and complete lack of follow-through from cash-strapped state and local governments. With a cumulative inflation rate between 1988 and 1994 approaching 84 million percent and all twenty-seven states undergoing some type of federal bailout and financial restructuring, grandiose judicial reforms—particularly various efficiency-maximizing measures—were either implemented barely or, in most cases, not at all.[4] The gap between what reformers promised and actually delivered was deep and profound.

Through very different paths and under radically different social and economic conditions, the results in Brazil paralleled those in El Salvador: a judiciary in an unprecedented state of crisis and one of the clearest examples of democratic decay in Latin America. At the state and federal levels, Brazil demonstrated declining confidence in the courts, increased cynicism about democracy and the rule of law, an increased tolerance for vigilante justice, a hardening of public attitudes that reflected a nearly complete lack of faith in the judiciary, and prominent sentiments that democracy was no real improvement over authoritarian rule. By the end of 1999, Brazil seemed to be on the verge of serious democratic decay, with the failure of the judiciary a critical factor contributing to the declining faith in the rule of law.

LEGAL PLURALISM IN BRAZIL

For most of Brazil's history, especially after the overthrow of the monarchy in 1889, the judiciary was characterized by what scholars have called a "legal pluralism" combining aspects of strict constitutionalism with a frequent irrelevance for most legal institutions.[5] Brazil's first constitution after separation from the monarchy was republican, federalist, and generally liberal, as was the democratic Constitution of 1946.[6] In both constitutions, the judiciary was explicitly modeled after the U.S. system, guaranteeing judges an irreducibility of salaries, ensuring non-transferal from one place to another, and even granting extensive powers of judicial review over acts of the executive and the legislature.[7] During this period, senior jurists issued a range of respected, well-reasoned opinions in line with prevailing notions of democratic jurisprudence; many federal judges explicitly drew on U.S. judicial rulings such as *Ex parte Milligan, Marbury v. Madison,* and *McColloch v. Maryland.*[8] David Fleischer and Robert Wesson write that in ensuing decades, the High Court, whatever its other possible flaws, was generally free from the intense politicization and recurring purges that characterized other judiciaries in the region.[9]

At the same time, the judiciary was characterized by a high degree of irrelevance for social and economic interactions for the majority of Brazilians. The courts frequently were criticized as elitist; academic training for judges was highly theoretical, the rigorous entrance requirements for federal judges ensured a narrow range of candidates from a relatively homogenous background, and the rigid formalism discouraged use by citizens of more modest income.[10] Meanwhile, throughout the country, local political and economic bosses relied less on the courts and more on personal police forces to impart private justice.[11] The quality of the courts—and the commitment of local chieftains to using them—varied widely by region, and allegations of frontier justice and lawlessness were commonplace.[12]

The Brazilian military regime that ruled Brazil between 1964–85 resorted to a number of the traditional means for reducing the personal and institutional independence of the courts. The primary approach to reducing judicial independence was through a series of so-called "institutional acts"—17 Institutional Acts and more than 100 Complementary Acts—that supplanted judicial authority and even the 1946 Constitution itself.[13] Institutional Act Number 1, for example, bluntly declared that the decrees of the junta represented the highest law of the land and henceforth carried the full force of constitutional edict, while Institutional Act Number 2, in addition to expanding the size of the Supreme Court from eleven to sixteen, declared that all acts of the high command would not be subject to judicial review. Armed with a sympathetic High Court, the military would periodically intervene in cases being heard before lower courts and transfer them to the Supreme Court on the specious grounds that the case presented a threat to national security.[14] Institutional Act Number 5 of 1968 unilaterally gave the president the power to remove or retire any sitting judge, while Institutional Act Number 6 of the same year reduced the number of Supreme Court justices back down to eleven—forcing the retirement of several justices that had been appointed by previous civilian governments.[15] When Congress failed to approve a military-backed constitutional amendment in 1977 that would have curtailed the purview of civilian courts and created an external oversight body to punish judges, (General) President Ernesto Geisel merely suspended Congress and declared that the judicial reform bill would be an amendment to the Constitution, and hence carry the full weight of law.[16]

Despite these steps, the judiciary was never as fully subordinated as was the judicial branch in neighboring military regimes in Argentina or Chile. Foremost among the reasons was the military's desire to maintain at least the façade of legalism and to avoid extreme levels of domestic repression, particularly in the early years (1964–69) and again toward the end of the regime (1980–85).[17] Indeed, one of the primary reasons for the court-packing scheme in 1969 was the high command's frustration with repeated Supreme Court decisions to free illegally detained students and to restore the political rights of professors deemed subversive by the military; the final straw was a Supreme Court decision in 1968 to declare unconstitutional key portions of the military's National Security Law.[18] This judicial assertiveness grew in fits and starts as the military pursued broader policies of a protracted "decompression" in the mid-1970s, allowing the courts to assert their authority on increasingly controversial issues and reestablish some degree of independence.[19] Supreme Court decisions against the government—itself a rarity in a time of military rule—were often, if begrudgingly, complied with. In several cases, both state and federal judges successfully held the state (but not specific military personnel) responsible for physical harm suffered by private citizens while in military custody, and in other cases federal courts would overrule the military's decisions on which criminal acts constituted crimes against national security.[20] Persistent pressure from the influential Brazilian Bar Association pushed the military government to be selective in overruling the courts, claiming increasingly more "political space" for the judiciary as the military government prepared to leave power in the mid-1980s.[21]

The result of these authoritarian and liberalizing tendencies was a judiciary viewed with a fair degree of skepticism and cynicism, but which nonetheless enjoyed some level of confidence among portions of the population. The civil courts were slow, but not hopeless. A 1981 survey of businessmen found considerable frustration with the slowness of the courts, but firms expressed the view that the courts were at least predictable. Approximately 60 percent of Brazilian firms surveyed said that they had taken the government to court at least once and 80 percent said that they would do so again, a reflection of a general belief that the civil courts did eventually function with some degree of independence, if only belatedly.[22] Turning to the judiciary more broadly, surveys conducted in 1984, one year before the military left power, found that 57 percent of Brazilians said that they did not trust the judiciary; asked to rate the performance of "the courts" on a scale of one to ten, the courts averaged a dismal 2.9—roughly the same rating as the legislature, which scored a 3.2. Worse yet for the prospects for democratic consolidation, according to Robert Shirley, the criminal justice system was held in particularly low esteem: nearly half of all respondents believed the solution to the failings of the judiciary was "popular justice," or lynch law.[23]

A TROUBLED BEGINNING FOR JUDICIAL REFORM

The failure of judicial reform to initially secure a more prominent role in democratic Brazil can be explained by three factors: the counterproductive role of President Sarney; the nature of Brazil's political class, particularly the Constituent Assembly tasked with reforming the judiciary; and the country's populist approach to judicial reform. All of these factors highlight the degree to which political forces shaped the nature and scope of the judicial reform process.

Brazil's return to civilian rule was facilitated in large part by the political role of Tancredo Neves, a respected centrist with a distinguished political career.[24] Neves's Brazilian Democratic Movement Party (PMDB) had been formally calling for judicial reform as early as 1982, and during the run-up to the indirect election, Neves had made broad pledges to create a more independent, efficient judiciary, including calling for a new, democratic Constitution once his administration took office.[25] After twenty-one years of military rule, early opinion about Brazil's democratic transition—and the more narrow issue of judicial reform—was consistently optimistic, almost euphoric.[26] Yet the optimism, and with it prospects for sweeping judicial reform, faded quickly: Neves died before taking office.[27]

Power fell to Neves's vice president Jose Sarney, whose commitment to judicial reform—and to democracy in general—was questionable. Sarney was chosen for the ticket primarily for reasons of political expediency and regional balance. He had been a loyal supporter of the military and was president of the military's official government party as recently as June 1984, and broke with the regime not for ideological reasons but because of a succession struggle among politicians seeking to be the military's electoral standardbearer.[28] Based on his non-elected status and pro-military credentials, Sarney lacked legitimacy from the outset in the eyes of his democratic coalition partners. Forced to accept Neves's cabinet—a heterogeneous group of ministers with whom he had little in common ideologically—Sarney's tenure was, from the outset, characterized by policy disarray. Faced with a four-digit inflation, a moratorium on foreign debt payments, a revolving door cabinet, and an increasingly restive military, judicial reform quickly faded to the background, particularly in light of Sarney's top political priority: using the long-anticipated constitutional review process of 1988 to defeat the growing support for adopting a parliamentary form of government and instead securing an additional fifth year in office for himself. This goal was all-consuming and ultimately would have implications for judicial reform. From the outset, political concerns—no matter how parochial—would define the parameters of the judicial reform process.[29]

A second factor shaping the Brazilian approach to judicial reform lies in the nature of the civilian political class that came to power in 1985 and assumed responsibility for drafting the new Constitution.[30] Unlike in neighboring Argentina and Chile, where opposition politics was banned during military rule, the Brazilian high command allowed regime opponents to operate openly—if they agreed to serve as the "loyal opposition" that would never challenge the fundamental legitimacy of military rule. Candido Mendes referred to this political arrangement as "inverted Darwinism"—guaranteed to produce "survival of the least fit"; that is, many opposition politicians under military rule were attracted less to the idea of building accountable government in Brazil and more to acquiring the extensive benefits associated with government service—so much so that they were willing to serve as the fig-leaf opposition to a military dictatorship.[31]

Judicial reform was thus placed in the hands of an uninterested president and an opportunistic political class, divided among thirteen regionally-based parties, few of whom had even given serious consideration to what a new Constitution and its judiciary ought to look like.[32] Legislators rejected the idea of calling an assembly with the specific purpose of drafting a new Constitution, and bypassed the idea of merely reforming or adjusting the more authoritarian features of the military government's Constitution of 1967. Instead, the new Congress elected in October 1986 simultaneously would conduct the affairs of ordinary legislation as well as those of drafting a new constitution. As Keith Rosenn explains, the decision was unwise from the beginning:

> Combining normal legislative powers and constitution-making powers in the same body made no sense, for the two functions interfered with each other. Congress is a highly political body with a short-term perspective and agenda. Constitutions should be elaborated by statesmen with a long-term and nonpartisan perspective. As a political player, Congress had a clear conflict of interests. It is not surprising that the constitutional document drafted aggrandized congressional power at the expense of other institutions and conferred numerous favors upon special interest groups.[33]

The third factor shaping the contents of the specific judicial reforms was the populist and statist approach of the Constituent Assembly in drafting the new Constitution. In a conscious effort to avoid charges of elitization that could eventually undermine the popular legitimacy of the Constitution, Brazil's framers opted for what Bolívar Lamounier calls the "Rousseauian option." To ensure that the drafting of the Constitution was as transparent and participatory as possible, legislators opened the process to civil society to propose constitutional amendments.[34] Congress was thus willing to defer much of the judicial reform to the so-called experts: the judicial lobby, the Brazilian Bar Association, and human rights groups.[35] Their specific judicial reforms, in and of themselves and without reference to the broader nature of the constitution, seemed sensible enough. Each is discussed briefly.

Increasing Independence

The 1988 Constitution restored a number of the protections that had been undermined during military rule. In an effort to strengthen individual independence, Article 95 declared that henceforth all judges would receive life tenure, with retirement at the age of 70; judges also could not be transferred from one jurisdiction to another and, in a clause modeled after Article 3, Section 1 of the U.S. Constitution, were guaranteed that judicial salaries could not be reduced. To boost the independence of the lower courts, the Assembly removed from the High Court the power to assume jurisdiction from a lower court on the grounds that the case posed an imminent threat to the public order, and also rejected efforts to introduce precedent into the legal system, on the grounds that it unfairly bound judges to a ruling of other courts and thereby reduced their individual independence.

Looking to insulate the judiciary from potential political influence, the courts were given near total control over their administrative, personnel, and disciplinary affairs. The full Senate could remove Supreme Court justices in a process similar to judicial impeachment in the United States, but lower court judges could be removed only by superior courts.[36] Finally, in an effort to protect the federal courts from the highly politicized budget process each year—the military government had centralized resource disbursement and often conditioned it on political loyalty—the Supreme Court was granted the power to prepare the annual budget for the federal court system each year; similar powers were given to the supreme courts at the state level. The federal Supreme Court then forwarded its proposals directly to the Congress, bypassing the executive branch altogether; if the courts chose to send the budget to the executive, the president could incorporate it into the overall budget, but not modify it. This laundry list of measures led many jurists to conclude that the Constituent Assembly had made dramatic strides in advancing judicial independence.

Increasing Access

Reformers created several mechanisms to increase access for both the average citizen as well as key political groups and organizations that had participated in the constitution drafting process. The outgoing military government had created in 1984 a nationwide system of small claims courts, although implementation had been sporadic because of local indifference and the lack of budgetary resources in many states.[37] To correct the lack of follow-through, the Constituent Assembly included explicit constitutional language that mandated the creation of a nationwide system of small claims courts, complete with self-representation, oral argumentation, and direct plaintiff/defendant interaction with judges. Mindful of the centralizing powers of military government and with state and local governments enjoying a political resurgence, the national assembly left to each state the specifics of how to create these courts, providing the broad outlines and even encouraging state governments to make various modifications. The Constitution included language that guaranteed that plaintiffs would be freed from having to pay the other side's court costs in the event that their lawsuit was defeated, and that guaranteed the presumption of innocence until all appeals had been exhausted and a conviction was final.[38] The reformers also expanded and constitutionalized a piece of ordinary legislation that had been passed in 1986, explicitly recognizing class action suits and building on the law by allowing individuals to bring these suits before the courts on a wider range of issues.[39]

Finally, various citizens' groups were given increased access to the courts. Under military rule, only the solicitor general could request the Supreme Court to rule on the constitutionality of a law. Under the 1988 Constitution, however, reformers created the Act of Unconstitutional Law (ADIN), a tool that expanded the ability to make such a request to include the president, Congress, state legislative assemblies, governors, the bar association, any party with representation in Congress, and labor unions and professional organizations with nationwide representation that had been in existence for more than one year.[40] The Supreme Court was obliged to hear the argument of the petitioning group, and could not deny standing to any ADIN.

Increasing Efficiency

Reformers focused most of their efficiency-creating measures on the federal court system and particularly the Supreme Court. Alarmed by the steady rise in the number of cases reaching the STF—each Supreme Court justice heard more than 1,000 cases in 1987—the Constitution created a separate Superior Court of Justice (STJ) to serve alongside the STF. The STJ was to function as a court of last appeals, freeing the STF to serve strictly as a constitutional court with a much-reduced caseload. Because the STJ would have thirty-three ministers, it would be able to handle a heavy work load and could help "decongest" the federal courts.[41] To better manage the caseload, reformers replaced the federal court of appeals that had been located in Brasília—which had forced litigants to travel long distances and created a backlog of cases—with a nationwide system of "regional federal courts" modeled after appellate courts in the United States.[42] Reformers argued that the creation of a nationwide system of small claims courts also would remove small-scale civil and criminal issues from the ordinary courts and hence assure access for those unable to afford lengthy trial delays.

REFORMS PRODUCE DISMAL RESULTS

More than a decade after the passage of the 1988 Constitution, it is difficult to argue that any of the judicial reforms achieved their desired results or improved public confidence in the courts. Judicial bottlenecks were worse than ever, times to disposition were increasing throughout the country, the average caseload per judge was worsening rather than improving, corruption scandals inside the judiciary had become commonplace, and the courts steadfastly resisted all reforms. Not surprisingly, public confidence had plummeted. By the late 1990s, polls revealed that public doubts about the judiciary were even greater than under military rule. One poll found that 73 percent of all Brazilians said they had "little or no confidence" in the judiciary, while 90 percent complained that justice was "too slow" and two-thirds said that justice was "not possible" for the average citizen.[43] Despite the intentions of the reformers, something clearly had gone wrong.

What went wrong? In a word, everything. Measures that on paper seemed sensible enough in reality exposed the profound flaws in the conventional approach to judicial reform. Reformers successfully created the independent judiciary they desired—but in the process swept aside the balancing constraint of accountability. In failing to tackle judicial efficiency, reformers did not anticipate the potentially disastrous results when an inefficient judiciary is, in turn, given excessive independence. And finally, neither the extremely modest efficiency measures nor the ambitious access strategies could be isolated from the broader political and economic forces in Brazil. The ultra-statist nature of the 1988 Constitution never gave the judicial reforms a fair chance and overwhelmed the courts with even the most trivial matters. The number of cases entering the court system swelled—creating the illusion of increased access—even as many of the access-creating reforms were never implemented. The unfortunate interplay between efficiency and access in Brazil is one of the strongest examples of the negative synergy that results from partial reform.

Independence

It is generally accepted that Brazil's judiciary has been genuinely independent since the 1988 Constitution. This aspect is reflected in the opinions of leading jurists as well as judicial rulings in sensitive political and economic cases since 1988.

Brazilian jurists acknowledge their independent status, noting that unlike the experiences in Argentina under Carlos Menem or Peru under Alberto Fujimori, there have been no efforts at court packing, no purges of judicial appointments, no attempts to reduce the retirement ages for judges, and no effort to pull back from the guarantees of judicial independence such as life tenure and non-transferability of judges granted in the 1988 Constitution. José Neri da Silveira, a respected Supreme Court justice, has written of the "administrative, financial, political, and disciplinary independence" of the courts, citing the Brazilian judiciary as "unique in Latin America."[44] Supreme Court Justice Carlos Velloso has favorably likened Brazilian judicial independence to that in the United States.[45] Former Supreme Court President José Celso de Mello Filho has echoed these general observations, stating that the Brazilian judiciary is arguably the "most autonomous" in Latin America, while Supreme Tribunal of Justice Minister Antonio de Padua Ribeiro has lauded the "self-governance" of the judiciary.[46] Leading Brazilian scholars of the judiciary concur with these broad observations, writing that the 1988 Constitution, whatever its other structural flaws, "gave effective, and not merely nominal independence" to the courts.[47] As Katrina Howell writes, Brazilian jurists and academics alike seem to agree on the "unprecedented power extended to the judicial branch" under the 1988 Constitution.[48]

This independence also can be gauged by looking at the degree to which the judiciary has carved out a sphere of authority for itself, because a striking aspect of post-1988 Brazil is that the courts have been capable of checking and restraining actions by the executive and the legislature. In contrast to most other Latin American countries, since 1988 the Brazilian judiciary has asserted itself regularly on important political issues involving the executive and Congress. To cite some of the more prominent examples, in 1992 the Supreme Court repeatedly gave the deciding word at crucial stages during the unprecedented congressional impeachment of President Fernando Collor, weighing in repeatedly at key junctures to determine whether and how Congress could move ahead with the admittedly vague impeachment proceedings—and when the legislature had to respect due process in judging the corrupt president. On repeated occasions, both Congress and the executive looked to the High Court to issue the final word on whether, when, and how to proceed, and both sides consistently, if begrudgingly, complied with the Court's rulings.[49] In other prominent cases, in 1994 the High Court upheld the ruling of a lower court that suspended the mandate of a prominent longtime senator for campaign financing illegalities, the first time in Brazil's history that the courts removed a legislator under democratic circumstances.[50] The courts also struck down various executive decrees of questionable legality issued by presidents Collor and Itamar Franco. In perhaps the most widely publicized showdown, in 1990 Collor issued Provisional Measure 190, a marginally modified version of a controversial executive decree that had been rejected by Congress only weeks earlier. With the legislature out of session and unable to overturn the dubious measure, the High Court ruled that the President was exceeding his constitutional authority by reissuing a measure so closely resembling one already rejected by Congress. The High Court ordered the president to rescind the decree, a ruling with which Collor complied. The decision has been cited as playing an important role in redefining the governmental balance of power and curtailing executive authority in Brazil, particularly at a time when each branch of government was struggling to define its roles and prerogatives in a still-nascent democratic setting.[51]

Finally, the independence of the judiciary is seen by examining its rulings on the economic policies of various administrations, because—for better or worse for Brazil's democratic consolidation—on repeated occasions the courts have ruled against the executive and enforced even some of the more ill-considered portions of the Constitution. The effects of these verdicts may have been disastrous for government efforts to reduce Brazil's perpetual hyperinflation, but they nonetheless attest to the ability of the courts to rule against the other branches and set the final word on constitutional matters. The experience of Collor's economic shock program known as "Collor I" is illustrative. In 1990, Collor introduced a heterodox shock program aimed at taming Brazil's 85-percent monthly inflation, and a prominent part of the package included Provisional Measure 168, a decree that included the introduction of a new currency and the mandatory freezing of all private bank accounts over $1,000. Faced with imminent legal challenges to the plan, Collor issued Provisional Measure 173, which preemptively blocked federal courts from issuing injunctions against the savings confiscation. The Supreme Court, while stopping short of overturning Provisional Measure 168, nonetheless ruled that citizens could petition lower courts to recover their frozen assets, a ruling that eventually triggered more than 20,000 petitions to federal courts throughout the country to recover confiscated funds and which contributed to the gradual unraveling of the ill-considered shock plan.[52]

Other examples highlight an institutional independence that generally is lacking in other regional judiciaries. For example, Brazil's Constitution mandates a national wage policy with a unique clause known as *isonomia*, which requires that any pay increase to one category of public-sector employees must be granted to all state employees. When the Franco administration granted a 28-percent wage hike to disgruntled military officers in 1993, regional federal courts ruled (and the Supreme Court upheld)—despite the arguments of then-Finance Minister Cardoso, who claimed that the across-the-board wage hike would bust the government's efforts to stabilize Brazil's 2,000 percent annual inflation—that the government was legally obligated to broaden the wage hike to include any public servant that petitioned for a pay raise.[53] Similarly, when the administration tried in 1993 to close the budget deficit by securing congressional approval of a controversial .25 percent tax on all financial transactions, lower courts overruled both branches of government, pointing out that, under articles 153 and 167 of the Constitution, no new tax could be collected in the same year that it is created. Many pundits criticized the court ruling for undercutting efforts to end hyperinflation, but the judgment was legally correct and forced the executive to devise alternative inflation-cutting strategies. Other rulings followed in subsequent years—such as decisions in 1999 on whether state officials were obligated to honor debt payments to the federal government and another on whether retirees were required to pay taxes on their government pensions, two highly important verdicts for the cash-strapped central government—and reinforced the notion that the Brazilian judiciary was able to ensure a fair degree of horizontal accountability among other branches and levels of government.[54]

Given that the courts have not seen their independence curtailed under the new Constitution, a more interesting question in contemporary Brazil is whether they have become too independent—whether the Brazilian judiciary in fact had become an entrenched bureaucratic oligarchy in need of restraint and devoid of all accountability to other branches of government and to the public. Indeed, it is striking that in a country in which consensus on most issues has been severely lacking since the return to civilian rule, one of the few areas of political or social agreement is that someone must "do something" about the judiciary. This notion is reflected in two broad ways: the opinions of leading political and intellectual elites, and the behavior of judges themselves, particularly by examining how they have managed their own budgetary affairs and how they have behaved in their professional conduct.

Across the political spectrum, opinion is commonplace that the judiciary has lost all accountability. Critics on the Left, who in the Constituent Assembly debates in 1987–88 argued for maximizing judicial independence, now lament that the judiciary is "the government branch most closed off and the least fiscally disciplined," "culturally attached to perks and nepotism," and "a power above the country."[55] José Dirceu of the social democratic Workers' Party argues that, "There is nothing more arrogant than the Brazilian judiciary" and José Genoíno, one of the leading intellectuals of the same party, has repeatedly complained that the judges behave as if they are "untouchable."[56] On the Right, opinion is equally harsh. Antônio Carlos Magalhães, Brazil's most influential conservative senator, has argued that the courts have become "a bastion of nepotism and corporatism."[57] Marco Maciel, a co-founder of the Liberal Front Party and vice president in the Cardoso administration, has argued that the courts are "indifferent" to calls for reform because of their extreme structural independence and "bureaucratic myopia."[58] Even respected centrist politicians such as Nelson Jobim, a federal deputy who served as justice minister from 1995 to 1996 before accepting a seat on the Supreme Court, has lamented the "lack of transparency" in the promotion and punishment process of judges and defended the idea of "external controls" on the judiciary.[59] The result of this growing sense that the judiciary has too much autonomy has been for Congress and popular organizations to seek greater oversight of the courts. During the constitutional review process of 1993, twelve of the eighteen proposals for judicial reform called for introducing some form of external oversight of the judiciary. Each proposal varied slightly—some called for publicizing internal disciplinary measures, others sought externally-appointed bodies to investigate the courts—but all shared the view that the judiciary had lost accountability.[60]

The reasons for this popular frustration are best understood by looking at the behavior of the courts and how senior judges have used the independence granted in the 1988 Constitution. Judges, empowered with setting their own wages, pension, staffing requirements, and budgets, have treated themselves—particularly their upper ranks—exceptionally well, with some of the world's most generous benefits. A Supreme Court justice earns US$10,800 monthly—more than the President himself—while an average judge of first instance earns more than thirty times the national minimum salary.[61] Judges do even better in retirement; Brazil's National Accounting Office has calculated that a typical judge of first instance earned US$2,393 monthly in 1994 when serving on the bench, but US$3,559 when he retired—the only country in the world in which a judge earns more in retirement than when serving on the bench.[62]

In addition to their generous pay and pensions, judges have established lavish institutional perks for themselves. Benefits for all federal judges include sixty days of paid vacation annually, a free furnished apartment, a car and driver, a gasoline allowance, and nearly $4,000 annually for every judge to pay potential medical and dental bills.[63] Senior judges also have budgeted an impressive support staff for themselves. In Brazil's five high courts—the Superior Tribunal of Justice, the Supreme Federal Tribunal, and the Supreme Tribunals of Labor, Military, and Electoral Issues—a combined total of eighty-eight justices have more than 5,000 staffers and clerks between them. More than forty-five functionaries support each individual Supreme Court justice, while sixty-five support each justice on the Supreme Labor Tribunal.[64] Indeed, the courts clearly have been immune to the broader budgetary trends sweeping the rest of state and federal governments. At a time when federal government was resorting to highly controversial and unpopular executive decrees in 1995–96 to cut government payrolls, the judicial branch hired more than 11,000 new employees—an average of thirty-two employees every day—to push up government spending, despite the objections of the President, his economic team, and Congress.[65] Brazilian officials reported that between 1987 and 1999, personnel costs in the judiciary rose by an astounding 760 percent, by far the greatest increase in real terms of any government branch.[66]

There also is a strong sense that judges are abusing their position by bypassing rigorous entrance exams and staffing these positions with unqualified family members and political appointments—and that they do so without fear of punishment. Examples to support this perception are numerous throughout the state and federal systems. When Senator Antônio Carlos Magalhães began soliciting allegations of judicial nepotism in 1995, he received more than 1,500 complaints in less than a year; when the senator launched a similar investigation in 1999, he received more than 3,000 complaints in the first month.[67] Despite the existence of anti-nepotism laws in many states and the presence of strict entrance exam requirements, scandals have become increasingly commonplace in which prominent judges have been caught hiring relatives without punishment. In the tiny northeastern state of Paraíba, audits in 1995 found that there were 565 judicial employees who had not taken the manda-tory entrance exam, 160 of whom were relatives of sitting judges.[68] In the state of Ceará, a recipient of various United Nations awards for innovative governance and considered one of the more efficiently administered states, forty-two of the 107 staff positions allotted for the state Supreme Court are filled by relatives of fourteen of the fifteen judges, while the former president of the state Supreme Court had hired seven of his children.[69] Other examples throughout the country abound but merely rein-force the same point.[70] Reports of judges actually being sanctioned for illegal behav-ior are rare—results of disciplinary hearings are secret—but journalists who have periodically obtained internal court records report that allegations of impropriety are shelved without effective follow-up in 90 percent of all cases; a typical ploy is for judges on the disciplinary bodies to investigate an allegation long enough so that the statute of limitation expires and the accused judge can be absolved.[71] When President Cardoso signed into law a bill in 1996 that prevented all federal judges from hiring relatives up to the "third level" (a Brazilian term that legally refers to a spouse, child, parent, grandparent, niece, nephew, aunt, uncle, or cousin) the reaction of the judi-ciary was swift. Judges claimed that the bill violated Article 37 of the Constitution—a nebulous clause granting all federal employees the right to hire the subordinate of their choice—and pledged to strike down the law at the first opportunity. Senior judges made sweeping charges that Cardoso was violating the separation of powers and plotting a "Fujicoup," a reference to the blatantly authoritarian purges of the courts conducted by Peruvian President Fujimori in 1992. Within days, judges throughout the country staged a one-day work stoppage to protest the administra-tion's allegedly dictatorial abuses.[72] A Senate decision to create a commission to in-vestigate reports of judicial corruption produced similar results in 1999: judges engaged in work stoppages, accused congressional leaders of "Nazism," declared that even investigating judicial behavior threatened Brazilian democracy, and refused to honor congressional subpoenas to testify before the legislature.[73]

Given this climate, it is not surprising that the courts do not administer their funds in an especially efficient or accountable manner. Allegations of wasteful spend-ing, while sometimes anecdotal, over time suggest a broader trend of bureaucratic dis-regard for accountability.[74] In 1994, for example, the federal courts had a budget of more than $500 million—but spent $843 million and billed the National Treasury for the rest. The Supreme Labor Tribunal alone—which boasted a less than impres-sive record of judging only 4,695 of the 78,695 cases brought before it in 1993—spent $400 million, more than both chambers of the entire 594-member Congress spent that same year.[75] Such reports of overspending are common. In 1993, the STJ launched a $4.5 million project to computerize its records; the project eventually was completed—two years behind schedule and a staggering $165 million over budget.[76] Similarly, a 1999 congressional inquiry into the federal labor courts found that the former president of the Regional Labor Court in Rio de Janeiro had authorized a series of construction projects at costs more than 340 percent above market rates, with relatives and friends receiving kickbacks in an elaborate overbilling scheme.[77] Symbolic of the waste was the building for the Supreme Tribunal of Justice (STJ) completed in 1995, a $170 million building with more empty offices than full ones. Attacked by the Brazilian Bar Association as indicative of a bureaucratic class that had become oblivious to the austere conditions confronting the rest of the country, the STJ building inexplicably included an indoor theater, exercise room, swimming pool, two restaurants, a bar, and a ballroom.[78]

EFFICIENCY AND ACCESS: A CYCLE OF FAILURE

Enhancing access—both for the person on the street and for various political groups—was one of the core goals of judicial reformers in the Constituent Assembly. As recounted in Chapter Two, the goal of access creation cannot be separated entirely from the concept of judicial efficiency, insofar as inefficient courts are the most costly for those unable to afford lengthy delays. Brazil after 1988 reinforces the notion of negative synergy: the initial surge in demands on the courts created by the statist Constitution generated a backlog of cases that the inefficient courts could not absorb—thereby undermining the efforts to create more genuine access. Meanwhile, none of the judiciary could be isolated from the larger political and economic forces that distorted the reform process along the way.

A first complicating factor was the nature of the Constitution itself. The openness that characterized the drafting of the judicial reforms was mirrored in the drafting of the entire document. No interest group was too insignificant to weigh in and no demand too marginal to include. The result was a shockingly convoluted process. Congress was flooded with 11,989 constitutional proposals from citizen petitions and civic organizations, particularly womens' groups, trade unions, industrialists, state and municipal governments, and environmentalists.[79] Responsibility for debating and merging these suggestions with Congress's own amendments was divided among eight congressional committees, each of which was composed of sixty-three members and an equal number of alternates and which was further subdivided into three subcommittees.[80] The final results of these twenty-four committees would be harmonized by the Integration Committee, a group of ninety-three legislators from all thirteen parties.[81] During the two-year process, the Assembly considered more than 61,000 amendments and, in October 1988, produced a 70-page, 245-article Constitution.[82]

The final contents of this approach were disastrous, combining sweeping pledges that were impossible to implement with minute, exacting provisions that were better left to ordinary legislation. Sarney, who had no real interest in judicial reform—as senator in 1977 he had tried to push through Congress the military's controversial judicial reform package—was all too willing to accede to the statist and populist demands in exchange for a fifth year in office. Among the more sweeping guarantees in the Constitution were pledges to eradicate poverty and inequality, end racism, and ensure regional economic equality. Other provisions included a 12-percent cap on real interest rates; severe restrictions on foreign investment in key economic sectors such as oil, mining, telecommunications, and shipping; tenure for all civil servants with more than five years of service; a constitutionally-mandated maximum work week of forty-four hours; annual paid vacations for all public and private sector employees, compensated with at least a one-third bonus over their regular pay; paid maternity leave; and a paid day off each week ("preferably on Sundays," according to Article 6). Other provisions included obligating the federal government to devote an unspecified amount of resources for the creation of a national amateur sports system, promotion of Afro-Brazilian culture, and the advancement of leisure as the national pastime. Congress left to ordinary legislation the task of specifying how and when these provisions would be enacted.[83] Almost immediately, the detailed, hortatory nature of the Constitution meant that many routine political and economic activities became constitutional challenges; the surge in the number of cases created the appearance of dramatically increased access simply because record numbers of citizens were being compelled to turn to the courts to conduct simple transactions.

Second, such a document predictably included provisions that paved the way for economic chaos that would prevent some judicial reforms from actually ever being implemented. State and local governments, reacting to decades of centralization under military rule, secured approval of a constitutional amendment that annually transferred more than half of all federal tax receipts directly to states and municipalities for discretionary use by governors and mayors. The arrangement forced the central government to run perpetual public sector deficits, contributing to a steady cycle of hyperinflation. Between 1988 and July 1994—when an economic stabilization plan dramatically reduced inflation—cumulative inflation in Brazil surpassed 84 million percent, producing what Bolívar Lamounier referred to as "hyperactive paralysis": constant policy innovations and repeated flurries of new programs—all of which gave the appearance of momentum but which concealed a lack of real progress on implementing the reforms essential for putting the country's economic house in order.[84]

Finally, the Constitution reflected two competing—and probably contradictory—prevailing political sentiments. On the one hand, Brazil's framers sought to constitutionalize, in national terms and in an enduring legal framework, a number of social, political, and economic rights that had been threatened or denied under military rule; hence, Brazil's Constitution is generally long on guaranteeing a number of so-called positive rights.[85] On the other hand, the framers demonstrated a strong reaction against the centralization that had come to characterize the military government. Coupled with heavy pressure from state and municipal governments, the framers offset many of their nationalist tendencies with an exaggerated deference to federalism and states rights (such as the aforementioned mandatory revenue-sharing scheme). The results were curious: a laundry list of sweeping positive rights were declared fundamental and mandated throughout the land—while the means and timing of their implementation were simultaneously left to state and local governments, on the grounds that they would need to be adjusted to local conditions. Against such a backdrop, it is not surprising that many of the judicial reform outputs looked nothing like the reformers intended.

Efficiency

The inadequacy (and the absence) of efficiency reforms, against such a tumultuous backdrop, created a near unanimous consensus about judicial efficiency and trial delays by the late 1990s. Editorials repeatedly denounce the courts for their lengthy delays, and polls show that more than 90 percent of the public describe the courts as "slow" or "very slow."[86]

Court statistics, while incomplete, nonetheless point toward the insufficiency of the 1988 reforms. Judges frankly admit that they have no firm grasp of how many cases are in the local, state, and federal court systems; many cases are resolved out of court but never removed from the dockets; some users file the same case in various regions hoping to get a prompt court date before at least one judge; and many litigants die while waiting for a trial date.[87] Former Supreme Court President Carlos Velloso has reported that the most accurate estimates approach 50 million total cases, some of which have been pending since the 1940s.[88] Since the late 1980s, approximately 400 new cases enter the judicial system each day, although only 40–50 percent are disposed of in any given year.[89]

The main efficiency measures—creation of a new federal court of appeals to help decongest the Supreme Court—cannot be said to have met their goals. Nine years after implementation of the reforms, the caseload of the Supreme Court, despite its narrower sphere of competence, was heavier than ever. The volume of cases went from 14,000 in 1987 to 24,000 in 1992, 28,000 in 1995, and 35,000 in 1996—and still, on 1 January 1997, the STF had an additional caseload of 10,000 cases pending.[90] A similar pattern prevailed with the STJ. The number of cases before the STJ went from 24,000 in the early 1990s to more than 40,000 cases by 1996, with a total backlog of some 60,000 cases.[91] Invariably, the increase in the number of cases affected the quality of the decisions. Unable to hear all the cases before the court, the thirty-three justices on the STJ would divide up the cases and individually render a verdict on behalf of the entire court; the other thirty-two justices would rubber-stamp the decision, assuming—but never verifying—that the verdict of the deciding justice was correct.[92]

These increases, coupled with the reformers' neglect of traditional efficiency reforms such as new case management techniques or an increased reliance on court clerks, produced predictable results. Lower court judges, distracted by the inevitable bureaucratic tasks of managing such affairs, devoted more than 60 percent of their time to routine administrative affairs rather than judicial decisionmaking.[93] Not surprisingly, times to disposition throughout the federal court system increased nearly 40 percent in less than a decade.[94] A further indication of the inefficiency is the degree to which this work load was distributed unevenly. The Supreme Military Justice Tribunal (STM) is cited as an example. Part of the federal judiciary responsible for hearing cases involving members of the armed forces, the STM in 1994 had a budget of $52 million, but held only eighty-two sessions lasting a mere 377 hours all year, and judged 418 cases, an average of only twenty-five cases per judge per year.[95] Meanwhile, state courts in Rio de Janeiro had some judges with active caseloads of more than 7,000, and some in São Paulo were managing as many as 10,000 cases at a time—despite a law declaring that no judge could consider more than 300 cases at a time.[96] The crisis of efficiency was so grave that one Brazilian author has calculated that, even if the country filled every judicial vacancy and every case could be disposed of in just one day, it would take judges a minimum of six years, working weekends and holidays, to resolve all lingering cases—assuming no new cases entered the system during this period.[97] The situation was so dire by 1996 the President took the unprecedented step of issuing a presidential decree in which the federal government conceded defeat on more than 250,000 suits of monetarily minor value against the federal government that were pending in court, whatever effects the costs of settlement might have on an already cash-strapped government.[98]

Access

The crisis of efficiency was due only in part to the relative absence of meaningful efficiency reforms; it was also due in large part to the reformers' approach to access and the distortions it created. If reformers thought that all access was good access, then they clearly met their goals. The surge in cases as the STF and STJ described earlier were replicated throughout the judicial system: federal courts saw the number of new cases entering the federal system increase by 100 percent between 1989 and 1991, while the caseload of the Superior Labor Court increased more than 60 percent between 1990 and 1992. New cases entering the São Paulo state judicial system increased more than 130 percent between 1988 and 1991.[99] For Brazil, the question is whether the increased tendency to turn to the courts reflected a growing public confidence in the ability to secure justice through formal legal institutions or whether it was the result of other factors.

In fact, the surge in cases seems to have had less to do with access creation strategies—many of which were never actually implemented—and more to do with the curious nature of the Constitution and the degree to which it managed to turn even minor disputes into constitutional challenges. The extent to which the 1988 Constitution produced a rise in allegedly "constitutional" issues is reflected in the growth of the Supreme Court's docket after 1988. Under the 1988 Constitution, the work load of the STF—some 14,000 cases in 1987—was supposed to be lightened considerably by transferring non-constitutional cases to the Supreme Court of Justice (STJ), the newly created court of last appeal for non-constitutional issues. Yet a decade after implementation of the reforms, the caseload of the Supreme Court, despite its narrower sphere of competence, was heavier than ever; the volume of cases went from 14,000 in 1987 to 35,000 in 1996.[100] The reformers' decision to deny the High Court the writ of certiorari—an effort to ensure that politically sensitive cases would not be shelved indefinitely, as occurred under military rule—left the Court no control over its own docket, forcing it to hear even trivial complaints such as bar fights, neighborhood noise disputes, and an impressive number of divorce settlements—the latter allegedly involving "constitutional" questions about which litigant was most likely to comply with the constitutional provision that private property would serve a "social utility." Sydney Sanches, a former president of the Supreme Court, has lamented that since 1988, "the Supreme Court has turned into a small claims court" that is obligated to hear the most mundane matters, the vast majority of which are not authentic constitutional issues.[101]

The ADIN was typical of the problems of access coupled with excessive independence and inefficiency. The ADIN had been intended to allow groups aggrieved by government decisions to petition against federal acts on constitutional grounds, an effort to protect against governmental violations of civil liberties—again, another reaction against two decades of military rule. Clearly the ADIN gave certain types of political and social movements unparalleled access to the courts; between 1988 and 1993 the courts received more than 100 ADINs. Looking specifically at the types of ADINs, however, a real question is whether they involved genuine constitutional issues or whether they were manipulated for partisan advantage to the detriment of the overall court system.[102] During this period, more than half of all ADINs were from political parties, and slightly more than two-thirds of them were filed by three ideological leftist parties (the Workers' Party, the Democratic Workers' Party, and the Brazilian Socialist Party) seeking to undo particular economic policies; only 1.6 percent of the cases actually involved an issue related to civil liberties, which had been the original focus of the legislation. As in the case with most of Brazil's access-creating measures, even this reform was less than met the eye: of the 113 ADINs filed by political parties between 1988 and 1992, the Supreme Court managed to rule on only six of them.[103]

An equally striking aspect of other access-creating reforms for the average citizen was that they generally were never implemented, or enacted only half-heartedly at best. Creation of the constitutionally mandated small claims courts had been left to each state much like an unfunded mandate. Yet during this period, most states nonetheless were bankrupt; all of them spent between 60 and 105 percent of tax receipts simply to meet payroll and pension costs and had few resources left for additional investments.[104] The results were not surprising: few state governors were willing to devote the scarce financial resources to creating new legal structures, particularly since the Constitution was vague about the timing of creation and silent on potential sanctions for failing to comply.[105] The results were ironic: "access" to the courts was increasing, even though many of the access-creating reforms were never actually implemented.

The statist nature of the Constitution, coupled with barely implemented access strategies and non-existent efficiency measures, created a series of judicial bottlenecks throughout the country. In 1993, Rondônia state reported that it had 75,367 pending cases in the courts of first instance—but only 439 total cases at the second instance, a reflection of the inability of courts to adjudicate on a timely basis and distribute its caseload more evenly. The state of Bahia was only slightly better—36,092 cases await-ing a trial date in courts of first instance, but only 2,484 at the second instance. In both states, the total number of pending cases had increased more than 50 percent over the previous decade.[106] By 1995, President Cardoso acknowledged that most states would never create these courts on their own initiative—despite the constitu-tional mandate—and secured approval of legislation that created a federal small claims court system.[107] Nearly a decade after the Constitution, the federal government was legislating for the states what they had failed to do themselves.[108]

A second factor contributing to the crisis of efficiency and access could be found in the judicial independence so fiercely defended by judges. Brazilian law required that any aspiring judge must first pass a rigorous professional entrance exam, a laud-able effort to avoid the selection of ill-qualified judges that was so common in Brazil's neighbors. Yet professional rigor had a downside: every year more than 80 percent of all applicants failed to make it past the first round of preliminary judicial examina-tions, meaning that the courts literally had difficulty finding qualified applicants to fill the vacant posts.[109] The ensuing lack of judges was apparent enough. Former Supreme President Sepúlveda Pertence has spoken of a "chronic deficit of judges" in the country, a view shared by his colleagues: according to a 1995 survey of Brazilian judges, more than 80 percent cited the lack of judges as a primary cause for lengthy trial delays.[110]

The evidence bears out the general shortage. In 1995, state and federal govern-ments combined for a total of 5,984 judges for a population of 158 million—a ratio of one judge for every 25,000 citizens, approximately the same ratio as that in 1950 and slightly worse than in 1980—and far below the OECD average of one judge for every 3,000 citizens.[111] Judicial officials indicated that of Brazil's 7,789 local, state, and fed-eral judgeships throughout the country, more than 1,800, or approximately 24 per-cent, were vacant in 1994. Not surprisingly, Brazil's rural western and northeastern states fared especially poorly. In Pernambuco, a state of more than 8 million inhabi-tants, 73 of the 176 townships did not have even one judge, while in Amazonas state, 31 percent of the towns did not have a single judge.[112] Brazil's more developed urban areas fared no better. Despite generally having better bureaucratic infrastructures, the judiciary has failed to keep pace with changing demographics. In 1980, São Paulo state had one judge for every 27,000 inhabitants; by the mid-1990s, after nearly a decade of democratic rule, the ratio had declined to one judge per every 29,000 in-habitants.[113] Nonetheless, judges fiercely resisted periodic calls to create a nationwide system of justices of the peace—which could have helped relieve some of the backlog—on the grounds that any structural reforms ought to come from the judiciary itself to avoid violations in the separation of powers. Extreme judicial independence, iron-ically, did not help boost efficiency. In many respects, the former undercut the latter.

Brazil also has fared poorly in improving access for the poor, women, and minori-ties. Even when Brazilians could gain access to a court, there was no evidence that the courts were more affordable than in the mid-1980s. The parochialism and lavish working conditions for senior judges had to be financed from somewhere. To pay for benefits such as generous retirement plans, average court costs increased in real terms since 1988. Twenty-six of Brazil's twenty-seven states added additional fees to court costs after 1988, funds earmarked for financing judicial medical plans and other expenses (such as weekend retreats for judicial personnel); these costs amounted to an additional 5 to 26 percent of court costs after 1988.[114] Other barriers include the excessive formalism of the courts—virtually all court proceedings remained written rather than oral. The story of respected scholar Dalmo Dallari in Chapter Two—of having to go to a local television station during the impeachment trial of Fernando Collor to translate for the public, who could not understand whether the justices were supporting or opposing the impeachment—points to the degree to which the average citizen continued to perceive court proceedings as too formal. It also is clear that on another sociological aspect of access—fostering the perception that average citizens have a fair chance of gaining justice if they turn to the courts—Brazil has not fared well. The record on access for women is one such example. Despite High Court rulings to the contrary, Brazilian state and local courts still invoke the so-called "defense of honor" laws that define a woman as the social property of her husband and that skew court proceedings against the woman by requiring a greater burden of proof in domestic violence cases.[115] One Brazilian NGO has reported that of the more than 2,000 spousal abuse and battery charges filed by women in Rio de Janeiro in 1990, none resulted in punishment of the accused. Similarly, in the northern state of Maranhão, of the more than 4,000 spousal abuse complaints filed between 1988–90, only 300 were forwarded for processing and only two men were actually convicted.[116]

FINAL THOUGHTS ON THE BRAZILIAN EXPERIENCE

Several conclusions stand out about Brazil's judicial reform efforts. First and foremost is that few judicial reform experiences in Latin America seem to have been clearer examples of failure. Reformers achieved unprecedented levels of structural and individual independence, but, in the process of reacting to more than two decades of military rule, swept aside the balancing constraints of accountability and transparency. By virtually any measure, the courts were irresponsible, inefficient, and inaccessible. With such a track record, it is not surprising that polls taken throughout the 1990s reflected a cynicism that far exceeded the dissatisfaction of the 1980s. Judicial independence, a near-universal topic of consensus during the constitutional debates of 1987–88, was increasingly under criticism: by 1994–95, 74 percent of the Congress declared itself in support of external controls on the judiciary, while 72 percent of the public expressed similar views.[117] Precise responses varied depending on the survey, but between 65 and 75 percent of the public consistently claimed that it was dissatisfied with the judicial system; 43 percent said that they had "little or no confidence" in the Supreme Court.[118] Nor were the courts seen as any more efficient: whereas nearly 60 percent of all respondents in the mid-1980s complained that the courts were "too slow," a 1992 survey found that 87 percent believed that justice was too slow—nearly identical to the 91 percent expressing that view in a separate poll conducted later that year and 94 percent expressing those views in 1999.[119] And despite the pledges to make the courts closer to the average citizen, the courts clearly were not perceived as any more accessible: 77 percent said that the courts were "inaccessible" for the average citizen, 81 percent described court proceedings as "onerous," 67 percent believed that the courts judged poor litigants more harshly than their wealthier counterparts, more than half disagreed with the statement that judiciary by and large "punishes those who are guilty of crimes and lets those who are innocent go free," 86 percent agreed with the statement that "there are some types of people who will never be punished for breaking the law," 80 percent said that the enforcement of the country's laws depended primarily on one's skin color and social standing, over 75 percent agreed with the statement that the country's laws "only benefit the powerful," and less than 4 percent said that they would be willing to take a hypothetical case to court.[120]

A second and more puzzling point focuses on why reform efforts subsequent to 1988 have not been more prominent or more successful given the overwhelming sentiment among legislators and the public that the courts are inadequate for the demands of a democratic society. Clearly, public contempt for the judiciary had reached unprecedented levels, and there was no shortage of reform proposals—some ninety-two judicial reform bills were pending in Congress by 1999.[121] Yet actual movement was curiously absent. A partial explanation for the apparent contradiction can be found in public opinion. As in the El Salvador experience, polls show profound dissatisfaction with the courts—but also a high degree of public disinterest. Asked to identify the most pressing national concern, a striking aspect is the consistently low prominence given to the judicial reform. A 1997 poll was instructive. After nearly a decade of failed judicial reforms, which witnessed increasing backlogs and trial delays, only one-tenth of one percent cited judicial reform as the top national priority; more pressing concerns were economic recovery, unemployment, personal security, health care, and education.[122] The logic was understandable enough. Faced with such pressing economic and social concerns, an inefficient court system may have been an object of frustration and even contempt—but was relegated to the back burner in the face of more immediate concerns. The case of the Cardoso administration is fairly representative of this point. Few Latin American presidents—and none in Brazil's recent past—more clearly understood the need for an independent, accountable, efficient, and accessible judiciary. Yet when Congress began investigating judicial corruption in 1999, Cardoso was at the forefront of those calling on Congress to shelve the inquiry, out of fear that the efforts would sidetrack legislators from passing fiscal reforms needed to assuage the IMF and international investors in the wake of the Asian financial crisis and the devaluation of the Brazilian currency.[123] In democratic Brazil, presidential candidates got elected by promising to "kill inflation with a single bullet" (Collor's pledge in 1990) and to deliver "first-world inflation rates" (Cardoso's pledge in 1994). No candidate is likely to get elected pledging incremental structural changes whose effects would, at best, be a decade away—and no politician is willing to risk trying.

Another reason that explains why the public's calls for judicial reform are so sparse—even though frustration is so high—is that the level of cynicism is now so great that the public appears to have given up on the courts altogether, reflecting a trend that James Holston and Teresa P. R. Caldeira have referred to as "the privatization of justice."[124] That is, there is little desire to focus political energies on the courts when they have become so irrelevant and have been replaced with other forms of justice. Some of the means of dispute resolution are benign and others clearly less so, but both show disregard for the formal legal system.[125] This tendency to administer justice on an interpersonal, extra-legal basis has accelerated since the 1980s, and with increasingly less benign connotations. The trend is clearest in the criminal justice system. Robert Shirley wrote in 1984 that one of the more disturbing trends for Brazilian democracy was the willingness of the public to resort to vigilante justice—nearly half the public expressed support for the idea in 1984—as a substitute for relying on the courts. A 1987 survey of the urban poor by the Brazilian Bar Association found that approximately half of respondents expressed similar attitudes, indicating a preference for "informal justice."[126] Yet by the 1990s, it was clear that the public had given up on the courts and was increasingly willing to tolerate egregious abuses of civil liberties if they meted out justice, no matter how primitively.[127] The inability of the criminal justice system to contain the rise of violent and non-violent crimes—and the widespread belief that the court system will merely return criminals to the streets—had fostered an increasing tolerance for vigilante groups in major urban and rural areas alike.[128] Recent years have witnessed a steady rise of self-styled "law and order" politicians who reject institutional or incremental reforms such as restructuring the courts and instead favor reinstating long-abandoned, hardline practices such as public executions and hangings.[129] Polls consistently reflect this hardening of public attitudes. For example, when a policeman in Rio de Janeiro unwittingly was filmed shooting an unarmed teenager execution-style in early 1995, polls found that 60 percent of city residents voiced support for the actions of the policeman, a position echoed by the state governor, himself a former human rights lawyer.[130] Several months later, when state police executed fourteen suspected drug traffickers despite published reports that the drug lords offered no resistance, the popular governor told reporters that he would "not accept any criticism" of the police, whose role he hailed as helping turn the tide against crime in the city.[131] Similarly, a 1993 poll conducted after police executed more than 110 inmates in a São Paulo prison uprising—the bloodiest police massacre in the country's history—found that 60 percent of the public supported the actions; a subsequent poll found that 56 percent of respondents agreed with the statement that the criminal justice system ought not extend human rights to criminals. Meanwhile, a hot line set up by state authorities in Rio de Janeiro seeking anonymous tips following the massacre of eight street children in 1993 had to be disconnected because the office was flooded by callers voicing approval of the actions of the anonymous off-duty officers.[132] By the late 1990s, with vigilante justice on the rise and the courts increasingly marginal to the average citizen, the attitudes toward democracy were not encouraging. Perhaps just as disconcerting was the fact that in one 1994 survey, 25 percent of low-income respondents believed that authoritarian governments were better able to hand out "equal justice;" 42 percent felt that authoritarian governments were better able to protect their citizens from crime and violence.[133]

Without more sustained pressure for judicial reform, the ability of the courts to resist reform efforts becomes much easier. As is clear from the foregoing discussion, the courts are clearly independent—excessively so—and have been reluctant to accept any measures that would enhance greater oversight. Some insight on the level of insularity and parochialism comes from a unique poll of judges conducted in 1995 by a São Paulo–based think tank. Recalling that more than 70 percent of the public and Congress support external controls on the judiciary and that more than 90 percent are dissatisfied with the pace of justice, the attitudes of judges are staggering. Asked if they supported some form of external controls, more than 85 percent said no; asked if judiciary was "in crisis," only 22.5 percent of judges said yes—a remarkably high level of satisfaction relative to that expressed by the public. Asked, then, who or what was responsible for the perception that the courts were in crisis, 64 percent of the judges blamed "the press."[134]

The degree to which excessive independence, lacking the balancing constraint of accountability, has undermined possible reforms of other aspects of the courts has been highlighted on various occasions: judges have consistently resisted virtually any reform measure, including those that, if implemented, would reduce the work load and enhance the efficiency and access of the courts. In the 1993–94 constitutional review process, when Congress began debating plans to establish external controls on the courts, judges and court employees descended on Brasília to pressure Congress, charging that such reforms would pose a threat to judicial independence.[135] In 1995–97, when progovernment legislators proposed a bill that would have introduced precedent into the Brazilian system—a well-intentioned effort to reduce the staggering number of duplicate cases clogging the federal court system—the reaction was swift: judges throughout the country publicly began comparing the measure with Nazi Germany and Institutional Act Number 5 of the military government, charging that having to follow the judicial rulings set by another court would stifle the individual independence of judges.[136] Without a public galvanized by the reform efforts, politicians faced a stark choice—and an unfortunately easy one at that: shelve pressing economic reforms and undertake a costly political fight against a well-organized opposition that can claim the rhetorical high ground of defending judicial independence, or stand aside and let the courts continue to administer their affairs as they see fit. The decision—regrettably, for the depth and quality of Brazilian democracy—has been an easy one.

NOTES

1. Brutus (Robert Yates) in *The Complete Anti-Federalist*, vol. 2, ed. Herbert J. Storing (Chicago: University of Chicago Press, 1981): 438.

2. José Genoíno, "O Contrôle do Judiciário," *O Globo*, 17 June 1995, 7.

3. Indeed, the Brazilian experience is unique in Latin America: it raises the unusual question of whether *all* access is *good* access; that is, are some types of access (small claims courts, for example) better than other types of access—such as the right to have a divorce settlement heard before the Supreme Court?

4. Throughout this chapter I refer to Brazil's twenty-seven states, for the sake of brevity, recognizing that there are twenty-six states and a federal district.

Inflationary arithmetic in Brazil is an imprecise science because civilian governments since 1985 have not relied on a single index to track inflation. Instead, governments typically have relied on various indices, usually citing the one with the lowest monthly rate and cobbling to-gether an annual rate of inflation based on disparate sources. I arrived at the figure of 84 mil-lion percent using the index provided by the University of São Paulo's Economic Research Institute (FIPE). Lincoln Gordon has noted, however, that other estimates are even higher. By using estimates from the Getúlio Vargas Foundation and published monthly in *Conjuntura Econômica*, Gordon has calculated that inflation in 1996 was 23.3 million times that of 1988, or a percentage increase of 2.3 billion. Whichever index one uses, all underline the point that extreme hyperinflation dogged Brazil until the economic stabilization plan was introduced in July 1994.

5. See Robert Damatta, *Carnivals, Rogues, and Heroes* (Notre Dame, Ind.: University of Notre Dame Press, 1991): 168–69; and Robert Shirley, "A Brief Survey of Law in Brazil," *Canadian Journal of Latin American and Caribbean Studies* 23 (1987): 1–14.

6. The exception was the 1930 coup that ushered Getúlio Vargas to power. Vargas gradu-ally remodeled the state along the lines of Mussolini's corporatist model and politicized the ju-diciary through dismissals and court-packing. See Marcus Wyler, "The Development of the Brazilian Constitution (1891–1946)," *The Journal of Comparative Legislation and International Law* 31 (November 1949): 53–60.

7. The nonstransferrability of judges was a respected tradition. When President Ku-bitschek moved the federal capital from Rio de Janeiro to Brasília in the 1950s, a debate en-sued over which constitutional article took precedence: the requirement that Supreme Court judges must be located in the capital city, or the clause ensuring non-transferal of judges. After some debate, the justices moved to Brasília. See E. D. Moniz de Aragão, "The Brazilian Judi-cial Organization," *Revista Jurídica Interamericana* 6 (July–December 1964): 258–59. For a dis-cussion of the early similarities between the Brazilian and U.S. federal court systems, see Amaro Cavalcanti, "The Federal Judiciary in Brazil and the United States of America," *Uni-versity of Pennsylvania Law Review and American Law Register* 60 (October 1911): 103–22.

8. Jacob Dollinger, "The Influence of American Constitutional Law on the Brazilian Legal System," *The American Journal of Comparative Law* 38 (Fall 1990): 803–37.

9. Robert Wesson and David Fleischer, *Brazil in Transition* (New York: Praeger Publishers, 1983): 84. The notable exception prior to the 1964 coup was the Vargas purge of the Supreme Court in 1931.

10. Henry J. Steiner, "Legal Education and Socio-Economic Change: Brazilian Perspec-tives," *The American Journal of Comparative Law* 18 (Fall 1971): 39–90.

11. In this respect, Brazilian federalism was less a reflection of the preferred ordering prin-ciple for the polity and more of an explicit recognition that the central government had little or no prospects for establishing a meaningful presence in major parts of the country.

12. The persistence of private justice in Brazil is traced in Maria-Victoria Benavides and Rosa-Maria Fischer Ferreira, "Popular Responses and Urban Violence: Lynching in Brazil," in *Vigilantism and the State in Modern Latin America*, ed. Martha X. Huggins (New York: Praeger, 1991): 21–32.

13. Upon seizing power, the armed forces did not renounce or suspend the 1946 Consti-tution. Instead, they merely issued the institutional acts as amendments that were said to su-persede the Constitution. This pattern persisted until the military introduced a new constitution in 1967.

14. Riordan Roett, *Brazil: Politics in a Patrimonial Society* (New York: Praeger, 1984): 127.

15. Maria Tereza Sadek, "A Organização do Poder Judiciário no Brasil," in *Uma Introdução ao Estudo da Justiça*, ed. Maria Tereza Sadek (São Paulo: Editora Sumare/IDESP, 1995): 12.

16. Maria D'Alva G. Kinzo, *Legal Opposition Politics Under Authoritarian Rule in Brazil* (New York: St. Martin Press, 1988): 171–79. This sensitivity to potential external oversight has been a recurring theme in Brazil, even under civilian rule.

17. Mark J. Osiel, "Dialogue with Dictators: Judicial Resistance in Argentina and Brazil," *Law and Social Inquiry* 20 (Spring 1995): 527. Apparently this decision not to purge the courts ran into opposition from the military's hardline faction. See John W. F. Dulles, *President Castello Branco: Brazilian Reformer* (Austin: University of Texas Press, 1980): 31.

18. See Beverley May Carl, "Erosion of Constitutional Rights in Brazil," *The Virginia Journal of International Law* 12 (March 1972): 157–91. Thomas Skidmore writes that during this period, the dominant faction in the military government had a "frenzy for law" and "penchant for formal legitimacy" and sincerely sought, however curiously, "to create a political system that would reconcile the military and constitutionalist ideas of the nation, the society, and the individual." See Thomas Skidmore, *The Politics of Military Rule in Brazil, 1964–85* (New York: Oxford University Press, 1988): 58.

19. Other aspects of this process included the gradual restoration of many civil liberties, the presence of an official opposition political party, the return of exiles, an amnesty law for political crimes, and at least symbolic debate of government proposals in Congress. As Javier Martinez-Lara points out, Brazil's liberalization and transition was "erratic rather than a linear movement. The restoration of democratic politics in Brazil was noteworthy for its uncertainties and length." See Javier Martinez-Lara, *Building Democracy in Brazil* (London: Macmillan Press, 1996): 27. The Médici government—particularly hardline Justice Minister Alfredo Buzaid—argued for institutionalizing the regime along the lines of the Mexican PRI. Later, liberalization in the late 1970s was abruptly interrupted by the April package. An insightful look at these trends as they developed can be found in Fernando Pereira, "Decompression in Brazil?" *Foreign Affairs* 53 (April 1975): 498–512. Congress is one example of the degree to which regime opposition was often more symbolic than real. For example, even though Congress convened for most of the period between 1967 and 1984, it regularly approved more than 95 percent of the bills proposed by the executive. See Abdo Baaklini, *The Brazilian Legislature and the Political System* (Westport, Conn.: Greenwood Press, 1992): 116.

20. Wesson and Fleischer, *Brazil in Transition*, p. 86. Osiel notes that in one prominent case, government lawyers argued that a naturalized alien was endangering national security by running a brothel, reasoning that prostitution threatened the Christian family which, in turn, undermined the "social order" and hence sowed the potential for subversion—particularly because the offending party was an immigrant. The High Court rejected all of these arguments. See Osiel, "Dialogue with Dictators: Judicial Resistance in Argentina and Brazil," pp. 534–35.

21. Maria Helena Moreira Alves, *State and Opposition in Military Brazil* (Austin: University of Texas Press, 1985): 160.

22. *World Development Report, 1997: The State in a Changing World* (Washington, D.C.: The World Bank, 1997): 46.

23. Shirley, "A Brief Survey of Law in Brazil," pp. 11–14.

24. Neves's record included three decades as a federal deputy and a brief stint as Prime Minister in the early 1960s, a range of contacts on the left and right, including contacts in the armed forces with whom he frequently met during the nervous transition, all of which allowed him to defeat the military's preferred candidate in the January 1985 indirect elections.

25. Gilberto Dimenstein, *O Cômplo que Elegeu Tancredo* (Rio de Janeiro: JB, 1985): 224–26.

26. A fairly representative piece from the international media that expresses this optimism is Ross Laver, "Beginning anew in Brazil," *Maclean's*, 21 January 1985, pp. 24–26.

27. Ronald Schneider argues that Neves was the only politician capable of holding together a movement as disparate and factionalized as the PMDB. See Ronald M. Schneider, "Brazil's Political Future," in *Political Liberalization in Brazil*, ed. Wayne Selcher (Boulder, Colo.: Westview Press, 1986): 228.

28. An early look at the uneasy relationship between these factions is Eul-Soo Pang, "The Darker Side of Brazil's Democracy," *Current History* 87 (January 1988): 21–24, 40–41. A more detailed look at the essentially nonreformist nature of Sarney and his supporters is Frances Hagopian, " 'Democracy By Undemocratic Means?' Elites, Political Pacts, and Regime Transition in Brazil," *Comparative Political Studies* 23 (July 1990): 147–70. The group of northeastern-based rightists opposed to the nomination of São Paulo's Paulo Maluf formed the so-called Liberal Front, a group of dissident conservatives that would ally with the Brazilian Democratic Movement Party (PMDB) of Neves. The Liberal Front, led by Marco Maciel, Jorge Bornhausen, and Antônio Carlos Magalhães, formed the core of what would later become the Liberal Front Party.

29. This brief summary does not do justice to the disarray and mismanagement of the Sarney government. During his five-year term, Brazil had three economic shock programs—all of which collapsed—three currencies, four finance ministers, three central bank presidents, and cumulative inflation of more than one million percent. Among the various accounts of this period, one of the best is Ronald Schneider, *Order and Progress: A Political History of Brazil* (Boulder, Colo.: Westview Press, 1991). A stern assessment of Sarney's economic mismanagement can be found in Riordan Roett, "Brazil's Transition to Democracy," *Current History* 88 (March 1989): 117–20, 149–51.

Sarney's own approach to constitutional reform was to appoint a commission of notables known as the Arinos Commission, which some critics have suggested was an attempt to sidestep the constitution-drafting process altogether. The Arinos Commission eventually produced a utopian draft covering more than 500 articles—one of which unexpectedly called for Sarney to give way to a parliamentary system. Not surprisingly, Sarney shelved the report. See "New Brazilian Constitution: Arinos Draft and Its Controversial Provisions a Likely Starting Point," U.S. Department of State, unclassified telegram Brasilia 00231, 2 February 1987. Reaction within Congress to the initial draft also was tepid. One prominent legislator told U.S. officials, "We will simply throw the Arinos Report in the wastebasket. Who are they anyway to tell us about a new constitution?" See "Proposals for Constitutional Changes Concerning Law and Order," U.S. Department of State, unclassified telegram Brasilia 06427, 11 June 1986.

30. See "Constitutional Assembly: Who Supports What," U.S. Department of State, unclassified telegram Brasilia 01331, 8 February 1987.

31. Thomas Skidmore explains the dilemma once the transition to civilian rule occurred: "Brazil was paying the price for its years of authoritarian rule. Those brave enough—or cynical enough—to enter politics in those two decades got a distorted apprenticeship in democratic governance. Legislatures with truncated powers, elections with changing rules, surveillance by multiple intelligence systems, media censorship and military intervention in virtually every institution—these were hardly designed to nurture a new generation of politicians skilled in the arts of identifying and representing citizen opinion. Rather, those years favored two types of politicians: the opportunists who could prosper in, or alongside, the government party; and the orators who eloquently excoriated the government for its subversion of human rights, democracy, and national sovereignty." See Skidmore, *The Politics of Military Rule in Brazil, 1964–85*, p. 267.

32. Martinez-Lara notes that at the time of the Constituent Assembly, none of the major parties had even produced position papers on what the new constitution ought to look like.

On the clientelistic nature of Brazil's fragmented party system, concise overviews can be found in Scott Mainwaring, "Brazilian Party Underdevelopment in Comparative Perspective," *Political Science Quarterly* 107 (Winter 1992–93): 677–707; and Scott Mainwaring, "Political Parties and Democratization in Brazil and the Southern Cone," *Comparative Politics* 21 (October 1988): 91–119.

33. Keith S. Rosenn, "Brazil's New Constitution: An Exercise in Transient Constitutionalism for a Transitional Society," *The American Journal of Comparative Law* 38 (Fall 1990): 776.

34. Rosenn notes that the process allowed for "an unprecedented amount of popular participation." See his article, "Brazil's New Constitution: An Exercise in Transient Constitutionalism for a Transitional Society," p. 777. The reference to the so-called "elitization" comes from Raymundo Faoro, "Constituente: a Verdade e o sofismo," in *Constituente e Democracia no Brasil Hoje*, ed. Emir Sader (São Paulo: Brasiliense, 1986): 117.

35. Celso Ribeiro Bastos, "A Constituiçao de 1988," *As Constituições Brasileiras: Análise Histórica e Propostas de Mudança* (São Paulo: Editor Brasiliense, 1993): 87.

36. A proposal was floated during the Constituent Assembly to establish a council of magistrates to oversee the administrative affairs of the courts, although it was quickly defeated by the so-called judicial lobby, which argued that such a measure smacked of authoritarianism. See José Ribas Viera, "O Poder Judiciário e A República: A Democratização Adiada," *Revista de Ciencia Politica* 33 (February/April 1990): 105.

37. Ada Pellegrini Grinover, "Deformalising Procedure in Brazil," *Civil Justice Quarterly* 7 (1988): 234–52.

38. Keith S. Rosenn, "A Comparison of the Protection of Individual Rights in the New Constitutions of Colombia and Brazil," *University of Miami Inter-American Law Review* 23 (Spring–Summer 1992): 669.

39. Under the 1986 law, standing to file a class action suit was limited to civic associations and some government agencies. Moreover, damages did not go to the plaintiff, but rather to a special fund that would reconstitute the damaged property. See Keith Rosenn, "Civil Procedure in Brazil," *The American Journal of Comparative Law* 34 (1986): 487–525.

40. "The Brazilian Judiciary Under the New Constitution: An Initial Look," U.S. Department of State, unclassified telegram Brasilia 07938, 7 July 1989.

41. The model for this approach was a similar constitutional court in Portugal. See Sadek, "A Organização do Poder Judiciário no Brasil," p. 15.

42. The TRFs were dispersed throughout the country—Porto Alegre in the south, Rio de Janeiro and São Paulo in the southeast, and Recife and Salvador in the northeast—with eventual plans to place a federal court in every state. "The Brazilian Judiciary Under the New Constitution: An Initial Look," U.S. Department of State, unclassified telegram 07938, 7 July 1989.

43. Figures are taken from "Justiça hoje é poder acima do pais," *Jornal do Brasil*, 7 May 1995, 1; "Second Thoughts on Democracy in Brazil," United States Information Agency, 22 February 1994; and João Batista Natali, "Maioria acha Justiça lenta e defende contrôle externo," *Folha de São Paulo*, 11 July 1993, 15.

44. José Neri da Silveira, "Aspectos institucionais e estruturais do Poder Judiciário brasileiro," in *O Judiciário e a Constituição*, ed. Salvio de Figueiredo (São Paulo: Editora Saraiva, 1992): 1–22.

45. Carlos Mario da Silva Velloso, "Seminario Ibero-americano," in *Justiça: promessa e realidade* (Rio de Janeiro: Editora Nova Fronteira, 1996): 13–32.

46. See, for example, the interview with Supreme Court President José Celso de Mello Filho in Policarpo Junior, "A lei e o limite," *Veja*, 5 March 1997, 9–11; and Antonio de Padua Ribeiro, "O Poder Judiciário: Algumas Reflexões," in *O Judiciário e a Constituição*, p. 33.

47. Sadek, "A Organização do Poder Judiciário no Brasil," p. 13.

48. Katrina Howell, "Politicized Justice? Judicial Review in Democratizing Brazil," Paper prepared for the XXIV 1995 Latin American Studies Association, 28–30 September 1995, p. 21. Brazilian judges also routinely speak out on political and economic policy debates well outside their purview. For a sampling, see "Pertence responde á ataques de ACM," *Correio Brasiliense*, 30 March 1999, 6; "Cadeia não é soluçáo," *IstoÉ*, 26 March 1999, 14; and Rosa Costa, "Pertence divulga nota contra acusações de ACM," *O Estado de São Paulo*, 30 March 1999, 8.

49. Collor was able to stall his impeachment at various stages by arguing—correctly—that Congress had never passed the implementing legislation needed to trigger into effect Articles 85 and 86 of the Constitution, which defined the grounds and procedures for impeachinent. As a result, the High Court frequently was called on to arbitrate the struggle between the two branches of government.

50. Then-President of the Supreme Court Octavio Gallotti highlights this ruling in Luiz Orlando Carneiro, "STF náo é instituto de opinião," *Jornal do Brasil*, 18 December 1994, 7.

51. Timothy J. Power, "The Pen is Mightier than the Congress: Presidential Decree Power in Brazil," Paper presented at the XVIII Congress of the Latin American Studies Association, 10–12 March 1994. For further discussion, see Timothy J. Power, "Politicized Democracy: Competition, Institutions, and Civic Fatigue in Brazil," *Journal of InterAmerican Studies and World Affairs* 33 (Fall 1991): 75–112.

52. The shock program would have crumbled eventually even in the absence of judicial challenges to the plan, although the court ruling undoubtedly contributed to its demise. See "A Cultura da Inflação," *Veja*, 11 July 1990, 46–53.

53. Brazilian law does not make judicial decisions binding on similar cases (the common law principle known as *stare decisis*). The Court does not rule that all employees deserve a raise; the ruling is made on a case-by-case basis and implies only that others may make a similar petition.

54. "Itamar: 'Venda da Cemig só com tropas federais,'" *O Globo*, 9 April 1999, 9; Lu Aiko and Ayrton Centeno, "STF autoriza Olívio a depositar parcela em juízo," *O Estado de São Paulo*, 15 January 1999, 1; and "ACM Attacks Future Court Head on CPI," *O Globo*, 20 April 1999, in FBIS-LAT, 21 April 1999.

55. "Justiça hoje é poder acima do pais," *Jornal do Brasil*, 7 May 1995, 1.

56. Jair Fegheli, a federal deputy from the Brazilian Communist Party, also complains that the courts are "the most hermetic, most closed power that exists." PT criticisms are taken from Olimpio Cruz Neto, "Genoíno leva a presidente do STF emenda propondo contrôle externo," *Folha de São Paulo*, 7 June 1995, 7; "Projeto de Genoíno é atacado por juízes," *Jornal do Brasil*, 8 August 1996, 4; and José Genoíno, "O Contrôle do Judiciário," *O Globo*, 17 June 1995, 7.

57. "ACM acusa judiciário de nepotismo e lentidão," *Jornal do Brasil*, 16 March 1995, 2; "ACM volta a tribuna do Senado e faz críticas ao Poder Judiciário," *Folha de São Paulo*, 5 April 1995, 6; and Marcelo Pontes, "ACM põe o Judiciário na berlinda," *Jornal do Brasil*, 6 April 1995, 2.

58. See Marco Maciel, "A arbitragem, sendo barata, rapida, e sigilosa, extrai do processo judicial a demora e o custo," *Folha de São Paulo*, 30 July 1995, 3; and "Os candidatos e a reorganizção do judiciário," *Folha de São Paulo*, 23 July, 1994. A telling indicator of the disillusionment with the courts was that in the 1994 presidential elections, the only area of consensus among the thirteen candidates—a group that spanned the Marxist Left to the ultra-authoritarian Right— was that some form of control over the judiciary was essential.

59. Daniella Sholl, "Contrôle do Judiciário volta com força total," *Jornal do Brasil*, 18 December 1994, 7; and Nelson Francisco Jobim, "Jobim defende reforma urgente do Judiciário," *Jornal do Brasil*, 29 April 1995, A5.

60. Luiz Orlando Carneiro, "Contrôle do Judiciário é alvo no 1 da revisão," *Jornal do Brasil*, 9 January 1994, 3; and Luiz Orlando Carneiro, "Conselho da magistratura volta a cena," *Jornal do Brasil*, 9 January 1994, 3. When Congress began considering constitutional reforms again in 1995, the two most prominent judicial reforms included measures to impose external disciplinary controls over the courts and another to establish an independent auditor to track the allocation of funds. See "Deputado propõe punição para juizes," *Gazeta Mercantil*, 9 May 1995.

61. José Mitchell, "Asociação faz lista de juízes corruptos," *Jornal do Brasil*, 27 March 1995, A4. To earn more than the President in a Latin American country is rare, as most countries have administrative laws stipulating that the chief executive shall be the highest-paid public sector employee in the country.

62. "O bom patrão," *Veja*, 2 July 1997, 23. Generous pension plans are not unique to the judiciary—it is a characteristic of all branches of the public sector—but the degree is exceptional. The typical executive branch employee retires at a salary nine percent higher than his average annual earnings and the typical legislative branch employee has a pension package approximately 19 percent higher than his pay during active service. The pension of a judicial branch employee is 33 percent higher than his salary during active service.

63. See Eunice Nunes and Silvana de Freitas, "Judges Stage National Mobilization Day," *Folha de São Paulo*, 26 February 1997, in FBIS-LAT, 3 March 1997; and Ricardo Miranda, "Abusos motorizados," *Jornal do Brasil*, 7 May 1995, 4. Miranda notes, for example, that the Supreme Court of Justice in Brasilia maintains a fleet of 128 cars—three times the number of ambulances owned by the entire hospital network in the Federal District.

Asked to justify the 60 days of paid vacation and the three-day work weeks, Decio Erpan, President of the Corregedores Gerais do Brasil, justified the benefits by explaining, "Don't airplane pilots sleep more hours than they fly? There are some activities, such as those in the judiciary, that demand great concentration and require greater rest."

64. Ricardo Miranda, "Mundo fechado e suntuoso," *Jornal do Brasil*, 7 May 1995, 3.

65. Maria Christina Fernandes, "Civil service and mandarins," *Gazeta Mercantil*, 2 June 1997, 19. Cardoso's first Planning Minister, Jose Serra, expressed irritation with the judiciary on various occasions. Frustrated at the government's inability to curtail excessive spending by the judicial branch, Serra complained, "I tried to limit the expenditures of the judiciary in the budget law, but I couldn't." He said that it was "an absurdity" that the courts could function "without limits on its spending." See "Serra endossa critica de ACM ao Judiciário," *Correio Brasiliense*, 12 May 1995, 4.

66. Gerson Camarotti, "Dossiê de ACM expõe gastos do judiciário," *O Estado de São Paulo*, 23 March 1999, 7. By contrast, spending for the executive branch increased 224 percent. For earlier estimates, see Antonio Kandir, "Justiça: ruim e cara," *Folha de São Paulo*, 21 April 1996, 2; and "Kandir vai a Pertence defender sum posição," *Jornal do Brasil*, 1 June 1996, 3. When 23 governors met with President Cardoso in August 1995, they went to Brasilia seeking not bailouts for their indebted state banks, but rather some type of help—either through an injection of financial aid or a constitutional amendment—that would allow the states to rein in judicial salaries that were consuming larger portions of state budgets. Dante de Oliveira, Governor of Mato Grosso, complained that "The judiciary has to share in the [austerity] reforms," while Pará Governor Almir Gabriel remarked that "these expenditures are increasing at a disproportionate rate." See "Salários da Justiça serão controlados," *Jornal do Brasil*, 9 Au-

gust 1995, 7; and Ilimar Franco, "Legislativo e Judiciário, vilões dos estados," *Jornal do Brasil*, 8 August 1995, 3.

67. "Gabinete de ACM passa a central de denúncias contra o Judiciário," *Jornal da Tarde*, 18 June 1995, 8. Reporting his findings, Magalhães stated, "Of 70 appellate judges, only three did not practice nepotism. The way the scheme worked was this: one judge would name the child of another judge to fill a slot on his staff, without calling attention to it, and vice versa. That way, it appeared in the Diario Oficial [Official Record] and still went unnoticed." For examples of this hiring scheme, see "De pai para filho," *Jornal do Brasil*, 7 May 1995, 4. Information from the 1999 inquiry can be found in Gerson Camarotti, "CPI investigará todas as denúncias, diz relator," *O Estado de São Paulo*, 13 April 1999, 6; and Eugenia Lopes, "Magalhães: CPI on Judiciary May Go Beyond 26 August," *Jornal do Brasil*, 10 May 1999, in FBIS-LAT, 11 May 1999.

68. "Nepotismo espalha-se como praga pelo pais," *Jornal do Brasil*, 9 May 1995, 4; and "Fim do nepotismo judicial," *Jornal da Tarde*, 29 December 1996, 3. For additional details on corruption in the judiciary in Paraíba, see Helio Gama Neto, "Corregedor afasta todos no TRT da Paraíba," *O Estado de São Paulo*, 25 June 1997; and "Brazil Labor Court Head Accused of Hiring Family," Reuter news dispatch, 10 November 1995. Nepotism is not limited to underdeveloped states. A retired judge from Rio Grande do Sul, one of Brazil's most developed and progressive states, has told the media that he is personally aware of fifty-four instances of nepotism on the state Supreme Court and that justices have an unspoken agreement to look the other way regarding such practices. See José Mitchell, "Ex-juíz denuncia nepotismo," *Jornal do Brasil*, 14 August 1995, 3.

69. Flamino Araripe, "No Ceará, o TJ tem 21 proprietários," *Jornal do Brasil*, 9 May 1995, 4; and "Juízes empregam parentes em tribunais," *Folha de São Paulo*, 11 September 1994, A9.

70. In 1994 an appellate judge in Rio de Janeiro named his son—a physician with no legal training—to serve as Director for the State Council of Magistrates, at an impressive salary of $4,000 per month; the President of the State Supreme Court in Espírito Santo named his 25-year-old son as an appellate court judge in the same state in 1995; and in Amazonas, Lafayete Carneiro, the President of the Federal Regional Court, named his son as Director of the same body—claiming that he needed to name someone he knew to the post because "a stranger would sell out the Court." See "Tudo em Familia," *Jornal do Brasil*, 9 May 1995, 4; and José de Arimetia, "Campeão de nomeações é TRT-PB, *Jornal do Brasil*, 9 May 1995, 4. A legislative proposal introduced in 1997 that called for establishing procedures for congressional impeachment of lower court judges was fiercely resisted by judges and killed in committee. See Isabel Braga, "ACM prega extensão do impeachment," *O Estado de São Paulo*, 25 June 1997, 3.

71. Carlota Araujo et al., "Juízes não enfrentam rigor dos tribunais," *Jornal do Brasil*, 12 May 1995, 4; and "Servidor não da trégua a corruptos," *Jornal do Brasil*, 12 May 1995, 4.

72. Vannildo Mendes, "Juízes fazem boicote a lei que combate nepotismo," *O Estado de São Paulo*, 28 December 1996, A4; and Vannildo Mendes, "FH proibe nepotismo na Justiça federal," *O Estado de São Paulo*, 27 December 1996, A7.

73. João Domingos and Ana Paula Macedo, "ACM defende CPI do Judiciário e juízes fazem greve," *O Globo*, 17 March 1999, 11; "Asociação diz que há risco de fujimorizção," *O Globo*, 17 March 1999, 11; Marcelo de Morães, "Magistrados atacam ACM," *Jornal do Brasil*, 30 March 1999, 6; and Mariângelica Gullucci and Sandra Soto, "Judiciáro condena atitude do chefe do Supremo," *O Estado de São Paulo*, 26 March 1999, 4. On the assertion that the congressional inquiry threatened democracy, see Hugo Marques, "Ministro vê risco institucional na abertura de CPI," *O Estado de São Paulo*, 24 March, 1999, 7.

74. Ricardo Miranda, an investigative reporter for the *Jornal do Brasil*, acquired copies of the budgets of several courts and provided a series of examples of questionable budget items. Miranda found that in 1994 the Supreme Court spent $20,000 of public funds for office parties—twice the expenses for similar purposes of the entire executive branch—and nearly $200,000 for purchases on unspecified "medical services." The Superior Military Tribunal spent more than $1,000,000 for office pillows and decorations and paid another $96,000 to a local travel company for tours of court personnel seeking to "familiarize" themselves with their own country. These and other questionable uses of funds are taken from Ricardo Miranda, "Judiciário sai do serio nas despesas extras," *Jornal do Brasil*, 7 May 1995, 4; and Francisco Gonçalves, "As togas voadores," *Jornal do Brasil*, 7 May 1995, 4.

75. Ricardo Miranda, "Um poder paquidérmico," *Jornal do Brasil*, 7 May 1995, 3.

76. Miranda, "Mundo fechado é suntuoso," 3.

77. For a survey of the scandalous details, see "As denúncias entre Mello Porto," *O Globo*, 10 August 1999, 1; Maria Lima, "Depoimento de juízes incriminan Mello Porto," *O Globo*, 1 June 1999, 1; and "CPI receberá dossiê sobre M.P.," *O Estado de São Paulo*, 8 May 1999, 5.

78. See "STJ inaugura sede faraónica," *Jornal do Brasil*, 24 June 1995, 4; Francisco Leali, "Um 'elefante branco' de US$169 milhões," *Jornal do Brasil*, 6 August 1995, 8; and Gustavo Paul, "A Justiça é luxo só," *Veja*, 17 November 1993, 44-45. In 1995, Federal Deputy Augusto Carvalho charged that many of the expenses—such as the $5,000 sofas in the waiting rooms of each justice—reflected an overbilling scheme designed to reward business friends of several senior judges. His allegations received considerable press coverage but were never proven. See "STJ inaugura sede que custou US$170 mi," *Jornal de Brasilia*, 24 June 1995, 5.

79. Martinez Lara, *Building Democracy in Brazil*, p. 100.

80. Each committee and subcommittee, in turn, had a president, two vice presidents, and a rapporteur.

81. Even establishing this process was subject was considerable debate and modification: merely agreeing on these internal rules was subjected to 1,636 amendments. Ironically, one of the senators responsible for producing this document was São Paulo Senator Fernando Henrique Cardoso, who would later spend most of his first term as president trying to undo much of the document.

82. For reasons of brevity, this description necessarily omits a number of important steps along the way. The Assembly first produced a document in 1987 that included more than 500 articles. Proponents of the final Constitution noted that its 245 articles had significantly streamlined the original Cabral draft, but the appearance of brevity was less than met the eye. For example, some sections of the Constitution, such as Article 5, included 77 subdivisions and 22 subsections. See Rosenn, "Brazil's New Constitution: An Exercise in Transient Constitutionalism for a Transitional Society," p. 780.

83. The Constitution required an additional 285 pieces of ordinary legislation and forty-one complementary laws to effectuate its implementation. See Keith Rosenn, "The Brazilian Constitution After Seven Years," Paper Presented to the XXXII Conference of the Inter-American Bar Association, Quito, Ecuador, 12-17 November 1995.

84. To the extent that any government or any administration could respond adequately to an economic crisis of such proportions, successive administrations in Brazil clearly fell short. During this 15-year period, the country experienced five presidents, thirteen finance ministers, fourteen Central Bank presidents, six economic shock programs, and four currencies.

85. Adam Przeworski, *Democracy and the Market* (Cambridge: Cambridge University Press, 1991): 84. Przeworski notes that across a range of emerging democracies in Latin America and

Eastern Europe, Brazil's Constitution by far goes the furthest in pledging the central government to provide a number of *ex ante* social rights.

86. Hugo Marques, "População apóia investigação do Judiciário," *O Estado de São Paulo*, 4 July 1999, 3.

87. See, for example, Denise Rothenburg and Tales Faria, "ACM aponta ás mazelas do Judiciário," *O Globo*, 18 June 1995, 8.

88. Andrea Hafez, "Armas contra a lentidão da Justiça," *Gazeta Mercantil*, 11 June 1995, A11.

89. Miranda, "Mundo fechado," 4.

90. Eduardo Oinegue, "Exhaustos meritíssimos," *Veja*, 26 March 1997, 109.

91. "O colapso da Justiça," *Jornal da Tarde*, 7 January 1997, A3; and Ricardo Miranda, "Milhares de procesos adormecidos," *Jornal do Brasil*, 7 May 1995, 3.

92. Supreme Court Justice Celso de Mello notes that "the amount of work affects the quality of the decisions," while Marcio Thomaz Bastos, a prominent São Paulo attorney, has argued that one consequence of the excessive work load is that judges have to rely excessively on the work of their clerks, because each judge does not have time to acquaint himself with the facts of most cases. See Oinegue, "Exhaustos meritíssimos," p. 110, and Eumanio Silva, "Suprema crise," *IstoÉ*, 27 November 1996, 42.

93. Edgardo Buscaglia, "Stark picture of justice," *Financial Times*, 13 March 1995, 11.

94. Edgardo Buscaglia and Pilar Domingo, "The Impediments to Judicial Reform in Latin America," Paper presented at the XVIII International Congress of the Latin American Studies Association, 28–30 September 1995, p. 5. Their statistics are from 1983–93 and reflect a 39.1 percent; the delays are higher if one takes 1988 as the base year. By contrast, delays increased only 2.3 percent in the decade 1973–82 under military rule.

95. Marcelo Moreira, "Justiça Militar gasta muito e julga pouco," *Jornal do Brasil*, 14 May 1995, 3; and Octacilio Freire "Excesso de tribunais emperra o Judiciário," *Jornal do Brasil*, 14 May 1995, 3. By 1999, experts had calculated that the typical justice on the Supreme Military Tribunal issued a ruling once every week. By contrast, a justice on the federal Supreme Court issued a ruling every twenty minutes. See Oinegue, "Os juízes como réus," p. 36.

96. Oinegue, "Exhaustos meritíssimos," p. 109; and Miranda, "Milhares de procesos adormecidos," p. 3. In 1998, Brazilian officials noted that the STF heard more than 30,000 cases and the STJ more than 100,000—while the STM heard only thirty cases, or two per justice. See Hugo Marques, "Ministro condena ofensiva contra Judiciário," *O Estado de São Paulo*, 20 March 1999, 7.

97. Drausio Barreto, *Justiça para todos* (São Paulo: Editora Angelotti, 1994): 67.

98. "Gordos Processos," (editorial) *Jornal do Brasil*, 4 January 1997, 8; and Vannildo Mendes, "União vai desistir de 250 mil ações jurídicas," *O Estado de São Paulo*, 26 December 1996, A4. Editorialists pointed out, however, that the measure still left nearly one million other cases pending against the federal government. See "Mãos atadas," *Jornal do Brasil*, 29 April 1997, 8.

99. Figures taken from Howell, "Politicized Justice?" p. 9; and "TST está a beira do colapso," *Folha de São Paulo*, 27 July 1994, 4.

100. Oinegue, "Exhaustos meritíssimos," p. 109.

101. Oinegue, "Exhaustos meritíssimos," p. 112.

102. According to Katrina Howell, the measure "allowed parties or interest groups whose interests have been defeated in the legislature to 'transpose a political conflict directly into a constitutional one.' . . . [P]olitical parties with only five percent representation in Congress, unable to forge a successful coalition to defeat a legislative act, can use the STF as a means to continue the legislative battle." See Howell, "Politicized Justice?," pp. 10–11.

103. Information in this paragraph comes from Marcus Faro de Castro, "Política e econo-mia no judiciário: as ações diretas de inconstitucionalidade dos partidos políticos," *Caderno de Ciência Política* 7 (May 1993): 1-26. See Marcus Faro de Castro, "The Court, Law, and Democ-racy in Brazil," *International Social Science Journal* 152 (June 1997): 246.

104. An early, skeptical look at this arrangement is found in Maria Isabel de Sa Earp Re-sende Chaves, Katia Maria de Souza Fialho, and Cecelia Maria Martins Antunes, "Juízado de pequenas causas: estudo comparativo entre Brasil, Inglaterra, Australia, EUA, e Canada," *Re-vista de Ciência Política* 33 (May/June 1990): 58-9.

105. "Só criminoso lucra com lentidão da Justiça," *Jornal do Brasil*, 11 May 1995, 4. Mato Grosso do Sul was one of the few states to experiment with conciliation and alternative sen-tencing, and reported a decline in case backlogs and prisoner-to-space ratios. See José Mitchell, "Exemplos de uma Justiça que da certo," *Jornal do Brasil*, 24 September 1995; and Vasconcelos Quadros, "Sentenças inovadoras," *Jornal do Brasil*, 24 September 1995, 8. A handful of states created small claims courts or expanded the special courts already in place prior to the Con-stitution; governors in Santa Catarina and Rio Grande do Sul, for example, instituted small claims courts—complete with orality, arbitration, self-representation, and no court fees—and re-ported reductions in case backlogs by the mid-1990s.

106. See Marcia Marques and Flavia de Leon, "Crise compromete atuação da justiça," *Folha de São Paulo*, 11 September 1994, 8.

107. "Cardoso sanciona Juízados Especiais," *Jornal do Brasil*, 27 September 1995, 5; and "Reforma Pragmática," (editorial) *Jornal do Brasil*, 29 September 1995, 8. The new courts were intended to handle matters below forty minimum wages ($4,000) and would include issues such as bar fights, common crimes, and consumer fraud. Lawyers would not be allowed to rep-resent litigants if the matter involved was valued at less than twenty minimum wages. See "Congress approves law creating special courts," *Gazeta Mercantil*, 19 September 1995, A10, in FBIS-LAT, 29 September 1995.

108. The lack of judges and court facilities obviously has implications for judicial efficiency, as well.

109. Francisco, "Sepúlveda não quer contrôle externo de salários de juízes," *Jornal do Brasil*, 17 March 1997, 3.

110. The judges poll comes from Sadek, "A Organização do Poder Judiciário no Brasil," p. 4; the Pertence quote comes from Marques and De Leon, "Crises compromete atauçao da Justiça," A8.

111. See "Gordos processos," (editorial) *Jornal do Brasil*, 4 January 1997, 8; and Luiz Or-lando Carneiro, "Não basta ter mais juízes. É preciso vocação" *Jornal do Brasil*, 8 May 1995, 3.

112. See Orlando Farias, "Amazonia, faroeste sem lei," *Jornal do Brasil*, 10 May 1995, 4; and U.S. Department of State, *Brazil: Human Rights Practices, 1994* (Washington, D.C.: De-partment of State, 1994). Judicial vacancy rates reached 51 percent in Sergipe, 53 percent in Acre, and 61 percent in Alagoas, and in several states ratios had actually worsened since the 1988 Constitution. See "Pequenas causas podem ser solução," *Folha de São Paulo*, 27 July 1994, 7; and Luiz Orlando Carneiro, "Justiça sofre de falta de juízes," *Jornal do Brasil*, 17 November 1995, 2. By contrast, only 20 percent of the judgeships were vacant in both São Paulo and Rio de Janeiro. The average judges served 37,000 habitants; Maranhão state had one judge for every 42,000 citizens and in Pará each judge served an average of 43,000 citizens. See "Ideal é 100 mil juizes. mas só ha 7,8 mil," *Jornal do Brasil*, 9 January 1994, 3; and "Pais tem 1,8 mil vagas abertas para juízes," *O Estado de São Paulo*, 16 February 1997, 3.

113. The figures are even more staggering if placed in a broader historical context. Robert Shirley has noted that in 1889, São Paulo had one judge for every 24,000 inhabitants—a ratio

that actually was better than in 1995, more than 100 years later. See Shirley, "A Brief Survey of Law in Brazil," p. 7.

114. José Mitchell, "Inocentes e culpados financiam lazer de juiz," *Jornal do Brasil*, 10 May 1995, A1, A4.

115. See Laura Sue Nelson, "The Defense of Honor: Is It Still Honored In Brazil?" *Wisconsin Journal of International Law* 11 (Spring 1993): 531–56; and James Brooke, "Brazil Tries to Curb Violence Against Women," *New York Times*, 17 November 1992, A14.

116. See Department of State, *Brazil: Human Rights Practices, 1993*, and *Injusta Criminal: A Violença Contra A Mulher No Brasil* (New York: Americas Watch/Projeto dos Direitos das Mulheres, 1991): 48–49. Initial research by a prominent Brazilian think tank has produced similar conclusions regarding blacks who use the courts. Sergio Adorno has found that blacks accused of the same crime as white Brazilians receive lengthier sentences and that—other factors being equal—blacks receive harsher sentences for killing whites than for killing other blacks. See Floriza Verucci et al., "O Judiciário e o Acesso a Justiça," in *O Judiciário em Debate* (São Paulo: IDESP/Editora Sumare, 1994): 9–30.

117. João Batista Natali, "Maioria acha Justiça lenta e defende contrôle externo," p. 15; and "Dificuldade para aprovar reformas," *Correio Brasiliense*, 5 February 1995, 4–5.

118. "Latin Americans Favor Democracy, But Democratic Institutions Rated Poorly," p. 10.

119. Compare João Batista Natali, "Maioria acha Justiça lenta e defende contrôle externo," p. 15; "Livres, leves, e soltos," *Veja*, 24 March 1993, 16; Gerson Camarotti, "ACM deve requerer hoje CPI do Judiciário," *O Estado de São Paulo*, 25 March 1999, 7; Hugo Marques, "92% dos brasileiros consideram a Justiça lenta," *O Estado de São Paulo*, 24 March 1999, 7; and "Brasileiros mostram insatisfação," *O Estado de São Paulo*, 8 April 1999, 4.

120. "Latin Americans Favor Democracy, But Democratic Institutions Rated Poorly," p. 3; "Second Thoughts on Democracy in Brazil," p. 10; Carlos Tautz, "The Color of Justice," *Latinamerica Press*, 6 July 1995, 4; Rubens Figueiredo, "Verdades e mitos sobre a cultura brasileira," in *Ouvindo O Brasil*, ed. Bolivár Lamounier (São Paulo: Editora Sumare, 1992): 105; "Livres, leves, e soltos," p. 17; "Pesquisa revela que cidadão não conhece os seus direitos," *Jornal do Brasil*, 3 December 1996, 5; and Rosa Costa, "Investigações devem ser iniciadas após a Páscoa," *O Estado de São Paulo*, 26 March 1999, 7.

121. Eduardo Oinegue, "Os juízes como réus," *Veja*, 24 March 1999, 38.

122. Helio Campos Mello, Eumanio Silva, and Luciano Suassuna, "O Presidente e o Candidato," *IstoÉ*, 18 June 1997, p. 26.

123. See, for example, Biaggio Talento, "ACM eleva o tom das críticas ao presidente," *O Estado de São Paulo*, 17 April 1999, 6; and Cristina Jungblat, Helena Chagas, and João Domingos, "STF e CPIs: Acordo no Alvorado," *O Globo*, 15 July, 1999, 1.

124. "James Holston and Teresa P. R. Caldeira, "Democracy, Law, and Violence: Disjunctions of Brazilian Citizenship," in *Fault Lines of Democracy in Post-Transition Latin America*, ed. Felipe Agüero and Jeffrey Stark (Miami, Fla.: North-South Center Press, 1998): 277.

125. Brazilians have always shown considerable flexibility toward the judicial system. Rosenn noted in 1984, a year before the transition: "The bending of legal norms to expediency occurs to some extent in all countries. It is especially common in Latin America, where the gap between the law on the books and actual practice is notoriously large. What is striking about Brazil is that the practice of bending legal rules to expediency has been elevated to a highly prized legal institution called the *jeito*. The *jeito* has become an integral part of Brazil's legal culture. In many areas of the law, the *jeito* is the norm and the formal legal rule is the exception." See Keith S. Rosenn, "Brazil's Legal Culture: The Jeito Revisited," *Florida International Law Journal* 1 (Fall 1984): 2–3.

126. See *Relatório de pesquisa: Formas comunitárias de intermediação de conflitos* (Rio de Janeiro: [no pub.], 1987).

127. The rise of vigilante justice in the impoverished state of Alagoas is recounted in "Execução extrajudicial, a marca alagoana," *Jornal do Brasil*, 30 June 1996, 3. Frustration with the failure of the judiciary to administer justice often dovetails with the persistence of police officers who earn low wages—sometimes below the national minimum wage—a combination that results in the participation of off-duty policemen in death squad activity.

128. Much of the violence takes place with either the tacit approval or the active participation of police officials; one 1991 survey of policemen in Rio de Janeiro state indicated that over 25 percent had offered to participate in off-duty vigilante groups at some point in their careers, while police in the rural state of Alagoas allegedly were involved in approximately 80 percent of the murders committed in that state in 1992. See U.S. Department of State, *Brazil: Human Rights Practices, 1992*; and U.S. Department of State, *Brazil: Human Rights Practices, 1993* (Washington, D.C.: Department of State, 1994): 23.

129. Mauro Silveira, Valter Goncalves, and Valdir Suzin, "A Bancada Dos Xerifes," *Manchete*, 9 December 1995, 62–65.

130. Governor Marcelo Alencar told journalists that the police were operating in a "war zone" and that their actions "must be understood in the context of an ongoing and tense combat between the police and criminals." See "Brazil shooting points to massacre—rights group," Reuter press dispatch, 12 May 1995.

131. Todd Lewan, "In Brazil, A Plaguing Question: Can Violence Stop Violence?" Associated Press release, 10 March 1995.

132. "O Inimigo das Ruas," *IstoÉ*, 4 August 1993, 57.

133. "Latin Americans Favor Democracy, But Democratic Institutions Rated Poorly," p. 9; "Second Thoughts on Democracy in Brazil," p. 10; and Edgardo Buscaglia and Thomas Ulen, "A Quantitative Analysis of the Judicial Sectors in Latin America," Paper presented at the Annual Meetings of the Law and Economics Association, 12–13 May 1995, 18–20.

134. See Sadek, *Uma Introdução ao Estudo da Justiça*, p. 9. A separate poll of judges conducted by the Brazilian Bar Association found that 89 percent said they were opposed to an externally-appointed council of magistrates. See "Juízes são contrarios ao contrôle do Judiciário," *Jornal de Brasilia*, 10 June 1995, 3. To the degree that judges acknowledge any need for reform, the tendency is to portray the courts' problems as manageable and unexceptional. One former Supreme Court president wrote in 1995 that "the judicial crisis is much less [serious] than the crisis confronting the other branches." Noting the mounting calls for external controls on the courts, the justice made the remarkable claim that, "At bottom, what they [the reformers] want is to control the decisions of the judicial branch, which represents a step backwards 100 years and would signify a return to the Africa of Idi Amin Dada." See Carlos Mario Velloso, "O Contrôle Externo do Poder Judiciário," *Revista Brasileira de Estudos Políticos* 80 (January 1995): 53–76.

135. "Lobby de juízes tenta impedir a reforma do Judiciário na revisão," *Jornal de Brasilia*, 17 March 1994, 4. Brazilian scholar Mauricio Godinho Delgado has written that this type of incident reflects an "unjustifiable corporatist resistance" to relatively minor, legitimate checks on government power. See Mauricio Godinho Delgado, *Democracia e justiça* (São Paulo: Editora Ltr., 1993): 54.

136. "Novo presidente do STF compara efeito vinculante ao AI-5," *O Globo*, 29 May 1997. *Gazeta Mercantil*, one of Brazil's most respected newspapers, wrote in an uncharacteristically sharp editorial:

> Many sectors are expressing opinions on important issues, sometimes passionately. That's democracy. Everyone has the right to express an opinion—workers, artists, intellectuals, businessmen,

politicians, students—with the possible exception of judges. The Judiciary being one of the main foundations of democracy, it behooves judges to be discreet in expressing their personal opinions on matters of public interest; in particular, they should avoid publicizing their views in the media. In practical terms, every time a judge talks to the media, he is prejudging the facts he is dealing with. . . . Indignation and irritability are not easily accommodated with the principle of justice.

See "Publicity-seeking judges," *Gazeta Mercantil*, 5 May 1997, 3.

When legislators pledged in 1999 to conduct a fact-finding inquiry into judicial corruption, judges again declared a work stoppage, with senior magistrates announcing that any congressional effort to expose judicial nepotism would be "unconstitutional." See Hugo Marques, "Para ministro do STJ, apuração é inconstitucional," *O Estado de São Paulo*, 30 March 1999, 8; and Rodimar Oliveira, "Juízes gaúchos se unem contra ACM," *Zero Hora*, 30 March 1999, 1.

Argentina: Opposite Paths, Same Results

[Interior Minister] Corach took out a paper napkin and began to write the names of judges that the administration controlled. He confirmed, for example, that Judge Bonadio was under his control and that Judge Tiscornia was part of the orbit of [Justice Minister] Jassan, although I certainly didn't need to have that written in front of me to know that.

> —Former Economy Minister Domingo Cavallo, recounting a 1996
> discussion in which Interior Minister Corach detailed the Menem
> administration's manipulation of the federal judiciary.[1]

A napkin wouldn't be enough. You'd need a tablecloth.

> —Interior Minister Carlos Corach, trying to explain why Cavallo's story was
> not true.[2]

Why should I be the only president in fifty years who hasn't had his own court?

> —President Carlos Menem, responding to a reporter's request that he drop
> plans to double the size of the Supreme Court.[3]

The Argentine experience would seem like a test case for many of the conventional assumptions about judicial reform. In many respects, Argentina represents a middle ground between the approaches of both El Salvador and Brazil. Presidents Raúl Alfonsín (1983–89) and Carlos Menem (1989–99) took office with broad popular support, a congressional majority united behind them, and ambitious yet manageable plans for a focused sequence of reforms. Unlike El Salvador's narrow approach or Brazil's more sweeping plans, Alfonsín and Menem carefully selected their reform variables and pursued well-defined, targeted objectives with clear reform inputs and a good sense of the desired outputs they should produce. Both experiences were case studies in the merits of narrow and incremental reforms. The fact that many of these efforts, particularly those of Menem, were backed by technical experts from the World Bank and key developed countries suggested that the country was well on its way toward a comprehensive overhaul of the administration of justice.

Yet after more than a decade of reforms, polls indicate that public trust in the judiciary is at an all-time low. Public approval ratings for the courts—near 60 percent at the time of the transition in 1983—hovered around single digits after a steady, decade-long decline. Court cases took longer than ever before, and the sentiment was rising that the courts did nothing for the average citizen; indeed, studies of anticipated case filings of Argentine courts found that Argentina is one of the few countries in the world in which times to disposition are increasing even as citizens are turning away from the judiciary and taking fewer cases to the courts altogether.[4] Worse yet, a series of major corruption scandals involving senior members of the judiciary—including a handful of Supreme Court justices and a revolving door of justice ministers—has fostered the perception the judiciary is corrupt, politicized, and even controlled by criminal mafias, a notion supported by more than 70 percent of the public.[5] By 1999, everyone from Argentine politicians to foreign investors, the Catholic Church, and the director of the International Monetary Fund agreed that the courts were the weakest link in Argentina's democracy.

What went wrong in Argentina's judicial reform programs? Stated as succinctly as possible, the reformers were wrong. A sequenced, staggered approach to judicial reform did not automatically lead to greater public trust and certainly did not translate into success on other reform variables. Alfonsín neither explained nor envisioned how increased independence would lead to a more efficient and accessible judiciary, while Menem never established how greater efficiency and access would somehow enable judicial independence to emerge from the process. In fact, in both cases the opposite occurred. Failure to address other structural flaws in the unreformed areas inevitably undercut and overwhelmed the tentative successes in the targeted area. In that respect, the Argentine experience—despite very different domestic environments, political conditions, and levels of national development—was not fundamentally different from El Salvador or Brazil. Despite the claims of reform experts, narrowly targeted incrementalism in judicial reform does not produce gradual improvement; it produces a negative synergy that contributes to a failed reform and democratic decay.

The experience of the Alfonsín administration is examined first. Alfonsín took office committed to strengthening institutional independence, with efficiency and access relegated to the back burner. His means for improving independence were fairly straightforward: selecting a civilian, democratic Supreme Court tasked with judging trials of military officers accused of human rights violations. The logic was familiar and similar to the Salvadoran experience: the responsible exercise of judicial power would build public confidence and establish an institutional sphere of authority for the courts, enabling them to ensure accountable government. Yet broader political forces and the negative synergy of partial reform combined to undercut his efforts. Faced with intense military opposition to the trials, Alfonsín faced a conundrum: he could push ahead with the trials and risk the consequences—most likely a coup—or he could scale back the prosecutions and target only the most senior military officers. By opting for the latter, Alfonsín alienated his political supporters, exposed individual judges to physical threats, and fostered the perception that courts were once again deferring to political considerations and that they were merely ratifying a political decision. What began as the "judicialization of politics," according to one Alfonsín aide, ended in the "politicization of the judiciary."[6] What should have been viewed as a success—civilian courts convicting active duty and retired generals was a first in Argentina and rare in Latin America—became a liability. The popular frustration with the results—coupled with the growing recognition that the courts were increasingly inefficient and inaccessible—created a crisis of confidence in the courts and a broad sense that the judiciary was less credible and less effective over time.

Through very different methods, Menem reached similar results. As part of his ambitious "modernization of the state" program, Menem stressed efficiency and access, arguing that both were essential to deepening investor confidence in the country. The administration launched an impressive number of initiatives lauded (and often financed) by the international community: alternative dispute resolution, mediation, free legal aid, expanded use of public defenders and prosecutors, and administrative reforms of the judiciary's internal bureaucracy. At the same time, Menem took a far less healthy approach to judicial independence; indeed, few democratically elected civilian leaders in Latin America in modern times did more to subordinate the judiciary to political influence. Ultimately, Menem wanted three achievements from his time in office: to effect real economic change and place Argentina on a path toward sustainable, long-term economic growth, to gain reelection and remain in office as long as possible, and to reward himself and his cronies—as lucratively as possible—for their time in office. Importantly, all three goals required a pliable and sympathetic judiciary, which Menem set out to create within weeks of taking office. By 1999, the courts had become so closely identified as a handmaiden of the administration that they were widely viewed as politicized and unreliable, with approval ratings in the single digits. The modest progress toward improved efficiency and access was overshadowed by the unreformed aspect of judicial independence.

By the late 1990s, the implications of failed judicial reforms for the quality of Argentina's democracy were familiar. The courts had clearly lost the reservoir of goodwill they enjoyed in 1983; the public increasingly expressed the opinion that the courts were corrupt and unreliable, prompting citizens to turn away from them and toward vigilante justice and authoritarian politicians, evincing increasingly less faith in the benefits of democratic institutions and processes. Finally, despite the impressive macroeconomic reforms implemented by the administration, a growing number of foreign investors were beginning to avoid Argentina precisely because of the politicization of the courts and the lack of "juridic security"—the belief that the courts were so politicized that they had become unpredictable, and that the judicial cost of doing business in Argentina had simply become too high.

THE RISE AND REVERSAL OF JUDICIAL INDEPENDENCE

Throughout the nineteenth century, the Argentine judiciary demonstrated an impressive degree of independence, repeatedly defending individual liberty, the separation of powers, and the primacy of constitutionalism. As early as the 1820s, the courts ruled—citing traditional Jesuit doctrine prevailing in the country—that separate spheres existed for the individual and the state and that there were certain areas government could not properly regulate; the courts repeatedly expressed this view in subsequent decades by issuing rulings that checked government encroachments against freedom of speech, thought, and religion.[7] In 1863, the Supreme Court struck down several executive acts as unconstitutional, a rarity in Latin America; the following year it issued a ruling that declared the judiciary to be the ultimate arbiter on constitutional questions and in 1887 struck down several legislative acts on constitutional grounds.[8] Throughout this period, many Argentine judges based their decisions on U.S. Supreme Court rulings and applied U.S. jurisprudence to specific Argentine cases.[9] By the early twentieth century, this tradition, coupled with healthy economic indicators, suggested that Argentina was well on its way to becoming a thriving democratic nation.[10]

Beginning in 1930—and particularly with the rise of the Peronist movement in the 1940s—Argentina's democratic tradition quickly and steadily eroded. Argentina became one of the clearest examples in Latin America of the majoritarian tendencies outlined in Chapter One: the two main political parties, both organized along populist-nationalist lines, sought access to government as a way to limit the other from participating in competitive politics.[11] Whenever either party gained access to public office, it pursued totalist, exclusionary policies against the other and pushed the constitutional order to its limits, ultimately triggering military intervention. The revolving door between irresponsible, short-lived civilian administrations and increasingly repressive military regimes produced predictable results for the courts. Between 1930 and 1976, the Supreme Court was replaced *en masse* on seven occasions and all but one justice was replaced on two other instances. Other administrations—civilian and military—repeatedly curtailed the independence of the courts by tinkering with retirement ages or simply placing the courts "in recess," prohibiting some judges from returning to the bench.[12]

These frequent purges clearly took their toll on judicial independence. The persistence of military governments usually left the courts with little recourse other than to acquiesce to de facto regimes—the Supreme Court actually recognized the legality of military governments five times since 1943—a tendency that eventually was elevated to an entire theory of jurisprudence in Argentina known as the "doctrine of de facto laws."[13] In Argentina, jurists repeatedly have upheld unconstitutional acts by de facto regimes on the grounds that "a government cannot be questioned in law because it is based on force"; any act of any government in power—such as the 1982 self-amnesty decree issued by the military before leaving power—was presumed to carry the full weight of constitutional law simply because it was issued by the agent exercising political authority at the time.[14] To be sure, there were periodic exceptions to the rule—the courts occasionally challenged (usually unsuccessfully) the military junta that governed the country from 1976–83—but on balance the courts in Argentina became progressively weaker over time.[15] By the time of the return to civilian rule in 1983, the courts were understandably held in low esteem. Respected intellectuals wryly noted that many Argentines turned to the judiciary only for the most cynical of reasons: as a way to freeze legal proceedings or drain a rival of financial resources by entangling him in costly, time-consuming proceedings.[16]

THE DEMOCRATIC TRANSITION AND THE REINVIGORATION OF JUDICIAL INDEPENDENCE

When Raúl Alfonsín assumed office in 1983, media pundits and internationally respected academics noted that few Argentine presidents appeared more likely than Alfonsín to display a strong commitment to democracy and human rights. Alfonsín had distinguished himself during the 1970s as an attorney defending students accused of subversive activity and representing families whose relatives had disappeared under military rule, while his own writings—both prior and subsequent to his presidency—seemed to buttress this impression.[17] Alfonsín argued that elections alone were insufficient for democracy, that democratic rule required greater attention to the ethical and qualitative nature of the regime, and that the state and its institutions had a moral obligation to protect the human rights of its citizens. Specifically, he highlighted the judiciary for its role in "controlling the exercise of power by the executive and legislative branches."[18]

From the outset, Alfonsín's primary emphasis on judicial reform was, not surprisingly, on strengthening the individual and institutional independence of the courts; measures to improve efficiency and access were intentionally and temporarily relegated to the sidelines. The means to achieve this goal were fairly direct and consisted of two main features. First, Alfonsín would select a new, less politicized Supreme Court to replace the military-appointed one; the new justices, in turn, would eliminate the "chilling effect" on lower court judges that had characterized previous military regimes and would also enforce greater professional conduct among lower court judges. Second, the more independent courts would be well positioned to assert judicial authority, thereby strengthening democratic rule. The primary vehicle for this goal would be through several criminal trials of military officers suspected of human rights violations committed during the previous government. The logic was similar to that in El Salvador: the responsible exercise of judicial power was the surest way for the courts to bring all sectors—particularly the armed forces—under the rule of law. It would strengthen government accountability, boost domestic and international confidence in the ability of civilians to govern effectively, and validate the principles of constitutionalism.[19] Alfonsín's legal advisers echoed the notion; while acknowledging the inevitable resistance that such trials would generate from the armed forces, they confidently claimed that the punishment of past offenders would help "deter officers from staging a coup d'etat" in the future and ultimately strengthen democracy.[20]

MEASURING THE RESULTS: THE LIMITS OF PRAGMATISM

How successful were Alfonsín's efforts to enhance judicial independence—and what were the results of neglecting efficiency and access in the process? The record, on balance, was not encouraging. By overpromising what judicial reforms he could deliver and what benefits they would produce, the President was left with a pair of unappealing options when larger political realities set in: he could push ahead with the military trials and risk the consequences—such as a coup attempt—or retreat from his goals, failing to satisfy the raised expectations of his followers and asking the judiciary to once again avail itself to broader political concerns. Alfonsín attempted to straddle the line between those choices and ultimately was not especially effective: the courts made some progress toward enhanced independence, but far less than Alfonsín pledged, and the concessions he made—while probably necessary to remain in office—undercut the credibility of the judicial reform program he had so aggressively promoted.[21] Meanwhile, his neglect of the other reform variables clearly had a cost: between 1983 and 1989, trial delays and court backlogs increased more dramatically than under military rule, and foreign investors increasingly noted the lack of juridic security and institutional capabilities of the courts—a theme that candidate Carlos Menem repeatedly would hammer home during his successful presidential campaign in 1989. On balance, the courts were undoubtedly more independent in 1989 than in 1983—but the failure to make simultaneous progress on other reform aspects virtually ensured that any progress on independence would not bolster public confidence in the judiciary.

Alfonsín clearly succeeded in his efforts to create a more professional Supreme Court staffed with independent-minded judges; the quality of the new Court is one of the main outputs the administration had to show for its efforts. Scholars point out that all five appointees to the High Court were respected jurists rather than party hacks and reflected a diverse range of legal thought. More impressive yet was Alfonsín's effort to reduce the sharp judicial partisanship that had characterized virtually all of his civilian predecessors. Alfonsín offered two of the five seats to judges that had even served in past Peronist administrations, the only Radical Party president ever to make such an offer. He even offered the presidency of the Supreme Court to respected attorney Italo Luder, the Peronist presidential candidate whom Alfonsín defeated in the 1983 elections—a move that represented an unprecedented bow toward bipartisanship and signaled that the President did not intend to turn the courts into a handmaiden of the ruling party.[22] The nomination and approval proceedings in the Senate went smoothly and were widely recognized as a noncontroversial process.

Once seated, the High Court issued a number of rulings that enhanced individual liberty, asserted judicial authority over the executive and legislature, defended the constitutional order, and reflected a fairly independent posture.[23] To take only several of the more prominent examples, the Court overturned a 1985 executive decree that had curtailed civil liberties during a period of urban unrest, arguing that the President could not suspend habeas corpus rights unless the country was in a legally-declared state of siege; it struck down another effort by the executive to enforce a foreign treaty via presidential decree and popular plebiscite when Alfonsín sought to circumvent the Senate. On other issues, the courts ruled that candidates could seek elected office without joining one of the established political parties and could run as independents, that workers were not obligated to pay union dues that would be used for political causes, and that a spouse could seek a divorce (previously illegal) in the event of physical or emotional abuse. Finally, in a vote roughly analogous to the Brazilian experience during the economic shock program Collor I (discussed in Chapter Four), the Court even struck down a portion of the government heterodox shock program known as the Austral Plan, arguing that the administration—even in times of economic emergency—could not use pension funds of public sector workers to finance government deficits and could not renege on workers' contracts and uni-laterally deindex pensions.[24]

A more complicated question centers on whether this more independent court was able to meet what Alfonsín had defined as a primary goal: to carve out a larger insti-tutional sphere of influence for the judiciary by having it arbitrate the administra-tion's efforts to assert civilian authority over the armed forces. On this count, the results were far less encouraging; indeed, Jaime Malamud-Goti, a close legal aide to Alfonsín, has acknowledged with hindsight that "the consequences have not been what we had hoped they would be," and that the trials of military officers actually "may have eroded democratic authority" rather than strengthened it.[25] The Alfonsín experience highlights the degree to which all aspects of the democratic consolidation process were not mutually reinforcing: to follow through with his ambitious pledges carried several risks—most narrowly to the individual independence of judges hear-ing sensitive cases, and, more broadly, to the stability of the civilian regime. Yet to backtrack inadvertently compromised the institutional independence of the courts by creating the impression that political considerations had once again taken prece-dence over judicial concerns.

At bottom, Alfonsín's judicial reform ambitions were oblivious to the larger politi-cal constraints in the country. As a candidate, Alfonsín had made sweeping pledges to punish those responsible for the massive human rights abuses that occurred be-tween 1976–83. He announced only three days after taking office that he would press ahead with the trials of military officers, and he secured early legislative approval of a bill that overturned the military's 1982 self-amnesty law, a move that the Supreme Court upheld that year.[26] While Alfonsín's preferred method for dealing with past abusers was to have the armed forces try and punish its own ranks, the President—recognizing fairly early on that the military did not intend to follow through in any serious way—gained approval of another bill (also upheld by the Supreme Court) that federal civilian courts would have the last word on trials involving allegations of human rights abuses.[27]

Yet follow-through was exceedingly difficult. Military and security forces who be-lieved they had fought a war against externally-financed Marxist aggression were not willing to face what they perceived as persecution by a left-leaning president pursuing vindictive, punitive policies. Confronted with staunch military opposition, Alfonsín repeatedly was forced to scale back his efforts and make broad concessions along the way for political expediency. Faced with several thousand cases involving members of the armed forces—a caseload that literally would have taken decades to pursue indi-vidually—and a growing, if belated, recognition of the tremendous difficulty in moving forward with even a handful of trials, simple pragmatism prompted Alfonsín to pursue charges against only the most senior commanders who led each of the three juntas.[28] In 1984 he gained congressional approval of the "Punto Final Law" that set a sixty-day limit to criminal investigations against military members. Following a military rebellion in Spring 1987—the third such uprising in less than a year—Alfonsín compromised again, sending to Congress the "Due Obedience Law" that restricted trials to those senior commanders who ordered the crimes.

These concessions had a profound impact on the implications for judicial reform and highlight the degree to which judicial reform cannot be isolated from the larger political forces in a polity. To pursue any prosecutions at all against a recalcitrant military clearly but inadvertently compromised the individual independence of many judges. Threats against judges became commonplace and forced widespread judicial resignations, and by 1987 the entire Supreme Court of Buenos Aires province had resigned under pressure from the military and its supporters.[29] More broadly, moving forward with the trials also put at risk the viability of the democratic regime; mid-level officers staged more than half a dozen rebellions during the President's last two years in office, for example, and Alfonsín actually left office six months early due, in part, to military pressure.[30] Yet efforts to scale back the judicial trials—such as the 1987 Due Obedience Law—also carried risks. They fostered the perception (even among Alfonsín's advisors) that the President had caved, that the courts were too weak to hold the armed forces accountable, and that the entire judicial process was being defined by political rather than legal considerations. Commenting on how the need to compromise undercut the credibility of the courts, Jaime Malamud-Goti, a close aide to the President, explained:

> There is an inevitable air of artificiality in establishing the boundaries of responsibility among members of a terror-ridden society. . . . For both parties [military and civilian], the trials were clearly political: far from being seen to administer justice, the judiciary was perceived to have merely adjusted to the political convenience of the executive. Accordingly, instead of reinforcing whatever authority the judiciary may have enjoyed, the trials had the opposite effect. Instead of contributing to bridging a fragmented society's multiple versions of reality, the courts generated the belief that the trials were a ploy to draw consensus from a compromised account of reality. . . . Such perceptions—that the justice system is compromised—deepen antagonisms between opposing groups.[31]

The results were discouraging, he concludes, and "suggest the inadequacy of talking only in pragmatic terms." Alfonsín's reversals, however necessary for the maintenance of the civilian regime, had the effect of "transforming the judicialization of politics into the politicization of the judges. . . . [W]hat actually took place was the politicization of the judiciary."[32] A judicial process that came to be viewed as settling for the politically expedient solution was unlikely to strengthen public trust in the courts. By the time the Court finally indicted five of the nine members of the first two juntas—a development that actually signaled some degree of independence—the results did not produce the expected boost in confidence for the judiciary. Instead, it produced derision and cynicism, as the courts were viewed as having merely ratified a previous and unpopular political decision.[33]

Meanwhile, Alfonsín's decision to downplay measures to enhance access and efficiency clearly had a cost. Between 1983 and 1989, the total number of pending cases in the federal court system rose from approximately 300,000 to nearly 600,000. The crisis of efficiency resulted in an increase in the number of cases per judges, increased times to disposition (up more than 20 percent, a rate that actually compared unfavorably even to the ineffectual military regime), and a worsening ratio of pending cases to resolved cases. Worse yet, researchers with the World Bank reported the increasing trial delays fostered such public cynicism that the judiciary actually experienced a decrease in the rate of filings per court by the late 1980s. Citizens were simply no longer taking their cases to the courts; they resolved their disputes informally, through extralegal means, or not at all. The courts were not accessible because they were inefficient, and the courts were so inefficient that they could not handle their work load even though increasingly fewer Argentines were taking their cases to the courts.[34]

The combined effects of unfulfilled expectations on independence, coupled with declining efficiency and access, were reflected in the polls. Early in Alfonsín's term, polls found that the public generally was optimistic; depending on the survey, between 45 and 55 percent of the public expressed confidence in the country's legal system, and approval ratings for the courts were higher than those for the police, military, unions, and businessmen, and on par with scores for Congress and the educational system. Indeed, many Argentines noted that public confidence in the legal system compared favorably to levels in the United States and France and surpassed approval ratings in Spain and Italy.[35] Yet by the end of Alfonsín's term, the trend line was clearly negative. Even though the federal courts had actually generated some meaningful, democratic jurisprudence—and even though the trials, while short of public expectations, were an important step forward for asserting the institutional role of the judiciary—the unmet expectations on independence, coupled with the deteriorating efficiency and access of the courts, fostered increased cynicism. Approval ratings for the courts dipped near 30 percent, with 80 percent describing the courts as inefficient and nearly half describing the courts as inaccessible.[36] Presidential candidate Carlos Menem would perceive the disillusionment and make it a central part of his campaign.

THE SECOND PHASE OF ARGENTINE JUDICIAL REFORM

In 1989, President Carlos Menem inherited a country clearly in need of reform. Inflation by early 1989 approached an annual rate of nearly 5,000 percent, wages were declining in real terms, and staggering debt servicing costs were stifling domestic productivity and investment. Factions of the armed forces had staged repeated rebellions in the past two years—not to topple the President but merely to humiliate him—and the efficacy of civilian institutions was increasingly in doubt.[37]

Upon taking office, Menem quickly outlined an ambitious agenda that sought to reverse sixty years of Argentine political tradition. Menem distanced himself from the non-aligned "third path" that had characterized his predecessors and began seeking the closest security and commercial relationships possible with the United States,

↳ not aligned w/ Commies or Capitalists

Western Europe, and Japan. More dramatically, he committed to an aggressive economic modernization campaign that included monetarist economic policies, privatization of state enterprises—some which were losing as much as $4 million daily—and reduced export subsidies and trade barriers. A crucial part of his efforts to modernize the state included reforming the judiciary, which Menem's advisors argued was necessary to overcome Argentina's persistent economic crises by guaranteeing investor confidence, attracting foreign capital, and reversing decades of declining domestic productivity.

The administration's main judicial reform goal was to enhance efficiency and access, which reformers saw as closely related to their goal of economic development. Consistent with its broader efforts to modernize and streamline the state, the administration introduced a nationwide system of records computerization intended to facilitate improved case tracking and case management. The administration introduced oral argumentation into the federal criminal justice system, arguing that orality would not only be more democratic than an inquisitorial system, but it also would be more efficient than the plodding, antiquated written system in use.[38] Menem secured funds to hire more than 200 new judges and introduced the use of public defenders to help decongest the courts. The administration began broadening the use of court clerks—judges spent 65–70 percent of their time conducting routine administrative affairs—to allow judges to devote more time to hearing cases.[39] Menem also created a national judicial studies center, modeled after the National Center for State Courts in the United States, that would conduct and disseminate research on successful reforms elsewhere. Meanwhile, the Justice Secretariat was upgraded to a full ministry and tasked with creating plans for a judicial training school that would devise rigorous professional criteria and provide post-entry training for judges.

Reform inputs to enhance access also were extensive. Menem launched one of Latin America's most aggressive programs to introduce alternative dispute resolution and mediation into the legal system. The program was intended to help low-income citizens avoid the time-consuming and costly process of seeking redress through the formal court system, and was envisioned as enhancing efficiency by removing a portion of cases from court dockets.[40] The program initially included four pilot projects involving ten courts and was later expanded to include ten more; during this period, the Justice Ministry began working with local NGOs and conducted an extensive public relations campaign to educate legislators, parties, and judges on merits of mediation.[41] Finally, the administration introduced the use of public defenders, and began using law students to provide legal counseling for the indigent. All of the programs were viewed as models for the region and most received extensive support from foreign governments and international lending institutions.[42]

Despite these ambitious and encouraging steps, by the end of the 1990s the courts were more unpopular than ever before. Business groups, domestic NGOs, international lending institutions, and the influential Catholic Church all regularly and sharply lamented the state of the judiciary.[43] A 1994 poll found that only 13 percent of the public expressed confidence in the administration of justice, and only 16 percent had confidence in judges. Half of all respondents described the state of justice as "bad" or "very bad," 80 percent could not identify a single positive aspect of the court system, 88 percent said the country did not provide equal access for everyone, 82 percent believed courts did little or nothing to protect the rights of the "common citizen," and 84 percent described the courts as "inefficient." Surveys throughout 1997 and 1998 found similar results: nearly 90 percent of the public had "little," "very little," or "no" confidence in the courts, and only 9 percent said they had any confidence at all.[45] Clearly, something had gone very wrong.

ACCOUNTING FOR JUDICIAL DECAY IN ARGENTINA

What accounts for the dramatic decline in popular faith in the courts at the very time that the administration was undertaking such impressive reforms? Two broad groups of factors are responsible, some unique to the projects themselves and others linked to broader political forces at play in the country. First, the efficiency and access reforms, while perhaps successful in their own right, were far too modest and narrow to affect the broader judiciary as a whole and public perceptions of it. Second, the Menem administration's constant politicization of the courts—and the growing perception that Menem was using the pliant judiciary to protect the corrupt activities of himself and senior government officials—fostered both negative synergy and increased public cynicism over time. Through very different paths, the judicial reform efforts of Menem and Alfonsín offered the same lesson: positive steps forward in one area of judicial reform did not naturally lead to progress in another, but the unaddressed and unreformed aspects of the judiciary invariably undercut the modest progress in other areas.

The efficiency and access-enhancing reforms, while clearly not a panacea for all of the problems affecting the judiciary, on balance produced modestly positive results. For example, the introduction of modern computerized case management tools improved handling of pending cases in the Supreme Court and was linked with an increased ability to reduce trial delays.[46] The use of oral argumentation and public defenders in the criminal courts was widely praised for introducing an element of transparency into court proceedings and reducing the concentration of power in the hands of the judge, a positive achievement in a country in which excessive authority in the hands of government officials often had been dangerous. Study groups found a general satisfaction with oral proceedings among users of the system; in his second term, Menem incorporated orality into civil, commercial, and labor courts, a move praised by private sector business leaders.[47] The mediation and ADR projects also met with some success. After initial skepticism among many judges, the number of cases removed from the courts and resolved through ADR more than tripled over a five-year period; many were longstanding or difficult cases that had been pending for as long as eight years.[48] The mediation centers were able to successfully resolve 65 percent of all cases in 1993 and 75 percent by 1997; indeed, ADR centers were sufficiently successful at the federal level that provincial governments began replicating them, as well.[49] Reformers also appeared to be reaching their targeted audience of low-income citizens. Approximately 90 percent of clients were low-income citizens and 60 percent were female, who traditionally have had lower incomes than men in Argentina.[50]

These modest steps forward were counterbalanced by several unanticipated aspects of the reform program, several of which highlight the notion that all judicial reforms are not necessarily mutually reinforcing—and that reform on all fronts is necessary to avoid undesired consequences. For instance, the use of orality in criminal courts may have been less prone to judicial capriciousness and inefficient, rent-seeking behavior, but the transition was not a smooth one. The introduction of new procedures, clearly less familiar than century-old methods, initially caused trial delays in the criminal courts to increase by a factor of eight; those criminal courts relying on orality quickly accumulated a backlog of cases seven times greater than criminal courts using written procedures, even though judges in the reformed courts had a lighter administrative work load.[51] Once judicial officials became more familiar with oral proceedings by the mid-1990s and time to disposition began to decline, reformers discovered yet another unanticipated result: faster trials resulted in faster convictions, resulting in more extensive prison overcrowding.[52] Other problems were more fundamental. Despite all of the attention and energies focused on the criminal justice system, criminal trials accounted for less than five percent of the total cases in the federal judicial system. Any progress could at best thus make only the smallest dint in the court system's overall caseload. Not surprisingly, the number of new cases entering the judicial continued to increase annually—from 720,000 in 1991 to 1.07 million in 1996—even though the courts continued to resolve only one-third of the new cases each year throughout this period.[53] As a result, the total backlog of cases more than doubled between 1989 and 1996.[54] Not surprisingly, the growing backlog adversely affected access-creation strategies by subjecting low-income citizens to longer delays that they could ill afford. Research conducted by Edgardo Buscaglia found a negative statistical correlation between family income and procedural times to disposition, essentially meaning that low-income families in Argentina experienced longer court delays than their wealthier counterparts during this period, thereby confirming the persistence of socioeconomic barriers to judicial access.[55]

Yet these problems with the specific reform programs cannot by themselves account for the huge decrease of support for the courts and the growing crisis of confidence in the courts, particularly at a time when many other indicators—economic growth, massive foreign investment, and growing international prestige—were so positive. Clearly something broader and more fundamental had to have been at play. That factor is not to be found in anything unique to Menem's approach to efficiency and access; rather, the cause for the crisis in confidence seems to be Menem's approach to judicial independence and accountability. Few civilian presidents in recent years did more to politicize the courts and to bring them under executive sway—legally and otherwise. At least three reasons seem to have motivated Menem: the desire to ensure that the courts would not undo portions of his controversial economic reform program; the desire to amend the Constitution to allow himself to run for immediate reelection; and the very real concern that an independent judiciary capable of checking the executive branch could hold the administration accountable for its extensive, flagrant corruption, thus sending Menem and his associates to jail. Each concern effectively undercut the credibility of the courts.

Economic Reform

As noted earlier, Menem's modernization of the state program focused heavily on sweeping reforms—many of which were implemented by executive decree—aimed at breaking up state monopolies and moving Argentina toward a free-market model in an abbreviated period of time. Menem had a congressional majority but was intensely wary of the judiciary, which had struck down portions of Alfonsín's Austral Plan in the 1980s. Reflecting this concern, a close Menem aide commented bluntly that, "Menem cannot be exposed to the risks of the New Deal," referring to decisions of the U.S. Supreme Court in the 1930s that overturned portions of Franklin Roosevelt's economic legislation.[56] Menem's first approach was to offer lucrative incentives, including ambassadorships to posts in Western Europe, to several justices affiliated with the opposition Radical Party. Failing that, Menem resorted to court packing, expanding the Supreme Court in 1990 from five to nine—on the grounds that he was so concerned with judicial efficiency that an expanded High Court would be better able to handle its growing work load. The quality of the new justices was debatable at the very least. All of them were identified as loyalists to the Peronist Party and several of them had unimpressive credentials: one was a former partner in Menem's law firm with an undistinguished track record; another was the brother-in-law of the head of the national intelligence service, whose most noteworthy previous assignment was president of the country's national tennis association.[57] Menem took several additional steps—such as issuing an executive decree firing the solicitor general and his entire staff, a first for any Argentine president—that helped bring the courts under greater presidential sway. He also doubled the number of judges and public prosecutors in the Buenos Aires province, moves that—when coupled with his creation of a new appellate court—meant that Menem had appointed more than 90 percent of all judges in Argentina's largest province.[58] The public apparently recognized these efforts as a cynical and blatant politicization of the courts: a 1994 survey found that 72 percent of Argentines felt judges were politically influenced by the government, while only 12 percent thought they were independent; another 69 percent said that Supreme Court decisions were "very politicized."[59]

In less than two years, the benefits of a Peronist-dominated Supreme Court were clear, particularly in the economic realm. To rapidly implement his painful market reforms, Menem relied heavily on emergency executive decrees—he issued more than 200 during his first three years in office, more than eight times as many as all of his predecessors since 1853 combined.[60] Even though many were of dubious legality—such as a measure enabling the administration to press ahead with major privatizations without an open bidding process and another allowing the executive to unilaterally establish prices for public utilities without consulting the proper regulatory agencies—no major decree was ever challenged by the High Court. Most notable was a Supreme Court ruling in the 1991 *Peralta* decision. In that case, the Court upheld the use of presidential decrees, but in the process went well beyond even the traditional jurisprudence of de facto laws. A majority of justices ruled that decrees were legitimate in times of economic emergency and that "in modern times" an "inefficient Congress" unilaterally abrogates its institutional authority and cedes it to the executive—on the grounds that Congress is too subject to special interests and that only the President can act above politics in the interest of the general will.[61] The contrast with Brazil is striking. In Brazil, the Supreme Court struck down economic shock programs and savings freezes as unconstitutional. In Argentina, the High Court ratified the decision with impressive haste. Judicial deference on economic matters would continue throughout Menem's two terms, despite frequent evidence that the administration was engaged in highly questionable dealings.[62]

Presidential Reelection

A second factor for the politicization of the judiciary was Menem's own quest for reelection. In important respects, Menem is heir to the intellectual tradition in which the leader professes a strong link with the masses, claiming to govern on behalf of the general will, skeptical of tolerating opposition to his governing agenda, wary of horizontal accountability, and prone to a desire to remain in office in perpetuity. In his quest to remain in office, Menem was, in many respects, far shrewder than Alfonsín, learning from the failures of his predecessor. After the 1985 congressional elections, for example, Alfonsín and his advisors, who in 1983 had extolled the virtues of democracy, began flirting with amending the Constitution to allow for reelection or the creation of a Prime Minister—which Alfonsín would fill—that would enable Alfonsín and the Radicals to remain in power indefinitely.[63] During this period, Alfonsín became intensely focused on staying in power, even as he became increasingly aware that a Supreme Court that periodically invalidated portions of his economic shock programs was unlikely to tolerate questionable legal methods to alter the Constitution.[64]

Menem, by contrast, would not repeat those failures. The packing of the Supreme Court was the first step, and Menem appointees publicly signaled that, should the President secure congressional approval of an amendment to seek reelection, it would not violate the "core clauses" of the Constitution. Wary of Menem's intentions but unable to present a viable candidate for the presidency itself, the Radicals agreed to support the constitutional amendment if Menem would agree to a larger set of constitutional reforms, including some that would depoliticize the judiciary: a nonpartisan council of magistrates to select and train judges, creation of a public ethics office that would investigate allegations of public sector impropriety, mandatory retirement for judges over the age of 75, and a law requiring all government employees—including judges—to annually declare their net worth and the value of their assets, an effort to identify which judges demonstrated an inexplicable wealth.[65] Menem also pledged to secure the resignation of two Supreme Court justices and to replace them with choices mutually agreeable to the government and opposition. Ironically, even the deal to depoliticize the courts in fact highlighted the persistent politicization of the courts: Menem could agree to the deal only because he was confident that he could order two justices to retire.[66]

Menem's follow-through, however, did little to ensure greater judicial independence. After securing approval of the reelection amendment (and reelection in 1995)

Menem, his brother (a federal senator), and his interior minister worked to gut the Council of Magistrates bill so that it was watered down and implemented only three years later.[67] Even after it was implemented in 1998, the administration looked for opportunities to politicize or circumvent the council—such as bypassing the council in filling judicial vacancies, encouraging the politicized Supreme Court to assume administrative functions reserved for the council, or using pro-government congressmen to pass legislation that would reverse disciplinary rulings made by the new body—preventing it from emerging as an effective counterweight to the executive.[68] For its part, the council showed little desire to check the abuses of the administration.[69] The public ethics office was created two years later but headed by an octogenarian loyalist of Menem, and the office's funding was entirely dependent on the executive. Nor did the turnover on the High Court produce any profound changes. One justice who resigned was made Justice Minister; his replacement was allegedly bought by the administration within months, and within two years was implicated in a government scandal to rake funds off an illicit $10 billion smuggling scheme inside the national customs union.[70] Four years after the pact with the opposition, Menem had secured his reelection and briefly toyed with pursuing a third term in office—even as more than 70 percent of the constitutional amendments he agreed to had not been implemented.[71]

Concealing Corruption

Third and perhaps most importantly, the administration apparently calculated that a pliable judiciary was necessary to conceal endemic government corruption that benefited Menem and a handful of his friends; in short, a politicized and responsive judiciary was necessary to ensure that Menem did not go to jail.[72] Government-sponsored criminal activity apparently increased during the Menem administration and reached audacious levels. Polls in 1996 found that more than 70 percent of the public believed that criminal mafias had penetrated the government, and corruption ranked as the second most important issue for voters after unemployment. Events bore out these general impressions. During Menem's first four years in office, the administration suffered nine scandals resulting in either the dismissal or resignation of twenty-nine senior administration officials, and by 1998 more than 100 government officials and their relatives had been investigated—and exonerated—by a sympathetic judiciary.[73] Most of the scandals involved administration officials looking to use their influence to manipulate government contracts and the privatization process to benefit themselves and business associates.[74]

To ensure that the judiciary did not hold the administration accountable for its actions, Menem and his associates clearly needed a more subservient court, and one of the clearest forms of extending administration influence was through corruption of judicial officials. Domingo Cavallo, the internationally respected former Economy Minister in the Menem administration, gave intimate details of the relationship between Menem, shady businessmen, and corrupt judges. According to Cavallo, Interior Minister Corach and Justice Minister Jassan organized a network of judges to manipulate judicial proceedings and shelve corruption investigations against administration officials accused of illicit participation in various privatization schemes—and to persecute honest officials who investigated these irregularities.[75] Cavallo gained considerable attention when he charged that Corach once wrote the names of several judges on a napkin and boasted that he could arrange in advance the outcome of any case before any of those judges. Corach, trying (ineffectively) to dismiss the charges, made the offhand—and unhelpful—comment that were he to list judges corrupted by the administration, such efforts would require a tablecloth, not a napkin.[76] Support for some of Cavallo's charges came in 1997 when Menem's sixth Justice Minister, Elías Jassan, was discovered to have made over 100 phone calls to a shady businessman named Alfredo Yabrán, despite Jassan's repeated denials to Congress and the press. The Justice Minister reportedly used the calls to alert the businessman to pending privatizations, discuss proposed legislation, and provide advance warning of pending regulatory changes.[77] Meanwhile, the press reported a constant stream of judicial scandals involving judicial appointees of Menem. One Menem appointee to the Supreme Court—who publicly stated in September 1995 that he would almost certainly never rule against the Menem administration—was accused of soliciting bribes to influence cases he was deliberating.[78] Another Menem appointee, Attorney General Angel Agüero Iturbe, was forced to resign in 1997 when it was revealed during his investigation of Yabrán's alleged criminal activity that he was in fact a business partner of the man he was investigating.[79] By the late 1990s, public cynicism about the judiciary was justifiably at an all-time high.

FINAL THOUGHTS ON THE ARGENTINE EXPERIENCE

Despite very different circumstances and under very different conditions than El Salvador and Brazil, the Argentine experience offers similar lessons about where reformers went wrong and what the failure meant for democratic consolidation in Argentina. At the narrowest level of specific approaches to judicial reform, the experiences of Alfonsín and Menem highlight the limitations of selectively reforming only particular aspects of the judiciary. Alfonsín followed a strategy advocated by many nongovernment organizations and focused narrowly on judicial independence, ignoring other aspects of reform; ultimately, however, the crises of efficiency and access became so severe that the President's achievements toward greater independence were overshadowed by the larger public sentiment that judicial reform had failed. Conversely, Menem concentrated on efficiency and access and ignored independence. Yet his politicization of the courts was so extensive that public cynicism only grew.

In this regard, the Menem experience especially demonstrates why focusing on only certain reform variables is an inadequate strategy for success—and the negative synergy that results when reformed variables are expected to coexist indefinitely with reformed aspects. Menem signaled that he expected partisan considerations to drive the behavior of judges, even as his laudable efficiency-maximizing measures aimed to uphold the rule of law in a predictable fashion, particularly for foreign investors who often based their investment strategies on the transparency of the host country's judiciary. Clearly some force had to give. Negative synergy affected the judiciary in two immediate ways. First, Menem's reluctance to follow through on his 1994 pledges to support a nonpartisan Council of Magistrates bill meant that the federal government had no legal authority to appoint federal judges between 1994 and 1997 in the absence of legislation to define the selection process. The result—more than 300 federal judicial vacancies nationwide—created a shortage of judges that added to trial delays and undercut Menem's efficiency-maximizing measures. Second, Menem discovered fairly quickly that while he may have been able to tell ill-qualified or un-professional judges how to *vote*, it was far more difficult to tell them how to *work*—how to conduct their affairs in a timely and efficient manner and how to implement his more forward-looking reforms. Observers noted with some irony that senior judges—even though they had "made it to where they are thanks to recommendations of the party in power"—had in some respects become "uncontrollable."[80] For exam-ple, they were able to block the creation of a judicial academy that would have devised and enforced standards of professional conduct; they undermined congressional ef-forts to create an administrative council that would have removed clerical chores from judges; they refused to follow legislation that required them to annually dis-close their personal assets; and they resisted government efforts in 1999 to reform the penal code.[81] In each instance, even politicized judges drew the line at the prospects of losing their institutional prerogatives and the budgetary resources that accompanied such responsibilities.[82] The unprofessional and politicized conduct Menem desired to affect certain rulings clearly had a cost in terms of efficiency. Judges rarely showed up for work—the typical judge in Argentina in 1996 worked only 130 days per year, while the average public sector employee in the country worked 231—and the extensive "judicial holidays" of the courts were widely viewed as an important factor contributing to the backlog of cases.[83] Even Supreme Court jus-tices had difficulty appearing for work, even though the administration wanted them to press ahead with rulings of pending cases involving foreign investment disputes.[84] Menem's track record of politicization required, in effect, that judges not take their jobs very seriously. When judges complied, efficiency and access suffered.

To a degree more striking than in El Salvador or Brazil, it also is clear that the lack of judicial independence and the growth of judicial corruption has served as a drag on economic development. This development is ironic because Menem—more than any other Latin American leader—moved so aggressively to implement market re-forms and create a macroeconomic environment hospitable to foreign investment. Yet the politicization of the courts that in 1990 was so essential for ensuring the via-bility of the economic reform process was a liability by the late 1990s.

The President thought that a politically dependent Supreme Court would be exactly what investors needed as a sign of certainty that things would not be changed by the federal courts. But what seemed to be so wise at that moment [1991] became a boomerang after the privatization process drew to a close in 1996. Investors, after the economic situation improved, were not so sure about investing in a country where the judicial process is dependent on presidential influence, thus creating a phenomenon known as 'legal uncertainty.'[85]

Thus, despite some of the most sound fiscal policies in Latin America and an impressive commitment to economic fundamentals, recent years have actually witnessed various instances of firms staying out of the Argentine market because of a lack of "juridic security"—the very real fear that their investments would be subject to politicized enforcement of the law and that judicial corruption made the operating environment unjustifiably costly.[86] By the mid-1990s, investors were increasingly critical of the role of bribery in winning government contracts; IMF Managing Director Michel Camdessus noted that even though the country's fiscal policies were sound, what Argentina really needed was to make the Justice Ministry "more important than the economy ministry," and respected journalists were repeatedly uncovering judicial corruption schemes involving major multinational investors, some of whom acknowledged that they were staying out of Argentina because of the unpredictable judiciary.[87]

In important respects, the failure of judicial reform also had negative implications for Argentina's post-transition democracy. The experience in Argentina, despite very different domestic conditions and under very different political circumstances, mirrored the pattern in El Salvador and Brazil: after more than a decade of democratic rule, the courts were increasingly less popular, raising concerns about the quality of democratic governance and the ability of civilian institutions to meet popular needs and expectations. Public confidence went from nearly 60 percent to 17 percent in 1993, 13 percent in 1995, and single digits by 1999.[88] Similar to the previous case studies, increasingly cynical voters were simply turning from the courts altogether, seeking instead alternative and often violent forms of justice as the courts became viewed as unreformable. Nearly half of the public say that they do not believe it is possible to mount an anti-corruption campaign to root out judicial corruption; illicit activity is thought to be too endemic in the courts to change or eliminate.[89]

Also similar to the other case studies, the failure of the courts to administer affairs in an efficient and timely fashion has contributed to a growing tolerance of vigilante justice, death squads, and law-and-order, populist candidates espousing quasi-authoritarian rhetoric, raising questions about the degree to which Argentina is successfully building a more democratic political culture.[90] Allegations of police brutality have risen dramatically even as Argentina has become further removed from military rule; political observers note that much of the violence has been met with approval by the middle class on the now-familiar grounds that the police are merely meting out the punishment that the courts will fail to administer.[91] Meanwhile, prominent politicians began calling for drastic measures—such as public beheadings and legalizing torture to inflict "prior suffering" before an execution—in an effort to deter crime.[92] According to Jaime Malamud-Goti, some aspects of political culture in democratic Argentina were beginning to resemble a milder version of the darker days of the 1970s: "There are strong indications that terror once again is gradually saturating Argentina's political life. . . . For advocates of individual rights, the Argentine situation in the mid-1990s is bleak. By and large, the citizenry is apathetic in the face of renewed police brutality."[93] The implications for democratic consolidation are not encouraging. A late 1996 poll found that 96 percent felt corruption high or very high in the country (66 percent cited judicial inefficiency as the main reason); worse yet, 64 percent of respondents agreed with the view that "honesty would not get them ahead"—hardly the foundations for a vibrant and healthy civil society.[94] Through different paths and different strategies, Alfonsín and Menem, and the failed judicial reform efforts they produced, contributed to democratic decay in Argentina.

NOTES

1. Domingo Cavallo, *El peso de la verdad* (Buenos Aires: Planeta Espejo de la Argentina, 1997): 261.

2. Stephen Brown, "Argentina's Cavallo Vows to Fight Court," Reuters press dispatch, 29 April 1997.

3. Mariano Grondona, "La justicia y los políticos," in *La justicia en crisis*, ed. Francisco Diez (Buenos Aires: Poder Ciudadano, 1994): 136.

4. Edgardo Buscaglia and Maria Dakolias, *Judicial Reform in Latin America* (Washington, D.C.: The World Bank, 1996): 9, 15.

5. Edi Zuniño, "El tiempo de la Justicia-less," *Noticias*, 14 December 1996, 26–30; and Edi Zuniño and Dario Gallo, "El Caso Yabrán: Gabinete en sombra," *Noticias*, 21 June 1997, 24–28.

6. Jaime Malamud-Goti, *Game Without End: State Terror and the Politics of Justice* (Norman: University of Oklahoma Press, 1996): 4.

7. Carlos S. Niño, "On the Exercise of Judicial Review in Argentina," in *Transition to Democracy in Latin America*, ed. Irwin P. Stotzky (Boulder, Colo.: Westview Press, 1994): 322.

8. See Niño, "On the Exercise of Judicial Review in Argentina," p. 316; and Phanor J. Eder, "Judicial Review in Latin America," *Ohio State Law Journal* 21 (Fall 1960): 575–77.

9. Alan T. Leonhard, "Constitutionalism and the Argentine Judiciary," *InterAmerican Law Review* 8 (January–December 1966): 245–56. In his classic study on Argentine constitutionalism, Santos Amadeo notes, "It may be said that the Argentine Court cites more frequently the commentators on the Constitution of the United States than does the United States Supreme Court itself." See Santos P. Amadeo, *Argentine Constitutional Law* (New York: Columbia University Press, 1943): 54.

10. Prior to World War I, for example, Argentina was a larger per capita exporter of beef and wheat than was the United States; had the world's third largest gold and silver reserves; and had the world's sixth highest per capita income—higher even than the United States. See Paul Lewis, *The Crisis of Argentine Capitalism* (Chapel Hill: University of North Carolina Press, 1990): Chapter 1; and Piero Gleisejes, "The Decay of Democracy in Argentina," *Current History* 87 (January 1988): 5–8, 49.

11. David C. Jordan, "Argentina's Bureaucratic Oligarchies," *Current History* (February 1972): 70–75, 113–114. The effects of this political tradition on the courts are tightly summarized in Atilio Cadorín, "Los riesgos de la adicción al poder," *La Nación*, 18 May 1997, 11.

12. See Robert Biles, "The Position of the Judiciary in the Political Sytems of Argentina and Mexico," *Lawyer of the Americas* 8 (1976): 287–318. Biles calculates that between 1953 and 1972, the typical Supreme Court justice served a mere 10.4 months. See also Felix Luna, *Argentina: de Perón a Lanusse* (Buenos Aires: Sudamericana/Planeta, 1984): 99. Even when governments tried to replace the most blatant political hacks—as when the military regime of General Jorge Videla replaced some of the unqualified candidates placed on the bench by the previous Peronist regime with more competent appointees—their efforts inadvertently

strengthened the traditional notion that any incoming government could not respect the judicial appointments of its predecessor. For a discussion of this period and Videla's actions against the judiciary, see David C. Jordan, "Argentina's Military Commonwealth," *Current History* (February 1979): 66–69, 89–90.

13. Mark Osiel details one example of this doctrine. Following the 1963 coup that removed President Illia from office, several Supreme Court justices were debating the constitutionality of the coup and whether to recognize the new military regime. One justice noted, "We can say, with Cicero, that we have saved the republic by violating the law," to which another justice replied—in line with the doctrine of de facto laws—"Cicero was wrong. He who saves the Republic cannot possibly be violating the law." See Mark J. Osiel, "Dialogue with Dictators: Judicial Resistance in Argentina and Brazil," *Law and Social Inquiry* 20 (Spring 1995): 495.

14. Carlos S. Niño, "On the Exercise of Judicial Review in Argentina," in *Transition to Democracy in Latin America*, p. 318. Niño notes that the High Court ruled in the 1940s that "decree laws enacted by *de facto* governments are valid on the basis of their origin, and because they have the value of laws, they are valid even when not ratified by Congress." During the 1976 coup, the Supreme Court ruled that the coup was a political question and hence beyond the legal purview of the High Court. An early look—but one which held up quite well in subsequent decades—is J. Irizarry y Puente, "The Nature and Powers of a De Facto Government in Latin America," *Tulane Law Review* 30 (December 1955): 25–72.

15. Some of the instances of judicial assertiveness are traced in Frederick E. Snyder, "State of Siege and Rule of Law in Argentina: The Politics and Rhetoric of Vindication," *Lawyer of the Americas* 15 (Winter 1984): 503–20.

16. Roberto Aizcorbe, *La Crisis Argentina* (Buenos Aires: Occitania, 1984): 195–98.

17. To be sure, there is a certain degree of revisionism when Alfonsín portrays his commitment to democracy. He consistently sidesteps the fact that toward the end of his term he sought to amend the Constitution to seek reelection and that when his plans faced congressional opposition, he considered a move that would have expanded the size of the Supreme Court from five to seven. Luigi Manzetti correctly notes that by the end of Alfonsín's administration, the President was ruling heavily by executive decree. See Luigi Manzetti, *Institutions, Parties, and Coalitions in Argentine Politics* (Pittsburgh, Pa.: University of Pittsburgh Press, 1998): 317.

18. Raúl Ricardo Alfonsín, "The Function of the Judicial Power During the Transition," in *Transition to Democracy in Latin America*, pp. 41–54. Alfonsín's main legal advisers clearly shared these views. See, for example, Andres José D'Alessio, "The Function of the Prosecution in the Transition to Democracy in Latin America," and Eduardo Rabossi, "The Role of the Judiciary in the Review of Human Rights Violations in Argentina," in *Transition to Democracy in Latin America*, p. 323.

19. Alfonsín admitted as much in his writings in the 1990s, noting: "The judiciary, and particularly the Supreme Court, must ensure that the Constitution and the laws are upheld. If they succeed, they will win the respect and following of the citizenry. If they fail, they will lose their prestige and their power; moreover, this failure will open the doors to anarchy and oppression." Raúl Ricardo Alfonsín, "The Function of the Judicial Power During the Transition," in *Transition to Democracy in Latin America*, p. 45.

20. Jaime Malamud-Goti, "Human Rights Abuses in Fledgling Democracies: The Role of Discretion," in *Transition to Democracy in Latin America*, p. 231.

21. Public frustration probably was somewhat greater, ironically, because judicial reform had not been a top priority for voters in the early 1980s. Less than 10 percent of the public assigned

a top priority to judicial reform; more pressing concerns were inflation, declining wages, unemployment, the foreign debt, declining social services, and crime. Once Alfonsín failed to deliver on his lofty rhetoric, cynical voters complained that the idealistic president had "wasted" too much time on judicial reform at the cost of neglecting more pressing issues. See Edgardo Catterberg, *Los argentinos frente a la política* (Buenos Aires: Grupo Editorial Planeta, 1985): 44.

22. Alejandro Carrio, *La Corte Suprema y su independencia* (Buenos Aires: Abeledo Perrot, 1993): 116. Luder rejected the offer, explaining the presidency of the Supreme Court was a post not important enough for a prominent politician such as himself—a reflection of the low esteem in which the Supreme Court was generally held.

23. Carrio, *La Corte Suprema y su independencia*, p. 148.

24. This paragraph relies heavily on Carrio, *La Corte Suprema y su independencia*, p. 136; and Eduardo Oteiza, *La Corte Suprema: Entre la justicia sin política y la política sin justicia* (La Plata: Libreria Editora Platense, 1994): 112–88.

25. Malamud-Goti, *Game Without End: State Terror and the Politics of Justice*, p. 4.

26. Specific details of the self-amnesty law can be found in "Human Rights in the World: Argentina," *Review of the International Commission of Jurists* 31 (December 1983): 1–6.

27. Rabossi, "The Role of the Judiciary in the Review of Human Rights Violations in Argentina," p. 337; and Oteiza, *La Corte Suprema*, p. 243.

28. Alfonsín justified these decisions years later on the grounds of pragmatism (it would have been impossible to try every enlisted soldier and officer) and on ethical considerations, writing that it was important that society understand that he was not pursuing vindictive policies against the armed forces. See Raúl Alfonsín, "Never Again in Argentina," *Journal of Democracy* 4 (January 1993): 15–19.

29. Malamud-Goti, "Human Rights Abuses in Fledgling Democracies: The Case of Discretion," p. 237.

30. Alfonsín's need for sensitivity toward the military during this early period is highlighted in Gary W. Wynia, "Democracy in Argentina," *Current History* 84 (February 1984): 53–56, 85–86; and Peter Snow and Luigi Manzetti, eds., *Political Forces in Argentina* (Westport, Conn.: Praeger, 1993): 112–18.

31. Malamud-Goti, *Game Without End*, p. 19.

32. Malamud-Goti, *Game Without End*, pp. 185, 198.

33. Public cynicism notwithstanding, international opinion at the time correctly noted that the convictions of the influential generals were a dramatic achievement when compared to past military regimes in Argentina and its neighbors. See Gary W. Wynia, "Readjusting to Democracy in Argentina," *Current History* 86 (January 1987): 5–8, 34.

34. Edgardo Buscaglia and Maria Dakolias, *Judicial Reform in Latin American Court: The Experience in Argentina and Ecuador* (Washington, D.C.: The World Bank, 1996).

35. Marita Carballo de Cilley, *¿Qué pensamos los argentinos?* (Buenos Aires: Ediciones El Cronista América, 1987): 68–73.

36. Alberto Ricardo Dalla Via, *Transformacion Económica y Seguridad Jurídica* (Buenos Aires: Libreria Editora Platense SRL, 1994): 21, 24; and Edgardo Buscaglia, Maria Dakolias, and William Ratliff, *Judicial Reform in Latin America* (Stanford, Calif.: Stanford University/Hoover Institution, 1995): 5.

37. A concise overview of the climate during this period is Gary W. Wynia, "Campaigning for President in Argentina," *Current History* 88 (March 1989): 133–36, 144–45.

38. The Justice Minister at the time explicitly declared that the new procedures would lead to "quicker trials." See Gregory W. O'Reilly, "Opening up Argentina's courts," *Judicature* 80 (March–April 1997): 237–41.

39. Edgardo Buscaglia, "Stark picture of justice," *Financial Times*, 25 March 1995, 15.

40. Harry Blair et al., *A Strategic Assessment of Legal Systems Development in Uruguay and Argentina* (Washington, D.C.: U.S. Agency for International Development, 1994): 17.

41. For a survey of the various types of ADR tried in Argentina, see Gladys Stella Alvarez, "Alternative Dispute Resolution Mechanisms: Lessons of the Argentine Experience," in *Judicial Reform in Latin America and the Caribbean*, ed. Malcolm Rowat, Waleed H. Malik, and Maria Dakolias (Washington, D.C.: The World Bank, 1995): 78–91.

42. Many of these examples are taken from *USAID Argentina and Uruguay Close-Out Report* (Washington, D.C.: U.S. Agency for International Development, 1995).

43. See, for example, "Los obispos y su visión de la Justicia," *La Nación*, 29 April 1997, 10; and "Camdessus pide segúridad jurídica," *La Nación*, 23 May 1997, 10.

44. The figures are taken from *Estudio de Opinión Acerca de la Administración de Justicia* (Buenos Aires: CEJURA, 1994). The study was conducted by the Gallup Institute.

45. Calvin Sims, "In Eyes of Argentines, Judges Often Biggest Lawbreakers," *New York Times*, 18 August 1997; and Adrián Ventura, "El último año judicial de Menem," *La Nación*, 3 February 1999, 3. The decline of popular support over time is reflected in Marita Carballo, "Confidence Down in Democratic Institutions," *La Nación*, 13 January 1996, 7, in FBIS-LAT, 6 February 1996.

46. Cristina M. L. Carjuzaa, "Desarrollo y proyectos del sistema de jurisprudencia de la Corte Suprema de Justicia de la Nación," *Jurismatica* 3 (April 1993): 25–34.

47. Adrián Ventura, "Agregarían otros juicios orales," *La Nación*, 26 August 1997, 5.

48. *Strengthening Democratic Institutions in Uruguay and Argentina* (Washington, D.C.: U.S. Agency for International Development, 1994): 4.

49. Buscaglia, Dakolias, and Ratliff, *Judicial Reform in Latin America*, p. 42, n.64. The 1997 figures come from a personal interview with officials at the Libra Foundation, August 1997, Buenos Aires, Argentina. See also Paul E. Mason, "The Benefits of Arbitration and Mediation for North-South Business Transactions," *Latin American Law and Business Report* 5 (May 1996): 4.

50. Blair et al., *A Strategic Assessment*, pp. 42–43.

51. *Strengthening Democratic Institutions in Uruguay and Argentina*, p. 4.

52. *Argentina: Human Rights Practices, 1994* (Washington, D.C: U.S. Department of State, 1994): 8.

53. "Un millón de causas ingresa cada año," *La Nación*, 14 July 1997, 1.

54. The total number of cases pending in federal system went from 800,000 in 1989 to 1.5 million in 1995. See Buscaglia, Dakolias, and Ratliff, *Judicial Reform in Latin America*, p. 5.

55. Edgardo Buscaglia and Pilar Domingo Villegas, "Impediments to Judicial Reform in Latin America," Paper Presented at the XIX Congress of the Latin American Studies Association, 28–30 September 1995, p. 13.

56. The official cited is Raúl Granillo Ocampo, a former legal aide to Menem, his one-time ambassador to the United States, and his seventh Minister of Justice. The quote is taken from Horacio Verbitsky, *Robo para la corona* (Buenos Aires: Planeta Espejo de la Argentina, 1993): 65.

57. See Horacio Verbitsky, "Argentines Tire of Menem's Politicized Justice," *The Wall Street Journal*, 13 March 1998, A14; Jorge Roullon, "Debatieron sobre la credibilidad de los medios y de la Justicia," *La Nación*, 13 August 1997, 13; and Adrián Ventura, "Pactos y peleas en una Corte Suprema afín al Gobierno," *La Nación*, 18 May 1997, 4.

58. Verbitsky, "Argentines Tire of Menem's Politicized Justice," p. A13.

59. *Estudio de Opinion Acerca de la Administración de Justicia*, p. 32. Even some High Court justices shared this view. Justice Augusto Belluscio remarked in 1993 that "prior to the increase in the number of its members to nine, the Supreme Court was independent," but now "it is demonstrating that it no longer is. . . . The court started going downhill as soon as the number of its members increased." See "Justice Says Supreme Court 'No Longer Independent,'" *Clarin*, 5 October 1993, 33, in FBIS-LAT, 6 October 1993.

60. Christopher Larkins, "The Judiciary and Delegative Democracy in Argentina," *Comparative Politics* 30 (July 1998): 423–42.

61. William Rogers, *La Corte Suprema de la Justicia y la Segúridad Jurídica* (Buenos Aires: Abeledo-Perrot, 1994): Chapter Two.

62. Adrián Ventura, "La Justicia, en favor de Menem," *La Nación*, 16 July 1999, 13.

63. Marcelo Cavarozzi calls this the "hegemonic dream" of Alfonsín. See Marcelo Cavarozzi and Maria Gross, "Argentine Parties Under Alfonsín: From Democratic Reinvention to Political Decline and Hyperinflation," in *The New Argentine Democracy*, ed. Edward C. Epstein (Westport, Conn.: Praeger, 1992): 182. According to the authors:

> The initial success of the Austral Plan and the government's impressive victory in the 1985 legislative elections stimulated the fantasy of possible party hegemony (along the lines of the Mexican PRI) in broad sectors of Radicalism. They believed that the moment had arrived for their party to constitute a so-called "Third Historical Movement" succeeding the national popular movements associated with the charismatic leadership of Yrigoyen and then Perón.

64. Cavarozzi and Gross noted the emergence of "the increasingly centralized discipline associated with Alfonsín's leadership, only comparable to Perón's characteristic leadership style. This change was not insignificant in a party that had always criticized Peronism for its absence of internal democracy." See their "Argentine Parties Under Alfonsín: From Democratic Reinvention to Political Decline and Hyperinflation," p. 177. Alfonsín flirted with expanding the Supreme Court from five to seven in 1987, but Congress and opposition parties forced him to scrap the idea.

65. "El costo del Pacto de Olivos," *La Nación*, 15 June 1997, 10.

66. One justice, Rodrigo Barra, stepped down to become Menem's sixth Justice Minister. Barra resigned in 1996 after revelations that he had once been a member of a militant Nazi Movement. See Dario Gallo, "Historia Prohibida," *Noticias*, 22 June 1996, 28–33.

67. Maria Fernanda Villosio, "El Consejo de la Magistratura, más lejos de convertirse en ley," *La Nación*, 21 April 1997, 9; Adrián Ventura, "La UCR presiona para aprobar la ley sobre la Magistratura," *La Nación*, 14 May 1997, 4; "El Consejo de la Magistratura," *La Nación*, 17 June 1997, 10.

68. Rather than allowing the Council to fill judicial vacancies, for example, Menem began reassigning sympathetic sitting judges to vacant posts, thereby sidestepping both the Council of Magistrates and Senate confirmation—a constitutionally dubious maneuver that the Council unsuccessfully protested. The High Court also continued to claim institutional prerogatives to manage the judicial bureaucracy, creating frequent standoffs. See Adrián Ventura, "Maniobra del Gobierno en la Justicia," *La Nación*, 19 February 1999, 1; Adrián Ventura, "El Consejo de la Magistratura se enfrenta con el Presidente," *La Nación*, 28 February 1999, 9; Adrián Ventura, "La Justicia volvió a ser esclava del poder político," *La Nación*, 1 February 1999, 8; Adrián Ventura, "Otra polémica entre la Corte y el Consejo," *La Nación*, 1 April 1999, 13; Adrián Ventura, "Prohíben a Menem trasladar jueces," *La Nación*, 21 May 1999, 12; and "Maniobra del PJ para protejer a dos jueces," *La Nación*, 8 February 1999, 10. In September

1999, the council did successfully suspend one corrupt judge for 180 days. See Daniel Gutman, "Ya funciona el sistema para renovar la justicia," *Clarín*, 3 September 1999, 3.

69. Adrián Ventura, "Un Consejo muy poco eficiente," *La Nación*, 7 July 1999, 22.

70. "Hidden Camera Does in a Corrupt Judge in Parallel Customs Scandal," U.S. Department of State, unclassified telegram Buenos Aires 01067, 27 February 1997.

71. These commitments are discussed in Rafael Bielsa and Eduardo Grana, *Justicia y Estado* (Buenos Aires: Ediciones Ciudad Argentina, 1996): 391–422; and Adrián Ventura, "La Corte y la reelección," *La Nación*, 10 February 1999, 3. In 1999, the Supreme Court exempted itself from some of the constitutional reforms, such as an amendment that required judges to retire at age 75. See Adrián Ventura, "Causas en busca de una solución," *La Nación*, 28 July 1999, 3; and Adrián Ventura, "Fayt continuará en su cargo," *La Nación*, 20 August 1999, 3.

72. Menem's political opponents make this charge publicly. See "Críticas a la demora por la Magistratura," *La Nación*, 19 August 1997, 8.

73. Verbitsky, "Argentines Tire of Menem's Politicized Justice," p. A14.

74. Roberto Pablo Saba and Luigi Manzetti, "Privatization in Argentina: The implications for corruption," *Crime, Law, and Social Change* 25 (1997): 363; and Silvana Boschi, "Armas: naufraga la jugada del Gobierno en la Corte," *Clarín*, 4 July 1999, 1.

75. "Corruption laid at Menem's own door," *Latin American Weekly Report*, 4 March 1997, 112. Cavallo claimed that "Cabinet members regularly called judges and prosecutors to give them instructions on how to handle important cases" and that Justice Minister Jassan was "the head of the mafia." See also Calvin Sims, "In Eyes of Argentines, Judges Often Biggest Lawbreakers," *New York Times*, 18 August 1997, 8; and "Minister Jassan Resigns; Criminal Connection Viewed," *Clarín*, 24 June 1997; in FBIS-LAT, 25 June 1997. The administration also relied on sympathetic judges to harass investigative reporters looking into allegations of government corruption. See, for example, Adrián Ventura, "La Corte apoyó a Menem en la causa contra Horacio Verbitsky," *La Nación*, 11 August 1999, 1.

76. Cavallo, *El peso de la verdad*, p. 261. Corach's not especially effective defense was reported in Brown, "Argentina's Cavallo vows to fight court." The minister's quote in full, was that, "A napkin wouldn't be enough. You'd need a tablecloth." A defense that scored more points politically was Corach's subsequent claim that corruption in Argentina was no worse than government corruption in the United States after January 1993. See "Corach: No Concern Over Transparency During Clinton Visit," Buenos Aires Todo Noticias Television, 8 October 1997, in FBIS-LAT, 8 Ocober 1997. The response of leading Peronist deputies also was not especially encouraging. They publicly berated Cavallo for being "a squealer," apparently preferring that the former minister keep his knowledge to himself. See Eduardo Van Der Kooy, "Rising Cost of Cavallo-Government Feud Seen," *Clarín*, 27 October 1997, in FBIS-LAT, 30 October 1997.

77. The affair was widely covered in the international press. Some of the better articles are Ken Warn, "Argentine justice minister resigns; Ruling Peronist party split into factions," *Financial Times*, 28 June 1997, 4; "The Yabrán Affair," *The Economist*, 1 July 1997; Pilar Bustelo, "Scandals Have the Peronists on the Run," *Business Week*, 13 October 1997; Marcela Valente, "Yabrán? The name does sound familiar, officials admit," InterPress Service press dispatch, 19 June 1997; Marcela Valente, "Justice Minister Resigns Over Reporter's Murder," InterPress Service press dispatch, 26 June 1997.

78. "Argentine Supreme Court Judge in Bribe Probe," Reuter press dispatch, 1 October 1997.

79. See Adrián Ventura, "Reasons for Iturbe Resignation Discussed," *La Nación*, 20 February 1997, in FBIS-LAT, 21 February 1997.

80. "Menemist-Cavallo Corruption Battle Viewed," *Clarín*, 13 October 1996, in FBIS-LAT, 15 October 1996.

81. Laura Zommer, "La Corte no levantará el secreto," *La Nación*, 29 August 1997, 15; Laura Zommer, "La Corte decide sobre el secreto patrimonio," *La Nación*, 28 August 1997, 17; "Granillo desairado por 26 jueces," *La Nación*, 16 April 1999, 11; and "La reforma judicial no conforma a todos," *La Nación*, 27 August 1997, 11.

82. Edgardo Buscaglia and Maria Dakolias, *Judicial Reform in Latin America: Economic Efficiency vs. Institutional Inertia* (Washington, D.C.: Georgetown University School of Business Administration, 1995): 16.

83. "Critican la duración de la feria judicial," *La Nación*, 14 July 1997, 1.

84. In 1996, all nine justices appeared for only eleven of the Court's thirty-three sessions, and some were absent nearly a dozen times. Menem appointees had the worst attendance rates. Adrián Ventura, "Atrasos en la Corte por las ausencias," *La Nación*, 3 October 1997, 2.

85. Saba and Manzetti, "Privatization in Argentina: The implications for corruption," p. 363. This issue emerged as an important theme in the 1999 presidential campaign. See Graciela Guadalupe, "Inversores: un voto de confianza," *La Nación*, 5 September 1999, 8.

86. Adrián Ventura, "Estudios jurídicos advierten sobre los negocios inseguros," *La Nación*, 28 September 1997, E2; Gabriela Origlia, "El costo de la inseguridad jurídica," *La Nación*, 6 August 1997, 1; "Criticó documento de EE. UU. sobre la Argentina," *Clarín*, 30 July 1997, 1; and Sebastian Edwards, "More IMF Austerity Won't Cure What Ails Latin America," *The Wall Street Journal*, 30 August 1996, 9.

87. Laura Zommer, "Se cae la causa por la aduana paralela," *La Nación*, 1 March 1999, 8; Mary Anastasia O'Grady, "Don't Blame the Free Market for Argentina's Woes," *The Wall Street Journal*, 30 May 1997, A13; "Camdessus pide seguridad jurídica" (editorial), *La Nación*, 23 May 1997, 2; Buscaglia, "Stark picture of justice," p. 15; and Ventura, "Agregarián otros juicios orales," 5.

88. Harry Blair et al., *A Strategic Assessment of Legal Systems Development in Uruguay and Argentina* (Washington, D.C.: U.S. Agency for International Development, 1994); Adrián Ventura, "Menem y la Corte, cerca del fin," *La Nación*, 12 May 1999, 3; and Patricia Garcia, "En la Teleraña," *Noticias*, 20 August 1995, 13.

89. Fernando Gonzalez, "El dedo en la llaga," *Noticias*, 15 June 1996, 24–29.

90. See, for example, Roberto Caballero and Adrián Murano, "El país del gatillo libre," *Noticias*, 10 April 1999, 84–90.

91. More than 80 percent of the public claims that it does not feel protected by the courts and police. See Alfredo Vega, "Robos: aumenta el clima de inseguridad," *La Nación*, 25 February 1996, 1; Adrián Ventura, "Aumenta la delincuencia: sus causas y sus efectos," *La Nación*, 25 February 1996, 17; and "Menem movilizó a todas las fuerzas de seguridad," *La Nación*, 16 April 1999, 3.

92. Deputy Norma Miralles argued, "There are some criminals who commit such atrocious crimes that shooting them is not enough, because they don't suffer. I would make them suffer more, because criminals should suffer in their own flesh what they do to their victims." See "Make Some Executions Painful, Peronist Deputy Asks," Reuter press dispatch, 21 August 1997. See also Adrián Ventura, "Adviertan que pueden aparecer los temidos escuadrones de la muerte," *La Nación*, 11 April 1999, 3.

93. Malamud-Goti, *Game Without End*, p. 147.

94. "Latest Gallup Poll Shows Argentines Believe Corruption Is On The Rise," U.S. Department of State, unclassified telegram Buenos Aires 00041, 3 January 1997.

Chapter Six

Chile's Coherent Approach to Judicial Reform

> The problem is so complicated that many members of the judiciary consider it unresolvable. But at the same time, they offer a glimpse of hope: by attacking simultaneously all of the factors involved, it is possible that justice might arrive on time.[1]

At this point, the obvious question is whether any reform strategy is capable of succeeding in Latin America. That is, is judicial reform possible in a period of only ten or fifteen years? Is concrete progress possible only over a much longer period? If so, are Latin America's frail democracies strong enough to withstand those delays and the accompanying strains caused by democratic decay? If governments struggle to reform only one or two variables at a time, would it make any sense to try to reform all three at once? And is there any combination of reform variables that can avoid the negative synergy exemplified in the failed examples of El Salvador, Argentina, and Brazil?

The Chilean experience offers tentative answers to some of those questions. The judicial reform experiment in Chile seems to violate all the principles inherent in the conventional wisdom of reformers. Presidents Patricio Aylwin and Eduardo Frei attacked all three reform variables simultaneously; there was no concentrated effort to improve one variable at the expense of another, no focused effort on a single component, and no exaggerated promises of what the reforms could deliver. Instead, reformers produced a steady stream of measures across all three variables at once, which, when combined, added up to impressive progress. They recognized that it made little sense to boost the independence of judges if the courts were too inefficient to exercise their newfound authority in a timely fashion; it was equally pointless, they argued, to build up the institutional authority of the civilian courts if the judiciary was so inaccessible that the public would not turn to it in any event. Efficiency-creating measures required independent and accountable judges dedicated to the rule of law rather than partisans subject to political manipulation. Finally, they understood that there was little logic in increasing access to the courts if judicial authority was exercised neither independently nor efficiently, as such efforts would only perpetuate public cynicism. The specific pieces of legislation may have been modest individually, but the logic and coherence were profound: only by attacking all three variables at once was it possible to nudge forward the reform process.

While any conclusions are tentative based on the short time frame of the Chilean example, by 1999 the results of this approach were encouraging. Efforts to pursue sensitive human rights cases through the civilian courts produced modest successes and several symbolically important victories that punished members of the former military government. Just as importantly, efforts to impeach several corrupt senior judges prompted the judiciary to undertake a thorough internal housecleaning and introduced into the courts a measure of accountability that had been missing in past decades. The efforts were also sustained, in part, by a fair degree of luck and happenstance: various senior judges—including some of the more powerful, antidemocratic justices appointed by the military—either retired or passed away in the early years of civilian rule. Efficiency-enhancing reforms laid the long-term foundation for more streamlined judicial proceedings by creating a national judicial academy and a public prosecutor's office. Until the deeper structural reforms take effect, reformers relied—and are relying—on an increased number of judges, procedural reforms to give judges greater control over the cases that come before the courts, and administrative reforms to remove from judges some of the burdens of routine paperwork unrelated to their primary duty. Meanwhile, an ambitious access to justice program—including the innovative use of mobile consultants and law students to provide access to the remote regions of the country—has given low-income citizens a stake in the formal justice system. Officials found that simultaneous reforms helped minimize the unintended consequences of other measures and in fact actually sustained each other. Periodic legislative setbacks—and Aylwin and Frei suffered a number of them—were tolerable to the public because reformers had other successes to show for their efforts. The broader perception that the courts were moving in the right direction was more important to gaining public trust than were the specific setbacks along the way. No setback was overwhelming and no isolated reform was undermined by unreformed aspects of the courts; in short, there was no negative synergy as in other case studies.

By 1999, polls reflected that the Chilean judiciary, while still facing deep public distrust, was nonetheless moving in the right direction. Approval ratings for the courts, which had hovered in the single digits in the late 1980s, ranged between 30 and 40 percent and steadily moved upward—hardly an overwhelming endorsement of the judiciary but a positive trend that helped sustain the reform momentum. Equally important is what the polls did not reflect. Despite a rise in crime rates and growing public concerns about security issues, there were few calls for law-and-order politicians, few populists espousing draconian or antidemocratic solutions, and few outbreaks of vigilante justice like those in the other case studies.

THE REVERSAL OF A RESPECTED TRADITION

Prior to the 1970s, Chile's tradition of judicial independence was undisputed. The country's democratic Constitution of 1925 included guarantees such as life tenure for all judges at all levels, irreducible salaries, and an explicitly nonpartisan appointment process that removed virtually any role for political parties in the selection of judges.[2] According to Arturo Valenzuela, during this period the judiciary was "a prestigious institution . . . respected for its neutrality and remoteness from the clamor of everyday politics"; it consistently attracted qualified applicants, maintained rigorous professional criteria, and was viewed as one of the most coveted career paths in the public sector.[3] Detractors rarely questioned the professional merits of judges.[4] Instead, most critics focused on charges that the courts were politically conservative and hence "socially distant" from the country's growing urban working class.[5]

The independence and integrity of the courts were severely undermined during the socialist administration of Salvador Allende (1970–73), highlighting the important role that judicial politicization can play in the breakdown of democratic regimes. Even though Allende was committed on paper to respecting a series of democratic guarantees—including judicial independence—his brief tenure was characterized by a series of judicial abuses. Government officials warned that they would use the levers of justice to punish political opponents and boasted that "the law has turned against its creators"; during his first speech to Congress, Allende claimed that, once Chile made its "peaceful transition to socialism," he would replace the court system with a new "Supreme Tribunal," selected by a "popular assembly" that would "assist the majority classes" in governing.[6] By his second year, Allende had begun creating special "neighborhood tribunals"—courts outside the formal judicial system and staffed by Socialist Party militants with little or no legal training—to rule on issues ranging from petty crimes and neighborhood disputes to squatters' rights and land confiscation; the defendant frequently was denied the right to an attorney in the process.[7] Meanwhile, senior administration officials repeatedly ignored various Supreme Court rulings that overturned government expropriations and nullified uncompensated land reforms; in some cases, Allende and his Justice Minister Jose Tohá ordered the national police force to ignore inconvenient judicial rulings.[8] By June 1973, the Supreme Court broke with its traditional silence on policy issues and issued a public letter warning that Chile was on the verge of lawlessness—"an imminent rupture in the country's legality"—a statement widely viewed as giving the green light for the military to take power three months later.[9]

Far more serious and enduring was the damage done under the military regime of Augusto Pinochet between September 1973 and March 1990; indeed, it is necessary to examine in some detail the institutional permutations Pinochet crafted because a key dilemma for civilian reformers was how to undo many of the contorted arrangements Pinochet left behind without politicizing or undermining the courts in the process.

At the most basic level, the courts—especially the Supreme Court—were extremely docile toward the military regime; the judiciary was regularly and repeatedly criticized for failing to vigorously pursue cases involving disappearances or illegal detentions and for accepting the military's version of controversial issues (such as disappearances) at face value.[10] Four factors accounted for the passivity: the simple fact that, under the circumstances, judges had little choice but to acquiesce to military rule and hence confine themselves to an extraordinarily narrow definition of their institutional role; the general ideological sympathy of senior justices toward the military regime; the fact that Pinochet actually respected the internal and administrative autonomy of the courts in apparent exchange for their political acquiescence; and, most importantly, the degree to which Pinochet created a number of unusual institutional arrangements that gave the High Court considerable influence over lower courts as well as other government bureaucracies and decisionmaking entities. Each aspect is treated briefly, as they represent legacies of the Pinochet era that civilian reformers had to undo upon taking office in 1990.

First, and perhaps most basically, the courts had little recourse other than to acquiesce. The military regime's invocation of a state of siege in 1973, which continued intermittently until late 1988, resulted in the familiar pattern of suspension of habeas corpus rights (the Supreme Court accepted only ten of more than 5,400 habeas corpus petitions during the first ten years of military rule) and rule by presidential decree, relegating civilian courts to the back burner.[11] Coupled with the military's moves to broaden the definition of treason to include a wide range of "political crimes" (such as "besmirching the dignity of the fatherland") and to place those cases under the purview of the military courts, the civilian courts were, in many respects, largely irrelevant to the actual administration of justice.[12] Indeed, observers noted that by the late 1980s, approximately 95 percent of all criminal cases in Chile were tried in military rather than civilian courts.[13] Not surprisingly, most judges were left with few options other than to confine themselves to a narrow range of activities, and they interpreted their roles in the narrowest, most mechanistic manner possible.

Second, many judges, alarmed by Allende's politicization of the courts, expressed broad ideological sympathy for Pinochet in the hope that he would restore respect for the judiciary and pave the way for new elections in 1976. Arturo Valenzuela and Pamela Constable note that Pinochet initially appealed to many judges with his frequent invocations of the importance of the rule of law and public homage to the courts.[14] Observers note that "the early relationship between the military junta and the Supreme Court was one of evident mutual respect and ideological affinity" and that the courts showed little zeal for investigating allegations of human rights abuses by the military government because it shared the anti-Communist worldview of the governing junta.[15] Supreme Court President Enrique Urritia Monzano demonstrated this tendency immediately after the 1973 coup, noting that he would gladly "place the courts in the hands of Pinochet" and declaring his "most intimate satisfaction in the name of the administration of justice in Chile."[16]

Third, and perhaps paradoxically given his blatant disregard for the separation of powers, Pinochet generally respected the administrative and internal autonomy of the courts. Pinochet—to a degree even more than the military generals in Brazil—was adamant about maintaining a façade of legalism to his regime, creating a dynamic similar to that in Argentina, in which the courts acquiesced to a series of de facto laws. Because the courts did not challenge the military's fundamental authority, Pinochet (in contrast to Allende, some judges argued) generally did not interfere in the judiciary's internal affairs; in fact, Pinochet's Constitution of 1980 strengthened the self-management of the judiciary that had been guaranteed in the Constitution of 1925.[17] The High Court managed the budget of the entire judiciary, its recruitment and personnel selection, and internal staffing patterns, with Congress and the President exercising virtually no influence in the process.[18] At the most basic level, then, Pinochet did not need to intervene in the judiciary: a sympathetic Supreme Court could instead influence the behavior of lower court judges because it possessed absolute control over the promotion and dismissal system, whose procedures were implemented secretly and with little predictability or written guidelines.[19] Nibaldo Galleguillos thus notes the "remarkably high degree level of autonomy bestowed upon the judiciary by [Pinochet's] 1980 constitution," while Lisa Hilbink correctly observes that "the functional autonomy of the judiciary is by many accounts extreme."[20] Even Pinochet's strongest opponents noted that "Pinochet did not overtly intervene in the Supreme Court when he came to power; he did not replace the justices, he did not threaten them, nor did he . . . use corrupt methods to assure the collaboration of the Supreme Court, at least not in the early years of his dictatorship."[21] In short, during this period the judiciary became quite acclimated to managing its own affairs, an autonomy that verged on insularity and unaccountability.[22]

Fourth, the Supreme Court acquired during that period a number of unusual institutional powers that were intended to preserve the vestiges of Pinochet's rule even after the military left power. Because he could rely on a pliable judiciary, Pinochet extended a number of powers to the High Court that made it an influential political actor capable of affecting other political institutions—not because of any compelling jurisprudence the courts produced but because of structural prerogatives granted to them by the executive that were intended to use the High Court as another agent of the military government. For example, the Supreme Court was granted the right to appoint three of the seven members on the Pinochet-created Constitutional Tribunal, a court empowered with the right of abstract review on draft congressional legislation involving constitutional questions; two other members were required to be "integral lawyers," prominent attorneys allowed to serve temporarily on the Supreme Court in the event of illness of a justice but whose selection was determined solely by the Supreme Court President and who served at his discretion.[23] Another member of the Constitutional Tribunal was to be selected by the powerful National Security Council—a body stocked with members of the Supreme Court and representatives of the military high command.[24] In addition, the Supreme Court was granted the right to fill three of the five posts on the Electoral Qualifications Tribunal, the body that monitors the eligibility of candidates each election year; regional electoral tribunals were staffed with one judge from a Court of Appeals and another two appointed by the Electoral Tribunal, which was stocked with Supreme Court justices. Finally, Pinochet's 1980 Constitution created nine designated, lifetime posts in the forty-eight-member Senate, reserving two seats for justices on the High Court.

In short, as Galleguillos notes, "Moreso than the military, the Supreme Court can appoint some of its members to the National Security Council, the Senate, all the positions in the Electoral Courts, and the majority of members of the Constitutional Tribunal." The result was a judiciary "that has too much power vis-à-vis the legislature" rather than too little.[25]

The results of these distorted individual practices and institutional arrangements, not surprisingly, created the widespread perception that the judiciary was in need of urgent reform.[26] Asked in 1987 who or which social and political actors could help solve the country's problems, "judges" ranked last among a list of twelve choices, an indication of the widespread popular disregard for the judiciary.[27] Surveys conducted shortly after the transition in 1990 found that 65 to 70 percent of respondents were dissatisfied with the judiciary; more than 60 percent said that the courts were "politicized" and 70 percent described them as "inefficient."[28] Lawyers who dealt with the courts were equally harsh; 73 percent of attorneys believed that the performance of the lower courts was "unsatisfactory" or "very unsatisfactory," while 70 percent expressed similar views about the superior courts.[29] Nor was the judiciary viewed as accessible. A survey of low-income Chileans found that 89 percent of respondents believed that the courts worked only for the wealthy; 96 percent said that they treat low-income citizens more harshly than wealthy Chileans, and 86 percent believed that they could get "better justice" if they had more money.[30] Meanwhile, the press was routinely filled with vivid examples of cases that had been pending for more than a decade, litigants waiting for years only to learn that their cases had been lost in a mountain of paperwork, and plaintiffs dying before their cases could reach a judge.[31]

A THREE-PRONGED APPROACH TO JUDICIAL REFORM

Presidents Patricio Aylwin (1990–94) and Eduardo Frei (1994–2000) took remarkably similar approaches to judicial reform; indeed, their efforts can best be understood as part of a single undertaking. They came from the same faction of the same party, relied on many of the same advisors and coalition partners, and worked closely with the same academics and NGO communities to fashion a reform strategy. The two leaders also are considered jointly because Frei presided over the final legislative approval of several reforms that Aylwin had initiated, and because Aylwin provided much of the institutional groundwork on which Frei would later expand and receive public acclaim.

Both presidents faced the same dilemma: how to pare back the institutional vestiges of authoritarian rule and replace them with more democratic and efficient structures when the author of the 1980 Constitution remained commander-in-chief of the armed forces—and who had created numerous procedural and practical obstacles aimed at blocking future politicians from altering the 1980 Constitution.[32] In short, even seemingly modest reforms were in fact quite ambitious, because, as Mark Ensalaco explains, of all Latin American militaries the Chilean military "was arguably the one that came nearest to establishing the constitutional and institutional bases for permanence."[33] The number of the "authoritarian enclaves" was impressive. Administration officials faced the simultaneous need to abolish the lifetime designated senators, assert civilian authority over the National Security Council, eliminate a highly skewed electoral system that favored parties sympathetic to the military regime, create easier mechanisms to amend the draconian constitutional clauses that severely curtailed civil liberties, and scale back a clause that guaranteed the military 10 percent of annual export earnings of the state copper company in addition to its regular budgetary allocations—a measure that gave the armed forces an extraordinary degree of autonomy.[34] With such an ambitious and controversial agenda, the approach reformers took was somewhat surprising: they sought to reform all three variables simultaneously, despite their crowded policy agenda, because they realized that the success of one measure often depended on the success of another.

Independence and Accountability

The reform inputs for independence and accountability were laid out from the beginning. Aylwin and Frei confronted the paradoxical need to scale back the autonomy of the courts while building up their institutional strength by somehow helping them produce jurisprudence capable of limiting abuses by other branches of government and garnering public respect. Aylwin (and later Frei) would first opt for court packing as a way to reduce the influence of military-appointed, life-tenured judges. They repeatedly referred to the U.S. experience in the 1930s and argued that it was an acceptable, if unfortunate, tactic for extraordinary times.[35] Failing that, they would seek the impeachment of the most irresponsible judges. Aylwin followed the familiar approach of pursuing human rights cases not covered by the military's 1978 amnesty law to demonstrate that the courts could enforce some degree of horizontal accountability; he also sought to carve out an institutional niche for the courts by scaling back the purview of the military courts and returning pending criminal cases to the civilian judiciary, on the grounds that it would help the courts exercise power independently of the military high command. A final measure was the creation of a judicial academy that would establish clear promotion criteria and disciplinary procedures for judges, thereby reducing the arbitrary authority that senior judges held over their subordinates and boosting individual independence. Frei would continue with some of these efforts in 1994, particularly efforts to alter the size and composition of the Supreme Court.

Efficiency

Aylwin and Frei pursued a series of efficiency-enhancing reforms to relieve court congestion and accelerate the pace of trials. The need for efficiency measures was somewhat less urgent because various layers of the judiciary had shown improvements in case management during the 1980s, but the courts nonetheless were in need of modernization. Moreover, reformers understood that several efficiency measures clearly had implications for independence and access.[36] For example, both presidents sought to create a public prosecutors office; such a reform would have removed burdensome investigative and prosecutorial responsibilities from judges—streamlining trial proceedings and thus improving access—while also curtailing the extensive powers that judges enjoyed.

Other measures were less sweeping but equally important. Reformers sought to give the Supreme Court control over its own docket by granting it the writ of certiorari. They also sought to introduce the use of precedent into the judicial system so that courts were no longer burdened with issuing repeat rulings, introduce oral argumentation into the courts to replace time-consuming written proceedings, and expand the use of alternative dispute resolution tools (such as mediation) to decongest the commercial courts. Finally, both presidents worked with prominent NGOs to develop better methods for tracking cases and identifying judicial bottlenecks.[37]

Access

Aylwin and Frei clearly recognized the need to make the courts more accessible, and advisors to both presidents explicitly linked access with the quality of democratic governance.[38] Some of the measures were traditional, such as increasing the number of judges.[39] Other measures were more controversial. Aylwin revived the push to create neighborhood courts staffed by attorneys and justices of the peace that would operate outside the formal court system. Other measures were both innovative and ambitious by Latin American standards. Aware of the need to produce immediate results, Aylwin and Frei sought to increase access by relying heavily on the Ministry of Justice to provide free legal services for the poor. Aylwin sought to strengthen those government institutions that provided services to the indigent in the hopes of keeping certain minor issues out of the courts, while Frei created a network of "mobile consultants" that would visit the indigent in rural areas in an effort to resolve their grievances before cases reached the courts.[40]

MEASURING THE RESULTS

Assessing the results can only be tentative after less than a decade of democratic rule—and the absence of up-to-date court statistics for the latter part of this period—although initial signs offer some grounds for encouragement. Even though both administrations suffered setbacks across all three variables, there are few signs of a worsening performance and in some instances concrete signs of improvement. The courts clearly are more accountable and on occasion have issued jurisprudence that has challenged key interest groups such as the military. Efficiency measures seem to have produced a stabilization in times to disposition and there is an informal consensus across the political spectrum that the reforms have provided the foundation for more proficient courts over time. Finally, an access-to-justice program has had an immediate impact on providing access for the poor without overburdening the courts with a flood of new cases. No specific reform measure has been an unqualified success, but all of the measures, when combined, have pushed forward the reform momentum, softened the effects of unintended consequences and potential negative synergy, and helped sustain the reform momentum.

Independence and Accountability

Reformers in Chile faced the need to simultaneously scale back and build up the powers of the judiciary: they had to reduce the influence and power of antidemocratic senior judges, while building up the judiciary as an independent force that was capable of defending the constitutional order and not merely a powerful authoritarian vestige of the old regime. Aylwin and his aides openly acknowledged the paradox: throughout military rule they had criticized the courts as being too politicized and possessing too little independence; once in power, they complained that the judiciary was insulated from change and possessed too much (rather than too little) independence.[41]

Aylwin's court packing scheme met with initial resistance—particularly from within the judiciary itself—but ultimately resurfaced and succeeded during the Frei administration in late 1997.[42] After an encouraging start in 1990—intellectuals affiliated with the conservative National Renewal Party indicated that they were not inherently opposed to the idea and proposed their own more modest court packing plans—the effort produced a predictably strong and negative reaction from within the courts.[43] The most conservative parties and Pinochet's lifetime designated senators charged that the governing coalition was trying to "decapitate the courts" and politicize justice; several justices warned that the proposed changes would undermine judicial independence and charged that the reforms duplicated the experience of the Allende administration. Some observers interpreted the remarks as an indirect signal to the military high command that it would welcome a coup.[44] Aylwin announced that he was shelving the plan.

Ironically, efforts to introduce greater accountability received an unintentional assist from more corrupt and unaccountable elements of the judiciary, including the Supreme Court President. In 1993, the administration impeached three justices for alleged neglect of judicial duties. Although the Senate convicted only one of the three judges, observers reported that the entire affair had a profound psychological effect throughout the courts and among the public: for the first time in 125 years, a judge had been removed for professional misconduct, a development that signaled to lower court judges that the impunity of their superiors was nearing an end.[45] Moreover, between 1994 and 1997, a series of corruption scandals surfaced involving several long-time members of the High Court. In one instance, allegations emerged that the Court President, under the influence of narcotics traffickers, intervened with lower court judges to ensure favorable verdicts. The scandals sufficiently outraged the far Right (which took a hard stance on crime and narcotics issues) and deeply offended portions of the moderate Right, which grew concerned that perceptions of judicial corruption could affect foreign investment patterns.[46] The Supreme Court President was impeached (but not convicted by the more conservative Senate), and the controversy forced him to step down a year later.[47] More importantly, the recurring allegations of High Court corruption prompted Congress to revive the court packing plan. In late 1997, Frei secured congressional approval of the constitutional amendment initially drafted by Aylwin, expanding the size of the Supreme Court from seventeen to twenty-one beginning in 1998.[48]

Finally, broader forces outside of the reformers' (and reform opponents') control intervened to help strike a greater balance between accountability and independence. Between 1990 and 1994, seven of the seventeen aging justices on the Pinochet-dominated High Court either passed away or retired because of poor health. In another instance, a justice retired and, because the list of candidates presented by the Supreme Court was politically unappealing to civilian officials, Frei left the seat vacant until a more moderate jurist assumed the presidency of the Supreme Court.[49] The vestiges of authoritarian influence were being chipped away, if only gradually. The solution was less than ideal but nonetheless produced a more balanced and democratic High Court. These justices, in turn, tended to exercise their authority more responsibly and democratically than did their predecessors, and generally appointed accountable judges to the Constitutional Tribunal, National Security Council, and Electoral Tribunals.[50] The turnover also enhanced judicial accountability. Between 1995 and 1997, the High Court removed a handful of corrupt lower-level judges on its own initiative, clamped down on judicial nepotism, and created an "ethics commission" that would allow external auditors to probe incidents of judicial corruption and misconduct.[51] The contrast was stark. In 1990, Pinochet's High Court warned that even publicly discussing court packing could usher in a state of lawlessness. By 1997, under public criticism and the ever-present threat of more impeachments, a more balanced Supreme Court—in an effort to salvage its image—was removing unqualified judges, streamlining court operations, and curtailing traditional perquisites such as generous vacation packages.[52]

Administration efforts to assert judicial independence by pursuing sensitive human rights cases produced a mixed bag of results that nonetheless pointed to an overall picture of slow progress.[53] Aylwin met with initial defeat when the Supreme Court rejected government arguments in late 1990 that the 1978 amnesty was unconstitutional, although the administration met with some successes on the more than 600 pending human rights cases involving abuses committed by the Right and Left.[54] The High Court upheld the 1978 amnesty in more than 500 of the cases, a modest record but one which enabled the administration to prosecute several lower-level officials who had served in the military regime.[55] Other efforts on human rights cases were more successful. The Supreme Court upheld administration arguments that common crimes no longer constituted a threat to national security and allowed the government to move more than 4,000 criminal cases from military to civilian courts, an effort that reestablished the primacy of civilian courts on issues involving routine criminal issues. In the two most important human rights cases in the country, the administration pressed ahead with the trials of Manuel Contreras and Pedro Espinoza, close aides of Pinochet who were the intellectual authors of the high-profile killing of a Chilean official in Washington, D.C. in the 1970s. In late 1993, a Supreme Court justice sentenced Espinoza and Contreras to six and seven year jail terms, respectively, a verdict the full court would uphold one year later.[56] The rulings were no small task: Pinochet had twice called Army troops to the streets during the trials and repeatedly warned that any effort to punish his colleagues for their role in fighting Marxist subversion would risk the full wrath of the armed forces.[57] Emboldened by the detention of Pinochet in London in 1998, the courts also reopened several human rights investigations—including "Operación Albania" and the "Tucapel Jiménez" cases involving crimes committed by members of the security and intelligence forces, declaring that both cases fell under the purview of civilian courts and removing them from suspect judges who had bungled previous investigations.[58] Lower court judges also successfully reopened a number of investigations that had fallen under the 1978 amnesty law without overturning the amnesty itself. The courts ruled that the amnesty covered only cases involving loss of life, and that loss of life could not be presumed in cases of kidnappings or those in which the body was never recovered. The ruling allowed the courts to pursue cases against a number of Pinochet's allies, including several Army generals and police commanders.[59] Throughout this period, appellate courts also regularly gave the final word on high-profile commercial disputes, challenging the administration's interpretation of environmental and commercial legislation and generally displaying a fair degree of independence from the executive.[60]

Efficiency

Efforts to create a judicial academy that would enhance court efficiency initially ran into strong opposition from the High Court. Just as the administration finalized plans to submit its controversial project to Congress in 1991, the Supreme Court claimed to have uncovered a plot to assassinate senior members of the judiciary and warned that the government was creating a "climate of insecurity" for judges, charging that the rule of law was endangered.[61] Because the rhetoric employed was so similar to that used in early September 1973 (when a similar plot was alleged to have been uncovered), the judiciary's reaction was widely viewed as an invitation for the military to reassume power.[62] Supreme Court President Correa Labra pronounced himself "thoroughly and completely" against the reform, and, when asked for his reaction to the proposal, publicly remarked, "I hate it. I feel contempt for it."[63] Rightist parties joined the fight, and the government shelved its idea—temporarily.

Upon recognizing the strong judicial opposition to reforms, Aylwin (and later Frei) learned fairly early on of the need to adroitly portray reforms in the least politically offensive manner. As noted in Chapter One, even seemingly minor or administrative reforms with clear benefits to society nonetheless may provoke strong judicial opposition if they redistribute powers enjoyed by judges or scale back institutional and personal privileges. After taking stock of the judicial opposition to a judicial academy (and later to a proposal to create a national public prosecutor's office), Aylwin and Frei sought to downplay the "political" impact that both measures would have on the senior judges' authority.[64] Instead, Aylwin began stressing that these reforms were necessary for reasons of modernization and efficiency—more neutral terms that, with some political groundwork, could be sold to parties across the ideological spectrum and which placed the judiciary in the uncomfortable position of opposing popular concepts.[65] The point is especially important because in Chile, rightist parties were extremely market-oriented and were strongly suspicious of discretionary powers granted to any government bureaucracies. As a result, they were supportive of virtually any measure that limited the potential for arbitrary or capricious state power. Frei tried a similar approach with the public prosecutor's office, repeatedly sidestepping any question of how the reforms would affect the personal power of judges, instead stressing that the measure would make the courts "more agile and efficient" and ultimately more accessible and "closer to the people."[66]

With a basic consensus over the need to create more "efficient" judicial institutions, the debate shifted to defining how the new bodies would look. Government officials, many of whom had spent time in exile in Western Europe, had been impressed by the transition from authoritarian rule in Spain and sought to replicate the Spanish National Council of Magistrates.[67] Conservative parties argued in favor of the integrity of the pre-1973 judiciary, noting that judicial academies had worked well in Spain and Portugal but had merely introduced new forms of politicization when tried in Peru and Venezuela, and floated various proposals aimed at leaving court administration within the judicial branch but not confined to the Supreme Court.[68] Over the course of the next three years, the administration held regular congressional hearings on the subject, solicited opposition views, and conducted an extensive outreach program with local universities to garner the support of the academic community.[69] By late 1994, the government secured approval of a nine-member academy, with representatives divided equally among the three branches of government.[70] There was less debate over the public prosecutor's bill, which gained approval with the support of all the six major parties in Congress.[71]

The question is whether these and other efficiency-maximizing inputs produced the desired or intended results. Of all the reform variables in all the case studies considered here, this assessment may be the most difficult. The two main institutional reforms—the judicial academy and the public prosecutor's office—have received praise from across the political spectrum, but will not be fully operational until 2002.[72] Other efficiency reforms, such as building ten new courthouses as part of a five-year modernization campaign, while laudable and probably providing the foundation for more efficient management over the longer term, have not yet had a significant impact.[73] For example, efforts to expand arbitration for commercial disputes have won praise from the local chambers of commerce and international investors and are slowly gaining confidence over time, although the total number of cases resolved through arbitration since 1992 is less than seventy, and it has not yet begun to have an appreciable effect on the total caseload of commercial courts.[74]

Other reforms have produced some positive results even if more time is necessary to establish long-term trends. Some indicators are fairly straightforward; for example, the annual docket of the Supreme Court, which had increased from 4,000 cases in 1980 to more than 6,000 in 1989, declined to less than 5,800 in 1993 because the Court had the authority to reject some cases as not involving constitutional questions.[75] Efforts to increase the number of judges initially had little effect—the Aylwin administration acknowledged that even though the number of judges in the country increased by 34 percent and judges were working longer hours, average times to disposition during the administration's first two years did not diminish by any statistically significant amount—although those regions of the country with the additional judges began to show modest but measurable improvements by 1994.[76]

The benefits of addressing independence and efficiency simultaneously also were clear; in fact, the simultaneous approach helped avoid some of the negative synergy that characterized efforts in other countries. Aylwin's efforts to boost the institutional independence of the civilian courts included transferring some 4,000 cases from military to civilian courts, nearly doubling the total caseload of the criminal courts literally overnight. But because the administration had begun conducting studies to identify structural bottlenecks in the judiciary, officials already had been devising plans to restructure the appellate courts even before the increased work load.[77] As a result, when the administration added fifty-four new judges in 1993, nearly all were placed in the appeals courts (rather than the courts of first instance) to assist with the increased caseload. By 1995, court statistics indicated that times to disposition in the appeals courts, which had slowly but consistently increased since 1981, remained constant despite the rise in cases.[78] Judges were able to handle the increased work load caused by the independence-enhancing reforms in part because the efficiency-maximizing reforms helped avoid a glut of cases as had happened in the Brazilian reform experience.[79]

Access

As with the other variables, reformers met with initial defeat. Aylwin's proposal to create a nationwide system of "neighborhood courts" to deal with petty crimes (vagrancy, vandalism, and other minor offenses) provoked considerable opposition from conservative sectors and the judiciary because the plan so closely resembled that which Allende had used to politicize justice.[80] The fact that members of the Socialist Party backed the plan added to their concerns. Amidst strong congressional and judicial opposition, Aylwin dropped the proposal in 1992.[81]

The administration then turned to other government services for low-income citizens, an effort that had some beneficial effects: they helped resolve an impressive number of grievances by administrative rather than judicial means and prevented the courts from becoming overwhelmed while they were still implementing their efficiency reforms. Aylwin administration officials increased the number of regional "judicial corporations"—government entities that provided free legal aid for the poor—from five to thirteen, including one in every region of the country, and saw the number of low-income clients served increase nearly 20 percent in four years.[82] Creation of a "women's rights center" serviced more than 3,000 clients in its first four years on a range of issues that otherwise were destined for the courts; a newly-created national labor directorate, roughly analogous to the U.S. National Labor Relations Board, aimed at mediating employer-worker disputes, resolved more than 75 percent of 4,000 labor disputes out of court. Finally, creation of a consumer affairs division in the Justice Ministry handled more than thirty complaints a day during its first year, a majority of which were resolved without recourse to the formal court system.[83]

More impressive yet was the "access to justice" program that both administrations pursued. In 1992–93, Aylwin created a program aimed specifically at providing judicial services to low-income citizens; Frei would later expand on the effort in 1995 by integrating it into his national poverty alleviation program. Facing limited resources, yet aware of the need to avoid creating a new bottleneck at the lower levels, Aylwin and Frei pursued a different reform path to boost access. The administration increased positions for law school students and graduates providing free legal consultations at the government's legal clinics from 200 in 1990 to 329 by 1992, 548 in 1994, 810 in 1995, and more than 1,000 by 1998.[84] The Frei administration incorporated these graduates into a comprehensive program of "mobile consultant units" (the teams included a social worker and a clerical assistant for record-keeping purposes) that would travel to low-income areas twice monthly to meet litigants, hear complaints, and provide legal advice in an effort to keep disputes out of courts. The program began in three communities in Santiago in 1993 and was expanded to nineteen in 1995 and fifty-four in 1998.

After four years, the program was having a significant effect on enhancing access for the poor without excessively burdening the courts. Studies conducted by U.S. consulting firms have given the program high marks, as has field research by U.S. scholars and a limited range of polls examining attitudes of the rural poor who have come into contact with the program.[85] More concretely, the program showed an increasing ability to handle a growing number of cases effectively. The Access to Justice program serviced 12,000 people in its first year, resolving 60 percent of those cases without recourse to the courts. The program serviced more than 34,000 Chileans in 1995 and 47,000 in 1996, settling 81 percent of those disputes through immediate resolution.[86] By late 1997, officials in the Justice Ministry calculated that the Access to Justice program had provided out-of-court resolution to nearly 100,000 cases; program officials noted that these were cases that otherwise would have gone to the courts of first instance. The social impact of the mobile consultants program was significant. According to a senior official involved in the program:

> The Judicial Council is good but its fruits are 10 years away. So we focus on access because we cannot do anything else now. The people sometimes think that justice is just for the rich and the businessmen. But we show the poor that modernism is not just for the rich and for the businessmen. One thing we hear from people who had experienced the access-to-justice program, again and again, is that "modernism works for me." Compare that to Argentina. Alfonsín focused on the human rights abuses of a dozen people or so. . . . Those types of problems still exist in Chile today, but we are focusing more on the public at large. And they see that justice works. They say, "Justice works for me."[87]

FINAL THOUGHTS ON THE CHILEAN EXPERIENCE

Any conclusions on Chile are tentative because its judicial reform experiment is the most recent of all the case studies, but the initial results offer grounds for cautious optimism. To be sure, Chile has the now-familiar patterns prevalent in other countries, or at least the faint outlines of them: more than 80 percent of the public believes that crime levels are increasing; more than half complain that judges are too lenient on delinquents; nearly half say that the main challenge for civilian leaders over the next decade will be to "maintain order"—all while many senior judges deny a crisis and blame other institutions for society's woes.[88]

These sentiments have not led, however, to a deep and popular conviction that the courts are irrelevant to the process of administering justice; instead, institutional crises have produced an opportunity for reformers to prod forward the reform movement.[89] In fact, some trends are encouraging. Polls conducted immediately after the transition in 1990 found that only 10 percent of the public had confidence in the courts, a figure that was 11 percent the following year and up to 21 percent by 1995. By 1997, approval ratings for the judiciary were 36 percent, hardly a stellar performance but a rating that actually was higher than approval ratings given to Congress, unions, and political parties.[90] And while there are no comprehensive nationwide polls of attitudes of the poor that can be compared with the 1991 surveys of Correa Sutil cited earlier, a diverse spectrum of observers agree that attitudes of low-income citizens are beginning to change.[91] Informal focus groups reveal that a growing number of rural poor say they know of someone who has come into contact with the judicial system in the past year, an important indicator because previous polling has revealed that those low-income Chileans who have had even a limited interaction with the courts, regardless of the verdict, tend to have healthier attitudes toward democracy. Whereas less than 8 percent of the poor nationwide had positive opinions of the judiciary in 1991, limited surveys of the poor in remote rural areas in 1994 found that 25 percent had a positive opinion, and 16 percent were "ambivalent"—again, not an overwhelming endorsement of the judiciary, but an indication that the gap between those with negative and positive opinions was beginning to narrow.[92] For their part, businessmen appear quite satisfied with the judiciary, giving it high marks for predictability, timeliness, and quality of judges.[93]

An obvious question centers on why the judiciary in Chile is slowly gaining confidence when, as noted above, both Frei and Aylwin suffered a fairly regular series of defeats on many of their initiatives to reform independence, efficiency, and access. Why, for example, will the public tolerate compromise and partial success on controversial human rights cases in Chile when a similar approach was so roundly condemned in Argentina? The answers seem to lie in two areas. First and most narrowly, reformers in Chile were careful to promise only what they could deliver and avoided raising exaggerated public expectations of what the judiciary could accomplish. Thus, José Zalaquett, a jurist on Aylwin's Truth Commission, noted that the government's approach was to "promise only the justice which is possible," while Aylwin pledged that he would seek "justice as far as possible."[94] The pledges were far more modest and less inspiring than those made by Alfonsín or even Duarte in the 1980s—but also more realistic and attainable, and less prone to public disillusionment when political forces intervened to force compromise.[95]

A second and more fundamental reason for public tolerance of such judicial setbacks lies in the comprehensive scope of the reform strategy itself. Because Chile is the only successful case study examined here, the conclusions are by no means definitive, but the results are suggestive. The public appears willing to tolerate compromised, gradual progress if there is the perception that the judiciary as a whole is moving in the right direction and the overall design of the reform is sound. As Louis Bickford has noted, various interest groups across the political spectrum—political parties, NGOs, civil society, and various government ministries—each assumed a stake in the process, giving reformers a sense of momentum and frequently placing opponents on the defensive.[96] Indeed, reform at times seemed so much like a *fait accompli* that many judges began to join the bandwagon if for no other reason than to head off a more radical restructuring from Congress or the executive.[97] The contrast with other reform efforts is striking. Alfonsín's entire judicial reform program amounted to a push for independence, so any compromise on that goal was devastating to the image of his judicial reform efforts. Aylwin and Frei made similar compromises on many human rights cases—neither ever fully overturned the 1978 amnesty law and both essentially gave up trying after their first years in office—but the backtracking was not fatal. Both men had other achievements to show for their judicial reform efforts and both could move to new initiatives. The public accepted slow but steady progress—even setbacks—as long as the overall direction of the reform program was positive.

As a result of this strategy of simultaneous reforms, Chile avoided much of the negative synergy that characterized other reform efforts. Efforts to move more than 4,000 human rights cases into civilian courts did not overwhelm the judiciary because the courts were slowly improving their efficiency and their ability to handle more cases in a timely manner. The efficiency-maximizing reforms, in turn, were sustained largely by an increasing number of judges who were willing to perform their functions in an independent, accountable manner and because the influence of antidemocratic senior judges was slowly waning. Efforts to ensure that the progress on independence and efficiency made an impact on the broader public were buttressed by the fact that the courts became more accessible; efforts to make the courts more accessible, in turn, required increased access to a number of auxiliary agencies such as the Justice Ministry. Efforts to encourage the public to turn to the legal system required that authority be exercised independently and efficiently—but also that reformers take steps to ensure that various social conflicts not clog the courts and that other government institutions and services provide alternative forms of dispute resolution. Chilean reformers did what conventional wisdom would advise against: they ignored the narrowly sequenced incrementalism and instead attacked all three variables simultaneously—and by 1999 had at least some progress to show for it.

NOTES

1. Francisco Artaza, "Slowness of Justice System Examined," *La Nación*, 13 June 1994, 8, in FBIS-LAT, 16 August 1994.

2. A standard defense of this tradition can be found in Osvaldo Illanes Benitez, "The Supreme Court of Justice in Chile," *Journal of the International Commission of Jurists* 2 (Winter 1966): 269–77. The author was Chief Justice of the Supreme Court at the time.

3. Arturo Valenzuela, "Origins, Consolidation, and Breakdown of a Democratic Regime," in *Democracy in Developing Countries: Latin America,* ed. Larry Diamond, Juan Linz, and Seymour Martin Lipset (Boulder, Colo.: Lynne Rienner, 1989): 171.

4. For example, a 1970 poll of attorneys found that less than two percent criticized the judiciary for having a low quality of judges or a lack of professional probity. See Steven Lowenstein, *Lawyers, Legal Education, and Development: An Examination of the Process of Reform in Chile* (New York: International Legal Center, 1970): 258.

5. Eduardo Novoa, "¿Justicia de clases?" *Mensaje* 187 (March–April 1970): 123.

6. Jose Antonio Viera-Gallo, "Law and Socialism in Chile," *Review of the International Commission of Jurists* 7 (December 1971): 44–47. Viera-Gallo served in the Ministry of Justice in the Allende administration.

7. These examples are taken from Neal P. Panish, "Chile Under Allende: The Decline of the Judiciary and the Rise of A State of Necessity," *Loyola of Los Angeles International and Comparative Law Journal* 9 (Summer 1987): 693–709. The creation of neighborhood courts is defended on the grounds that they brought "popular justice" closer to the masses in Jack Spence, "Institutionalizing Neighborhood Courts: Two Chilean Experiences," *Law and Society* 13 (Fall 1978): 139–82.

8. Paul Sigmund, *The Overthrow of Allende and the Politics of Chile, 1970–76* (Pittsburgh, Pa.: University of Pittsburgh Press, 1977): 206, 210. In October 1972, the Supreme Court took the unusual step of delivering a letter to the President pointedly reminding him of "the absolute necessity of instructing his cabinet to instruct, in turn, their subordinates to adhere strictly to the decisions that, in the exercise of their constitutional attributions, emanates from the ordinary courts of justice."

9. Cited in Panish, "Chile Under Allende," p. 702. Allende responded to the letter by noting that he would decide on a case-by-case basis whether he would enforce judicial rulings: "The government, as warrantor of peace and public order, should analyze each case and make its own judgments on the merits as to whether or not it will grant the assistance of the public force to carry them out."

10. See, for example, Hugo Fruhling, "Repressive Policies and Legal Dissent in Authoritarian Regimes: Chile, 1973-1981," *International Journal of Sociology and Law* (Fall 1984): 351. Fruhling writes that, "The Courts acted as if government officials were always telling the truth, particularly when they denied having detained somebody." Fruhling's charge seems well-founded. Between 1973 and 1983, for example, the Supreme Court denied more than 4,000 habeas corpus requests—more than 98 percent of all such petitions. Judicial officials justified their position by invoking an exceedingly narrow interpretation of their duties. Asked why the courts so often rejected habeas corpus requests, former Supreme Court President José Maria Eyzaguirre stated simply, "If the Minister of the Interior states that the person on whose behalf the application is made is not detained, the application cannot be entertained." See "United Nations Report Describes the Deterioration of Judicial Independence," *Centre for the Independence of Judges and Lawyers Bulletin* 9 (April 1982): 11.

11. Pinochet issued more than 4,100 decree laws during his regime. See Watson Galleher, "State Repression's Façade of Legality: The Military Courts in Chile," *Temple International and Comparative Law Journal* 2 (Fall 1988): 183–98. For a concise overview of the authoritarian features codified in the 1980 Constitution, see Roland Bersier, "Legal Instruments of Repression in Chile," *Review of the International Commission of Jurists* 34 (June 1985): 54–60.

12. William D. Zabel, Diane Orenlichter, and David E. Nachman, "Human Rights and the Administration of Justice in Chile: Report of a Delegation of the Association of the Bar of

the City of New York and of the International Bar Association," *The Record of the Association of the Bar of the City of New York* 42 (May 1987): 431–84.

13. Thomas Andrew O'Keefe, "The Use of the Military Justice System to Try Civilians in Chile," *New York State Bar Journal* 61 (November 1989): 43–47. These military courts often were condemned by international human rights organizations for employing antidemocratic features, such as denying the right to confront one's accuser.

14. Arturo Valenzuela and Pamela Constable, *A Nation of Enemies* (New York: W. W. Norton and Co., 1991): Chapter Five. They note:

like many other Chileans, they [senior judges] were too convinced of looming economic chaos and ideological enslavement to question the violent overthrow of an elected government. . . . In turn, Pinochet and his men paid careful homage to the dignity and prestige of the judiciary—especially the Supreme Court, whose seventeen members were assigned state cars and chauffeurs. Instead of trying to change the courts, as impatient US leaders had done, the regime played to judges' vanity and conservatism, thus ensuring the collaboration of all but a few, stubborn iconoclasts. "During the administration of Salvador Allende, the president insulted the courts; his press insulted us every day," recounted [Supreme Court President] Urritia's successor, José Maria Eyzaguirre, in 1978. In contrast, he said, "the current government has never insulted the courts."

15. A revealing quote came in 1981 from then-Supreme Court President Israel Borquez, who complained that he was growing weary of being asked to identify human rights abuses committed by the regime, noting, "I'm fed up to the teeth with this issue of missing people." See Eugenio Hojmon, *Memorial de la dictadura* (Santiago: Emisión, 1989): 104.

16. *Chile: A Time of Reckoning* (Geneva: International Commission of Jurists, 1992): 78.

17. One exception was the clause on the retirement age for judges. All judges on the bench at the time of the Constitution were granted life tenure; all judges appointed subsequently faced a retirement age of 75. See *The Political Constitution of Chile*, Articles 73–80.

18. Pablo Ruiz Tagle, "Análisis comparado de la función judicial," *Estudios Públicos* 39 (1990): 131–62.

19. Sergio Dunlop, a former president of the Chilean Association of Magistrates, noted that because the Supreme Court was responsible for promotions and internal discipline, lower court judges were "unwilling to stand up to their superior, sacrificing their careers and knowing that to fight would be useless." Judge René Garcia Villegas made similar observations: "If the Supreme Court was on its knees, committed body and soul to the military regime, what could the lower levels do, if they depend on the highest court alone for their tenure and promotion?" See Monica Gonzalez, "Hay jueces de la Suprema que tienen 30 o 40 parientes colocados en el Poder Judicial," *La Época*, 9 May 1989, 12.

20. See Nibaldo Galleguillos, "Checks and Balances in New Democracies: The Role of the Judiciary in the Chilean and Mexican Transitions: A Comparative Analysis," Paper Presented at the 1997 Meeting of the Latin American Studies Association, 17–19 April 1997, 8; and Lisa Hilbink, "What Is the Role of the Judiciary in a Democracy? The Judicial Reform Debate in Chile and Proposals for Future Research," Paper Presented at the 1995 meeting of the Latin American Studies Association, 28–30 September 1995, p. 5.

21. Jorge Correa Sutil, "The Judiciary and the Political System in Chile," in *Transition to Democracy in Latin America: The Role of the Judiciary*, ed. Irwin P. Stotzky (Boulder, Colo.: Westview Press, 1993): 89–90.

22. This lack of accountability led to charges of widespread nepotism within the judiciary. See Beatriz Aliste and Eva Von Baer, "Santos en la Corte," *Qué Pasa*, 3–9 February 1998, 20.

23. Integral lawyers were widely regarded as mouthpieces for the Supreme Court President and in many cases were personal associates of General Pinochet. One study examining the voting patterns of the integral attorneys between 1981 and 1984 could not find a single example in which they voted against the government. See Antonio Martinez, "Los 'allegados' de la Justicia," *Hoy*, 16-22 December 1985, pp. 15-17.

24. The National Security Council is important because under Pinochet's 1980 Constitution, future presidents could dismiss military commanders only with the concurrence of his NSC. The clause was an effort to ensure that civilian presidents could not abruptly remove any service chiefs—and that he would be required to consult with those same commanders before taking any actions.

25. Galleguillos, "Checks and Balances in New Democracies: The Role of the Judiciary in the Chilean and Mexican Transitions: A Comparative Analysis," pp. 2, 5.

26. Asked in a 1987 survey to identify the three top problems facing the country, respondents mentioned the lack of confidence in the judicial system three times more frequently than the lack of democratic elections. See *Estudio social y de opinión pública en la población de Santiago* (Santiago: Centro de Estudios Públicos, 1987): 125-27.

27. Antonio Alaminos, *Chile: transición política y sociedad* (Madrid: Siglo XXI, 1991): 40. Institutions ahead of "judges" were, in order, the Church, human rights groups, universities, unions, radio, the press, television, "the government," parties, businessmen, and the military.

28. "Criticos resultados arroja encuesta sobre la Justicia," *La Época*, 6 January 1991, 21.

29. Carlos Peña González, "Los abogados y la administración de justicia," in *Proposiciones para la reforma judicial*, ed. Eugenio Valenzuela S. (Santiago: Centro de Estudios Públicos, 1990): 376.

30. These results come from *Justicia y marginalidad: percepciones de los pobres*, ed. Jorge Correa Sutil (Santiago: Corporación de Promoción Universitaria, 1993): 17-25.

31. Mauricio Carvallo, "La Justicia llega tarde," *Hoy*, 25-31 July 1988, 29-33.

32. In one famous 1990 quote, Pinochet warned that any effort to change "even one comma" of the Constitution could bring the military back to the streets. See Anthony Holland O'Malley, "Chile's Constitution, Chile's Congress: Prospects for Judicial, Legal, and Constitutional Reform," *Canadian Journal of Latin American and Caribbean Studies* 15 (1990): 85-111.

33. The point is worth stressing because many scholars suggest that Aylwin and Frei had a relatively easy time implementing their agendas since Chile enjoyed economic prosperity and presidents thus did not face the distractions that leaders in Brazil and Argentina confronted. See Mark Ensalaco, "In with the New, Out with the Old? The Democratising Impact of Constitutional Reform in Chile," *Journal of Latin American Studies* 26 (May 1994): 409-29.

34. For discussions of the constraints imposed by some of these arrangements, see José Luis Cea, "Chile's Difficult Return to Constitutional Democracy," *Political Science* 20 (Summer 1987): 665-73; and Rhoda Rabkin, "Redemocratization, Electoral Engineering, and Party Strategies in Chile, 1989-1995," *Comparative Political Studies* 29 (June 1996): 335-56. The latter article is especially insightful, arguing that however undemocratic the electoral law may be, it has fostered centrist coalition building, just as the authors of the constitution had intended.

35. Reformers made the clear distinction between their efforts at court packing—when they faced holdover from a previous military regime—and those efforts in neighboring Argentina, where Menem confronted holdovers from a previous democratic opponent. See Owen Fiss, "The Right Degree of Independence," in *Transition to Democracy in Latin America: The Role of the Judiciary*, pp. 55-72.

36. Juan Enrique Vargas Viancos and Jorge Correa Sutil, *Diagnóstico del sistema judicial chileno* (Santiago: Corporación de Promoción Universitaria, 1995): 42.

37. José H. Yañez, "Servicios solicitados y prestados por la administración de justicia en Chile," in *Proyecto de capacitación, formación, perfeccionamiento, y política judicial* (Santiago: Corporación de Promoción Universitaria, 1991): 139.

38. Jose Guzmán Vial, a close legal aide to Aylwin, argued that it made little sense to equip the courts with more computers and more modern technologies if the benefits were not made available to the economically marginal; he noted that a state could not be democratic "in which millions of citizens live in and suffer from judicial marginality. . . . The reality is that a large portion of the population has no real probability of having their conflicts resolved in an easy, understandable, and efficient manner." Manuel Guzmán Vial, "La modernización del sistema judicial," *Mensaje* 400 (July 1991): 241.

39. More than 100 towns did not have a single judge in 1990. In addition, a judicial reorganization of 1986 had pared the number of nationwide labor courts from fifty to thirteen. See Santiago Carvajal A., "Descripción y análisis de la situación de los derechos humanos en las zonas rurales indígenas de Chile," in *Derechos humanos y servicios legales en el campo*, ed. Diego Garcia-Sayan (Lima: Comisión Andina de Juristas, 1987): 181–200; and Raúl Branes, "Access to Justice in Chile," in *Access to Justice: A Worldwide Survey*, Vol 1, ed. Mauro Cappelletti and Bryant Garth (Milan: Pott A. Giuffre Editore, 1978): 345–70.

40. As discussed in the concluding chapter, the aggressive use of the Justice Ministry to assist reform efforts is unique in the four case studies and suggests that solutions for judicial reform lie outside as well as within the judicial system itself.

41. Jorge Correa Sutil, a prominent legal adviser in the new coalition government, remarked that it was necessary to inject some political considerations into the judiciary in an effort to depoliticize it:

[Chile] is probably the one country in Latin America with a longstanding tradition of judicial independence. . . . That tradition, now that Chile is recovering its democratic history, is at odds with democracy. It may be time for the new government to intervene with measures that had traditionally, and correctly, been viewed to run counter to judicial independence, in the name of democracy and on behalf of a new concept of judicial independence.

See Correa Sutil, "The Judiciary and the Political System in Chile," p. 102.

42. On judicial resistance to reform efforts, see the thoughtful study by Louis Bickford, "Democracy, Stakeholdership, and Public Policymaking in Chile," 1990-1997: the Case of Judicial Reform," Paper Presented at the XXII Congress of the Latin American Studies Association, 24-26 September 1998, pp. 20-23.

43. The plans of National Renewal called for increasing the size of the Supreme Court from seventeen to thirty, on the condition that at least one-third of the new court would consist of members of the old court and another one-third would be selected by current justices. See Eugenio Valenzuela Somarriva, "Proposiciones para una reforma al poder judicial," *Mensaje* 400 (July 1991): 242.

44. Santiago Television Nacional de Chile, 2 March 1992; and Santiago Television Nacional de Chile, 7 March 1991.

45. *Chile: Unsettled Business: Human Rights at the Start of the Frei Presidency* (New York: Human Rights Watch/Americas, 1994): 4.

46. Francisco Dagnino, "La Mandeja Se Desenreda," *Hoy*, 13 July 1997, 6; and "Chile: The justice and the politicians," *The Economist*, 22 August 1997, 24-25. Some elements of the Right also were offended by the allegations of judicial corruption, because they believed, rightly or

wrongly, that the Pinochet regime had made a concerted effort to avoid government corruption. See Hugo Guzmán, "RN propone drásticos cambios," *La Tercera*, 28 June 1997, 28.

47. See "El Contraataque de Jordan," *Qué Pasa*, 19 July 1997, 16–17; Roberto Candia, "El Curriculum de Jordan," *Qué Pasa*, 7 June 1997, 16–20; "Polémica en Chile por crisis judicial," UPI press dispatch, 30 June 1997; "Se inicia en Chile juicio político al presidente de la Corte Suprema," AFP press dispatch, 1 July 1997; and "Presentan acusación constitucional contra Presidente de Corte Suprema," *Notimex*, 1 July 1997.

48. "Aprobadas reformas a la Corte Suprema," *El Mercurio*, 15 October 1997, A1, A12.

49. "Nuevo titular de la Corte Partidiario de Revisar Ley de Amnistía en Chile," Agence France Press release, 5 January 1998. The average age of an appointee under civilian rule was 65, while the average age of a Pinochet appointee was 74, leading pundits to speculate that the democratically appointed judges would outlast those selected during the military regime. See "Radiografía Suprema," *Qué Pasa*, 8–14 July 1997, 3.

50. See "Remaking Chile's Constitutional Tribunal—Frei Scores Big Upset Victory," U.S. Department of State, unclassified telegram Santiago 00876, 11 March 1997; and "Bancada Judicial," *Qué Pasa*, 23–29 December 1997, 13.

51. "Judicial Branch Under Investigation for Drug Trafficking," Santiago Television Nacional de Chile, 10 March 1995, in FBIS-LAT, 10 March 1995.

52. Gisela Von Muhlenbrock, "Discretion and Corruption: The Chilean Judiciary," *Crime, Law, and Social Change* 25 (1997): 335–51; "C. Suprema Creó Comisión De Control Ético Judicial," *El Mercurio*, 27 June 1997, A1; and Jazmán Jalile M., "Ministro Roberto Dávila: 'Modernizar la justicia es un proceso universal,' " *La Tercera*, 3 March 1998, 1. Polls found that more than 70 percent believed that was a "protection network" for narcotraffickers inside the Supreme Court and 60 percent said that they believed there are corrupt judges. See "Veredicto popular," *Qué Pasa*, 24 May 1997, 20.

53. Although less of a priority for both administrations, there also was a general sense that the courts issued genuinely independent, democratic rulings on a growing range of economic issues during this period, in many cases overruling actions taken by the administration. See Genaro Arriagada, "La Judicialización de los Procesos Regulatórios," *Estrategia*, 1 September 1997, 22.

54. "Suprema Declaró Constitucional Decreto Ley de Amnistía del '78," *El Mercurio*, 25 August 1990, A1.

55. The lower court ruling is discussed in Alejandro Salinas Rivera, "Two Examples of Battling Impunity in Chile," *Review of the International Commission of Jurists* 53 (December 1994): 13–18. The final Supreme Court decision is detailed in Robert J. Quinn, "Will the Rule of Law End? Challenging Grants of Amnesty for the Human Rights Violations of a Prior Regime: Chile's New Model," *Fordham Law Review* 62 (February 1994): 905–60. The administration successfully argued at the Appeals Court level, based on several obscure constitutional clauses that placed international treaty obligations above domestic law, that some 30 of the more egregious human rights violations could be reopened. The Supreme Court would later strike down that judgment on the grounds that such an interpretation could reopen the entire 1978 amnesty law, although it upheld arguments that families of the victims were justified to compensation for their losses and that the courts were obligated to provide a full accounting of the disappearances of the relative.

56. Don Podesta, "2 Generals Convicted of Killing of Letelier; Chileans to be Jailed for Washington Murder," *Washington Post*, 13 November 1993, A19; and "Justice Denies Pressure Will Affect Ruling on Letelier," Madrid EFE, 27 April 1995, in FBIS-LAT, 29 April 1995.

57. In one famous speech, Pinochet warned that any effort "to touch even a hair on the head of any one of my men will bring the tanks into the streets." See Brian Loveman, "¿Misión Cumplida? Civil-Military Relations and the Chilean Political Transition," *Journal of Interamerican Studies and World Affairs* 33 (Fall 1991): 35–63.

58. José Ale, "Doce victimas en busca de justicia," *La Tercera*, 23 March 1998, 6; José Ale, "Formalizaron petición para que siga Dolmestch en caso Albania," *La Tercera*, 23 December 1998, 11; José Ale, "Caso Tucapel Jiménez: piden la extradición de ex agente de la CNI," *La Tercera*, 17 March 1998, 3; and Jazmín Jalile M., "Designado tribunal en juicio oral contra Arancibia Clavel," *La Tercera*, 10 March 1998, 17.

59. "Justicia Investigará Hasta Clarificar Participaciones," *Estrategia*, 7 April 1999, 7; José Ale, "Procesando ex-jefe metropolitano de CNI," *La Tercera*, 16 September 1999, 1; and Pedro Vega, "Corte rebajó cargos a general (R) Gordon," *La Tercera*, 22 September 1999, 1.

60. Eugenio Tironi, "El suprapoder," *Qué Pasa*, 4–10 April 1997, 23.

61. It is worth noting that the administration was able to present plans for a judicial academy so quickly because key advisors had been discussing the issue well before the transition occurred. See Manuel Guzmán Vial, "Reflexiones sobre el poder estatal y el poder judicial," *Estudios Sociales* 50 (1986): 71–88.

62. Aylwin challenged the courts to produce any evidence of the alleged plot, offering to provide the requisite security for any and all endangered judges. The High Court never produced any documentation to support its claims. See Santiago Radio Chilena Network, 13 March 1991; and Santiago Television Nacional de Chile, 7 March 1991.

63. Santiago Radio Nacional de Chile, 14 March 1991. Correa Labra's attitudes toward reform are demonstrated in the following 1992 exchange with a journalist:

Correa Labra: The government is wrong. We are right. All we need is more judges and we will resolve the problems. There is no crisis, simply too much work.
Reporter: That is all it will take? More judges?
Correa Labra: That is right. Tell me something. Can you imagine a judge handling 5,000 cases? Answer me.

See Santiago Television Nacional de Chile, 2 March 1992, in FBIS-LAT, 4 March 1992.

64. Senior judges initially opposed the idea, apparently because they believed that fewer responsibilities for judges would translate into reduced respect (and smaller budgets) for the judiciary. See Humberto Nogueira A., *El poder judicial Chileno: su crisis actual y vías alternativas de solución* (Santiago: Instituto Chileno de Estudios Humanos, 1987): 17.

65. Robert Vaughn, "Proposals for Judicial Reform in Chile," *Fordham International Law Journal* 16 (1992–1993): 589. Vaughn correctly noted, "Because of the highly charged nature and political character of some aspects of the debate, arguments often are couched in more neutral terms of 'judicial efficiency.' "

66. Frei's quotes come from "Promulga Presidente Eduardo Frei ley que crea Ministério Público," *Notimex*, 8 September 1997; and "Promulgada en Chile reforma judicial que crea el Ministério Público, AFP press release, 8 September 1997.

67. Spain employed a 20-member council composed of twelve jurists and eight members selected equally from both chambers of Congress, subject to a three-fourths approval. The coalition's proposal envisioned an academy composed of outside academics, members selected by Congress, and appointees of the Supreme Court.

68. The initial proposal that served as a baseline negotiating stance for the Right can be found in *Proposiciones para la reform judicial*, ed. Eugenio Valenzuela S. (Santiago: Centro de Estudios Públicos, 1991): 119.

69. "Ivan Lavados and Juan Enrique Vargas, "La Gestión Judicial," *Estudios Sociales* 78 (1993): 203-25.

70. *Plan de Acción, 1994-2000* (Santiago: Ministério de Justicia): 1-3.

71. "C. Suprema: 'Historica Creación de Min. Público,' " *El Mercurio*, 31 August 1997, p. C2; and "First Judicial Reform Ratified," *Chile Information Project News*, 21 November 1994.

72. Training for prosecutors began in 1998, followed by a two-city pilot project in 2001, and nationwide introduction in 2002. Several reforms aimed at decongesting the courts—introducing plea bargaining and alternative sentencing, and decriminalizing issues such as debt collection—also will be phased in over a multiyear period. See "Aprobada Transcendental Reforma al Juicio Penal," *El Mercurio*, 31 August 1997, A1; "Frei Signs Judicial Reform Law," *El Mercurio*, 9 September 1997, in FBIS-LAT, 11 September 1997; "Congress Approves Historic Justice Reform," *Chile Information Project News*, 1 September 1997; and "Chief Justice Calls for Broader Reform," *Chile Information Project News*, 3 March 1998.

73. "Courts Overcome Distaste for Judicial Reform," *Chile Information Project News*, 28 September 1998. The plan called for the construction of forty courts spread throughout all regions of the country.

74. The number has increased from two in 1992 to twenty-eight in 1997, with increases each year. See "Hacia una Justicia Comercial Privada?" *La Estrategia*, 20 October 1997, 41; and Robert Layton, "Changing Attitudes Toward Dispute Resolution in Latin America," *Journal of International Arbitration* 10 (January 1993): 123-41.

75. Jenny Del Rio, "Draft Law Gives Supreme Court New Powers," *El Mercurio*, 6 November 1994, A1, A20, in FBIS-LAT, 8 November 1994.

76. Carlos Cerda, *Duración del procedimiento sumario los juzgdos de Santiago* (Santiago: FONDEYCT, 1993): 5; Juan Enrique Vargas Viancos and Jorge Correa Sutil, *Diagnóstico del sistema judicial chileno* (Santiago: Corporación de Promoción, Universitaria, 1995): 36, 57; and "Undue Delays in Supreme Court Criticized," *Chile Information Project*, 13 January 1995.

77. The administration, working closely with a prominent NGO, produced a comprehensive study of judicial bottlenecks that found that throughout the 1980s the courts of first instance had been disposing of cases more quickly than had the courts of appeal.

78. Reformers point out that the ratio of cases entering the system to cases being resolved actually improved between 1990 and 1994, although they acknowledge that a longer time series is necessary. See Vargas Viancos and Correa Sutil, *Diagnóstico del sistema judicial chileno*, pp. 36, 57.

79. Some credit also must go to Aylwin's efforts to boost the administrative capabilities of the Judicial Administrative Corporation. Between 1990 and 1995, the Corporation emerged as a fulltime organ dedicated to managing the administrative affairs of the courts, such as preparing budgets, ordering supplies, maintaining facilities and paying bills, and integrating the use of computerized records. The innovation is important because judges in Chile spend on average 65 percent of their day doing administrative functions. See Luis Manrique Reyes, "Modernization of Judicial Systems in Developing Countries: The Case of Chile," in *Judicial Reform in Latin America and the Caribbean*, ed. Malcolm Rowat, Waleed H. Malik, and Maria Dakolias (Washington, D.C.: The World Bank, 1995): 195-200.

80. The creation of neighborhood courts is defended in Jaime Williams, "Reforma a la administración de justicia en Chile," in *Memoria: Conferencia Iberoamericana sobre reforma de la justicia penal* (San Salvador: Ministério de Justicia, 1991): 24.

81. The reaction was overdrawn. Leaders of the Socialist Party had undergone an ideological renovation while in exile and were far more moderate than their counterparts in the 1970s. See Katherine Hite, "The formation and transformation of political identity: leaders of the Chilean

left, 1968-1990," *Journal of Latin American Studies* 28 (May 1996): 299-329; Alan Angell and Susan Carstairs, "The exile question in Chilean politics," *Third World Quarterly* 9 (January 1987): 148-67; Alejandro Dario Molina, "PS: el marxismo 'light,' " *Ercilla*, 7 November 1990, 8-11; and Patricio Silva, "Technocrats and Politics in Chile: From the Chicago Boys to the CIEPLAN Monks," *Journal of Latin American Studies* 23 (May 1991): 401. By the late 1990s, members of the Chilean Right were actually backing a proposal similar to the neighborhood courts, arguing that the plans were consistent with their broader goals of decentralization. See Eugenio Guzmán and Claudio Osorio, *Hacia un nuevo munícipio: segúridad ciudadana justicia vecinal* (Santiago: Instituto Libertad y Desarrollo, 1998): 11-15.

82. Mirtha Ulloa Gonzalez and Macarena Vargas Pavez, "Políticas públicas y necesidades de justicia de los sectores pobres," *Estudios Sociales* 83 (1995): 51-97. The administration also created a career track for public defenders—the posts previously were staffed by students and recent law school graduates—although this program, like the public prosecutor's office, will be phased in over several years.

83. *Primera Feria Nacional de Asistencia Jurídica: Justicia para Todos* (Santiago: Imprensa Gráfica Nueva, 1994).

84. A typical law student handles between 80 to 110 cases in a six-month period. See *Corporación de Asistencia Judicial de la Región Metropolitana, 1995* (Santiago: Corporación de Asistencia Judicial de la Región Metropolitana, 1996): 17.

85. Michael Samway, "Access to Justice: A Study of Legal Assistance Programs for the Poor in Santiago, Chile," *Duke Journal of Comparative and International Law* 6 (Summer 1996): 347-69.

86. *Acceso a la Justicia: Program de Asistencia Jurídica* (Santiago: Ministério de Justicia, 1997, unpublished mimeo).

87. Off-the-record interview with Chilean official, Ministry of Justice, Santiago, Chile, 9 September 1997.

88. A slim majority favors the death penalty. See "Las cifras del miedo," *Qué Pasa*, 7 June 1997, 22-23; "Government reacts to rising crime," *Chile Information Project*, 7 April 1998; Mará Eugenia Oyarzun, "Me duele lo que ocurre con el Poder Judicial," *La Tercera*, 30 May 1997, 17; "German Valenzuela Erazo: 'Gobierno se apoderó del Poder Judicial,'" *La Tercera*, 1 August 1998, 33.

89. Bernadita del Solar, "Jorge Correa: 'El sistema judicial solo funcionó bien hasta los años 60,' " *Qué Pasa*, 5-11 August 1997, 9.

90. "Problemas de imagen," *Qué Pasa*, 24 May 1997, 21.

91. See, for example, Eduardo Jara, "Discurso de Clausura," in *Asistencia Legal en America Latina*, ed. Marco A. Lillo de la Cruz (Santiago: Centro de Desarrollo Jurídico, 1996): 143-47.

92. *Seminario: Justicia y Marginalidad Rural* (Santiago: Corporación de Promoción Universitaria, 1994). Thirty-one percent has a positive opinion of judges—a rate nearly three times higher than in CPU's 1991 survey of the indigent.

93. In fact, some polls indicated that businessmen gave the courts a higher approval rating than did the general public. See Cristian Bofill, "Detrás del Escándolo," *Qué Pasa*, 27 May-2 June 1997, 8; Soledad Alvear, "El Mercado Exige un Sistema de Justicia Imparcial y Eficiente," *La Estrategia*, 20 October 1997, 5; Bernadita del Solar and Claudio Vera Acuna, "Los desconocidos de siempre," *Qué Pasa*, 14 June 1997, 54-58; and "El Reparto de Botín," *Qué Pasa*, 12 August 1995, 52-57.

94. David Pilling, "Military Whitewash? Chileans Worry Army General Will Be Cleared of 'Disappeared' Deaths," *Montreal Gazette*, 15 August 1993, B4.

95. Both men are often criticized for their "blandness," although one recent article suggests that their more cautious approach reflected a sign of democratic maturity that has been missing in some of Chile's neighbors. See Gerardo L. Munck, "Democratic Stability and Its Limits: An Analysis of Chile's 1993 Elections," *Journal of Interamerican Studies and World Affairs* 36 (Summer 1994): 1–35.

96. Bickford, "Democracy, Stakeholdership, and Public Policymaking in Chile, 1990–1997: The Case of Judicial Reform," p. 39.

97. "150 jueces piden cónclave extraordinário," *La Tercera*, 17 July 1997, 33.

Chapter Seven _____

Judicial Reform and
Democratic Decay

This study began by looking at the relatively unexplored area of comparative judicial reform in Latin America, seeking to identify the implicit and explicit assumptions of reformers, test whether they had met their objectives in specific case studies, and assess the impact on the democratic consolidation process. The traditional framework, as outlined in Chapter One, has taken a narrow, technical approach to judicial reform and at first glance seems sensible enough: it intuitively fits with what we know about limited state capabilities in the developing world and in Latin America specifically. According to conventional wisdom, governments undertaking a judicial reform program ought to define their goals and their means as narrowly as possible and concentrate on a minimum number of variables, usually efficiency-maximizing reforms that lend themselves to supposedly easy fixes—such as more computers for court personnel and more training for judges—and whose benefits are so inherently desirable that they represent a collective good for society. Progress on one variable provides a foundation to build upon and is thought to lead to successes on other variables. The merit of such a strategy, reformers suggest, is that a targeted, sequential approach is better than a broad-based effort that strains state capability and risks getting bogged down in too many initiatives at once.

Yet the case studies examined here, to one degree or another, expose the fundamental weaknesses of this approach on at least three basic levels. First, it is not possible to isolate one variable of the judicial system from other variables and to implement the reforms in an isolated, sequential fashion. In fact, the case studies here suggest the opposite is true: all aspects of the judicial system are so closely related that failure to reform one variable often produces a negative synergy that complicates and undermines the reformed aspects of the judiciary. Second, just as it is impossible to isolate one reform variable from another, so too is it impossible to isolate any or all of the variables from the broader political and economic forces at play. That is, the independent variables of independence, efficiency, and access are in fact not as independent as they seem; they are shaped and constrained by broader forces in a polity. Third, the reason that it is impossible to isolate the judiciary from broader forces is that, at bottom, reforming the judiciary is not a merely technical or administrative reform with alleged benefits that are universally desired. Rather, judicial reform is inherently political in nature, involving a series of political calculations and confrontations along the way. Each point is worth briefly recapping.

In the cases of El Salvador, Brazil, and Argentina, a striking feature is the degree to which a narrowly defined incrementalism failed as a viable reform strategy. Each country represented a range of reform combinations, none of which were especially effective. The negative synergy was first examined in El Salvador. Duarte's well-intentioned efforts to boost some aspects of individual independence and judicial efficiency were supposed to lead to a judiciary that would eventually develop the capability to rule against other branches of government, develop more structural independence, and gain the citizenry's trust to help nurture support for the rule of law. Efforts of the Cristiani administration following the end of the civil war justifiably claimed to be even more ambitious by focusing on the long-ignored aspect of structural independence. Even though some of the reforms—particularly those after 1991—clearly were positive steps toward a more professional and accountable judiciary, the public hardly seemed to notice. Both administrations failed, in part, because reformers never made a concerted effort at access creation. The neglect is curious and almost inexplicable. In a country that spent most of the 1980s attempting to implement an extensive land reform program that would incorporate the average citizen into the formal economic system, no corresponding effort was made to integrate Salvadorans into the formal legal system and to bring the rule of law closer to the typical Salvadoran. By the late 1990s, distrust of the courts in democratic El Salvador was as great as during the height of the civil war in the 1980s. More than $60 million of international judicial reform aid—including extensive training for judges, sophisticated criminal codes, more computers, and modern court facilities—failed to have an appreciable effect on strengthening public confidence in the rule of law.

Through different means and under different circumstances, a similar pattern prevailed in Brazil. Authors of the 1988 Constitution created an independent judiciary, as well as a number of measures to ensure access, yet a decade later were unanimous that they had produced unintended results: a judiciary devoid of accountability and accessible to no one. The failure to make the courts more efficient meant that the access-creating strategies were essentially meaningless. Again, the perils of partial reform and negative synergy stand out. Without enhanced efficiency in the courts, unfettered access for everyone produced, not surprisingly, access for no one. Meanwhile, the failure to include a degree of accountability to balance the enhanced independence provided virtually no incentive for the courts to implement reforms on their own. Indeed, an overly independent judiciary was able to consistently resist any measure that would have reduced its traditional perquisites or increased its accountability, efficiency, and access.

The Argentine case study was the third example of the negative synergy that results from focusing on a partial, narrow approach to reform. Alfonsín staked his entire judicial reform program on enhancing the structural independence of the courts by pursuing a series of controversial human rights cases against members of the former military junta, and he actually achieved some symbolically important victories by securing indictments of high-ranking junta members. Yet these very real achievements were overshadowed and undermined by his simultaneous failure to make virtually any headway on efficiency and access. Compromises on the scope of military trials that otherwise may have been acceptable to the public seemed intolerable when combined with the perception that the performance of the courts as a whole was decaying rather than improving. Modest progress on judicial independence, when unaccompanied by other reforms, ultimately produced more cynicism, not less.

The Menem experience offered many of the same lessons by following the opposite approach. Menem focused on what Alfonsín ignored, launching impressive reforms of efficiency and access (and doing so with the enthusiastic backing of reformers at the World Bank and AID) while ignoring judicial independence and actually undermining it in an effort to conceal the most egregious instances of administration corruption. By the end of his second term, Menem's positive achievements on efficiency and access were rejected by the public in the face of his simultaneous politicization of the courts. Even Menem belatedly learned the degree to which partial reform produces a negative synergy: ill-qualified, partisan judges with no real overriding interest in the rule of law could not be reliably counted on to implement some of his more innovative efficiency-maximizing reforms. Menem wanted a judiciary that was efficient and accessible but politicized, and he eventually learned that the unstable equilibrium could not exist indefinitely.

The sole case study that clearly was not a failure—and may even constitute a success—was Chile. Chilean reformers followed an approach that was virtually the opposite of that advocated by international development agencies, even as some of those agencies were funding some of the specific project components. Reformers set out to create a better balance between independence and accountability, streamline efficiency, and enhance access, despite the risks of becoming overextended and bogged down in the face of simultaneous reforms. To be sure, there were legislative setbacks and outright defeats along the way, but by 1999—in the relatively short span of just over nine years—reformers had some degree of progress to show for their efforts. Anticorruption campaigns and impeachments had made the courts more accountable, while efforts to establish more rational criteria for promotions, training, and dismissal for judges through a judicial academy enhanced the individual independence of lower court judges who for years had been intimidated by the Supreme Court. Efforts to boost the structural independence of the courts by giving them jurisdiction over cases that had been in the military courts, while substantially increasing work loads for the civilian courts, could be handled because the courts were gradually becoming more efficient. The courts were able to become more efficient, in turn, because a surge of cases—more than 100,000 in seven years—were resolved through an innovative access to justice program that developed alternative forms of dispute resolution and thus integrated low-income citizens into the legal system. By the late 1990s, the image of the Chilean judiciary—while still far short of an overwhelming endorsement by the public—was slowly, perceptibly gaining trust over time, the only case study that did not reflect growing distrust and that actually showed some signs of improvement. Gradual, comprehensive reform achieved what more ambitious, narrowly defined reforms could not.

A second flaw in the traditional approach is the assumption that judicial reform is somehow separate and discreet and can be isolated from larger social forces at work in a polity. Just as one variable cannot be isolated from another, the judiciary as a whole cannot be reformed without reference to broader political and economic trends. Even assuming momentarily that the reform strategies in El Salvador, Brazil, and Argentina may have been sound on their own merits, a striking feature is the degree to which their ultimate success or failure nonetheless seemed reliant on larger forces. For example, laudable reforms in El Salvador, even if they had been structurally sound, were virtually assured of failure in a climate in which political forces on the Right and Left shared no commitment to the rule of law. Judicial reform aimed to build a lasting democratic consensus in El Salvador, even though it became clear that a democratic consensus must precede rather than follow judicial reform. In the case of Brazil, even if judicial reforms had been adequate, the exaggerated statist impulses of the 1988 Constitution distorted the reforms by turning a disproportionate number of minor civil and criminal issues into questions of potential constitutional importance; appellate courts and even the Supreme Court were quickly overwhelmed with divorce settlements, bar fights, neighborhood noise disputes, and a host of other marginal cases glutting the system. Reformers could have devoted more attention and more resources to address these flaws, but cumulative inflation rates of 84 million percent between 1985 and 1994 did not create an environment conducive to rational, long-term planning in the public sector. Even in the more successful case of Chile, adverse political forces frequently prevailed: Aylwin and Frei met with a number of legislative defeats during the reform process because some politicians simply did not place a priority on judicial reforms and because some political forces were blatantly hostile to the idea. In Argentina, Menem's own political goals—to remain in office and out of jail—defined the parameters of judicial reform. Reformers in Chile and in Alfonsín's Argentina learned that a recalcitrant military limits the success of strategies to enhance judicial independence—a lesson Alfonsín learned most clearly when the military made his life so difficult that he left office six months before his term expired.

The third and final flaw in this traditional approach is the notion that judicial reform is merely a technical, apolitical institutional reform. Sustainable, meaningful reform cannot be achieved through total quality management or tinkering with wiring diagrams and missions statements that are devised in an aseptic, apolitical manner. Judicial reform, like virtually all bureaucratic reform, is deeply political. It involves altering power relationships between various branches of government and between levels of the judiciary itself, restructuring institutional arrangements and introducing new patterns of conduct, providing new services to new constituencies, and reexamining resources and how they are allocated. In short, an independent, efficient, and accessible judiciary is not necessarily a collective good desired by the public and the judiciary alike. In fact, it is likely to be resisted by any number of opponents: politicians accustomed to stocking the courts with the party loyalists, interest groups accustomed to a privileged relationship with the state, judges reluctant to have their actions subject to greater oversight and accountability, and court personnel skeptical of enforcing new patterns of professional conduct. Edgardo Buscaglia has accurately described the "institutional inertia" that confronts judicial reformers:

> The main obstacles to an effective legal reform in Latin America stem from the vested interests which may be threatened by any profound alteration in the system as it exists and from which they have benefited. . . . Reforms may also imply a loss of discretionary powers, an increase of mechanisms in control, or even greater accountability at any level of the justice apparatus that will be regarded with considerable distrust by the affected judges, prosecutors, and clerks. Finally, measures which establish merit-based systems, where there were none to begin with, will be spurned by individuals or groups who benefited precisely from a more clientelistic or political award system.[1]

This point is made clear by comparing the responses of various actors in the reform process. Perhaps most striking—particularly given the traditional assumption that the judiciary is a natural ally in the reform process—is the reaction of senior judges in the various reform cases examined here. A common theme across all four cases is that reforms were strongly resisted by the judicial branch itself. In El Salvador, Supreme Court President Gutierrez Castro actually instructed judges that they did not have to comply with congressionally approved judicial reforms because he had not authorized them; in Chile, members of the High Court went even further in 1991 and 1992 and hinted they would acknowledge the legality of another coup if the armed forces would step in and stop measures such as judicial reform.[2] In Argentina and Brazil, the opposition was less dramatic but no less real. Judges in Argentina took the lead in opposing measures that would introduce standardized post-entry training for judges, and they threatened work stoppages if Congress tried to force judges to declare their incomes and assets on an annual basis.[3] In Brazil, efforts to introduce a career track for judges prompted senior judges to openly compare the Cardoso administration with Nazi Germany and to repeatedly stage national protests and work stoppages to block the proposed reforms.[4] Given the track record, the constant opposition of senior judges to judicial reform suggests a need for reformers to reconceptualize how the reform process ought to be implemented and who ought to lead it. Contrary to conventional assumptions, the judiciary is not necessarily a supporter of reform and may actually be an outright opponent.

The case studies demonstrate that the notion laid out in Chapter One—that judicial reform is a universally-desired collective good in society—also is false. Because judicial reform affects core political interests, it should not be surprising that leading political forces oppose reforms for various reasons. In El Salvador, judicial reform was opposed first by the armed forces and political parties on the far Right who resisted the prospects of being held accountable to the rule of law; by the mid-1980s it was opposed by parties and movements on the far Left for much the same reason. In Brazil, reforms were shaped in large part by the fact that the President took little interest in the process; in Argentina under Menem, reforms were distorted by the fact that the President took an interest far too intense in the process—and for reasons that could hardly be described as democratic. In Argentina under Alfonsín as well as in the successful case of Chile, the armed forces also placed limits on the scope of judicial reforms. In short, reforming a judiciary is clearly more difficult—and more political—than it would initially seem.

Along these lines, it is also clear that while political will is a *necessary* precondition for launching a judicial reform, it also is not *sufficient*. The successful case of Chile—and the ability of successive presidents to build multiparty coalitions spanning the ideological spectrum behind the reforms—clearly was the critical variable in igniting the reform process.[5] Yet this experience should not create the mistaken impression that merely building a political consensus is sufficient grounds for ensuring success. In the case of Brazil in 1988, most of the thirteen parties in Congress backed the reform process and collaborated openly with NGOs and human rights organizations, while neither the President nor the armed forces appeared especially opposed to the idea. Despite this consensus, the reforms ultimately represented a step backward rather than forward for Brazilian democracy. In short, the consensus that emerges from the reform process cannot be aimed at implementing merely *any* type of reform. Instead, it must be sound on two fundamental levels. It must be comprehensive and reform the entire judiciary rather than only portions of it, and the reforms themselves must be aimed at reinforcing a specific type of regime—one that is accountable to the public and to itself, that lays the foundations for a vibrant private sector capable of checking abusive government power and sustaining civil society, and that incorporates the average citizen into a system based on the rule of law. Reforms in Chile met both criteria. Brazil's reforms met neither.

SOME EARLY LESSONS FROM FAILED REFORMS

There are important lessons both in the failed and successful reform projects. No two experiences are identical, but for those observers interested in strengthening democratic consolidation through judicial reform in other parts of Latin America—or even the developing world more broadly—certain parallels emerge between those case studies examined here and reform efforts elsewhere.

First and most basically, these case studies suggest that while no strategy is assured of meeting with success, some reform paths—particularly those partial reforms that produce negative synergy—almost certainly will fail. The point is important because despite the poor record on judicial reform of El Salvador, Brazil, and Argentina, those same strategies continue to find a receptive audience elsewhere in the region. For example, the Wasmosy administration in Paraguay (1993–98) and the Chamorro government in Nicaragua (1990–96)—like the Duarte administration in El Salvador—launched programs to enhance judicial independence, with only passing consideration given to efficiency and access and no real role for accountability—the latter an especially worrisome trend given the longstanding problem with judicial corruption in existence in both countries.[6] Efforts in Peru under President Alberto Fujimori closely resemble the experience under Menem in Argentina: notable attempts to enhance access and efficiency, aimed at boosting investor confidence and providing justice for routine, man-on-the-street issues, have been accompanied by judicial purges, court packing, and politicization of the judiciary. Similarly, Fujimori, like Menem, has learned that politicization has a cost: ill-qualified, politicized judges cannot be relied on to implement efficiency-maximizing reforms and in many cases demonstrate such unprofessional work habits—such as regularly failing to show up for work—that efforts at efficiency and access are severely undermined.[7] If the patterns of the case studies here are correct, then reformers in each of the above projects are virtually assured of failure because they eventually will encounter a negative synergy that resembles the complications experienced in other failed judicial reform programs.

There are indications that these patterns do occur when examined over a broader series of countries. Recent events in Colombia repeat the broad outlines of the Brazilian reform process. The Colombian Constitution in 1991, heavily influenced by the same ultrapopulist spirit that produced the Brazilian Constitution of 1988, sought to dramatically enhance independence and access while relegating the issue of efficiency to another time. Indeed, the Colombian Constitution even included an innovative feature known as the *tutela*—roughly similar to the ADIN in Brazil—that allowed citizens who believed their rights had been violated to have their case heard before the Supreme Court within ten days. Not surprisingly, just as in Brazil, unfettered access for everyone, when coupled with extreme inefficiency and judicial resistance to change, produced access for no one. By 1997, more than 110,000 *tutelas* had gone to the Supreme Court and justices complained that they spent 60 to 80 percent of their time on these cases, even though the Supreme Court President complained that "about 90 percent of these cases are frivolous."[8]

Another lesson for reformers is that efforts to improve the administration of justice must be accompanied by reforms of other agencies that support and complement the formal court system. If broader forces and institutions do matter in shaping the success of a program, it is worth asking what some of those other forces may be and how they may be used to sustain the reform process; military obduracy and economic crises, as the case studies suggested, may be the most obvious, but are not necessarily even the most determinative. Indeed, a striking contrast between the three failed case studies and the Chilean example is the constructive role played by auxiliary agencies in the reform process. Chilean reformers took pains to actively solicit the participation of the executive branch, particularly the Ministry of Justice, in the process. Justice Ministry officials worked closely with the judiciary and the main political parties, for example, to institute an aggressive Access to Justice program that provided meaningful access for the poor while giving the efficiency-creating strategies time to take effect. The experience stands in contrast to the role played by the justice ministries in Argentina and Brazil, where the post served virtually no role in judicial reform and instead has been little more than a patronage position raffled off to partisan loyalists and ill-qualified hacks. Menem, for example, had seven justice ministers in his first eight years, several of whom were corrupt business cronies. Brazil had twelve justice ministers in its first fourteen years of civilian rule, including a mixed bag of drunkards, political opportunists, and one-time financial backers of death squads. Given the constant turnover, it is not surprising that the Justice Ministry was not able to play a more constructive role in the reform process in those countries.

A similar logic applies to police forces. Chilean reformers could rely on a relatively professional, efficient, and respected police force, in stark contrast to its neighbors. The growth in Brazil's backlog of cases between 1988–99 was due not only to the inefficient judiciary's inability to cope with the burdens of the statist Constitution but also to police inefficiency and corruption. Police forces, like judges, struggled with the increased caseload, and in many states police closed less than 20 percent of their investigations in an average year.[9] In El Salvador, even the most independent judge could not produce a sound verdict if his investigation relied on evidence gathered by inefficient and politicized security forces. And in Argentina, the most independent, accountable, efficient, and accessible judge could hardly be expected to reach a sound verdict when the police were tasked with investigating crimes that had been committed by members of their own ranks.[10] Again, these experiences offer lessons for other governments undertaking judicial reform programs. Despite notable efforts by the administration of Mexican President Ernesto Zedillo to depoliticize the judiciary—such as instituting a new selection process for the Supreme Court that closely resembled the Salvadoran model under the Peace Process—there is a growing recognition that it is pointless to press for greater judicial independence and accountability if the police forces are increasingly tainted by narcotics corruption and unwilling to cooperate with judges in sensitive criminal investigations.[11]

If larger forces do in fact play a role in facilitating or slowing reform efforts, more caution ought to be given to the traditional assumption that more money and more resources are by themselves solutions to the judiciary's problems. Clearly, more funds are critical for hiring more judges and prosecutors, purchasing more computers, and building more courts that can serve more people; more money was an essential component of the reform efforts in Chile, where Aylwin and Frei increased the judiciary's funding from 1 percent of the national budget to over 3 percent in 1997. Conversely, the decline of the judiciary in Argentina can be explained, in part, by the fact that federal outlays for the judiciary in Argentina have been fairly consistent since the military government in the mid-1970s—approximately 1 percent of the federal budget—and actually less under Menem, despite a 10 percent increase in population during this period. Even though more money may be necessary, however, it clearly is not a panacea. Most Latin American countries already devote more funds to the judiciary as a percentage of the national budget than do developed countries in Western Europe and Japan.[12] As the case studies of Brazil and El Salvador demonstrate, merely increasing resources that will be managed by an unaccountable or politicized Supreme Court reinforces and strengthens the power of entrenched reform opponents and enhances the discretionary power they hold over lower court judges. Political will to use increased resources efficiently and effectively must precede the actual increase in outlays; more money alone cannot serve as a catalyst for reform and in fact may amount to throwing good money after bad.[13]

Finally, the focus on institutions should not conceal the fact that formal processes and institutional mechanisms are not necessarily *the* determinative element in a reform effort.[14] That is, there is no ideal structural arrangement that best promotes or guarantees successful judicial reforms. Democratic-minded reformers could work around imperfect institutional arrangements (as in Chile) just as antidemocratic forces can exploit sound institutional reforms (as in El Salvador) to their advantage. Some institutional setups are sufficiently neutral that they may be exploited by authoritarians and democrats alike. The self-selection process of judges in Chile was an enemy of judicial reform when the Supreme Court was controlled by pro-military justices, yet the same process was an asset for reformers once the High Court was controlled by more democratic elements. The concentration of power in the hands of the Supreme Court President in El Salvador was an impediment to reform in the 1980s, but those same powers were a force driving greater accountability when in the hands of a more responsible successor. A council of magistrates that would take the power of judicial selections out of the hands of politicians and put that prerogative into the hands of judicial authorities was a logical step in Argentina, but would have made little sense in Brazil, where judges already demonstrated an inability to conduct their affairs in an accountable manner. In looking to launch a reform effort, judicial reformers often take office with a zealous drive to undo all of the institutional vestiges of their predecessors. Yet they would do well to distinguish whether it is the institutional structure or merely the individuals exercising judicial authority that are in need of change.

JUDICIAL REFORM AND DEMOCRATIC DECAY

There are several implications for the broader question of how judicial reform in Latin America has contributed to the process of democratic consolidation. In reviewing efforts to advance democracy throughout the region, a striking feature is the degree to which the judiciary has emerged as one of the critical "fault lines" in nascent democratic regimes. Alongside real progress on various institutional planes— in areas such as regularizing elections and modernizing statist economies—has been the absolute failure to make greater headway in narrowing the gap between the role that the judiciary ought to play and the role that it actually does.[15]

The failure to make the administration of justice more predictable and transparent clearly has caused a drag on economic development so crucial to helping citizens meet their basic daily needs and enabling them to afford meaningful participation in their community's affairs. Indeed, further delays in reforming the judiciary appear likely to exact increasingly higher costs on developing countries as they struggle to adjust to globalization and the changes in the international economy.[16] The importance of the judiciary also will continue to grow as developing countries move away from statist, mercantilist economies—in which transactions are based primarily on political concerns—toward more open, liberal-capitalist models, in which commerce is regulated by technical and legal considerations.[17] The emergence and expansion of trade agreements such as the North American Free Trade Agreement and the Southern Cone Common Market require standardization and harmonization of trade rules and regulations—and an ability of the courts to enforce the increasingly complex rules of economic competition across a range of technical issues.[18]

The failure to make greater headway on judicial reform also suggests that the countries examined here—particularly El Salvador, Brazil, and Argentina—are each much earlier in the consolidation process than has been traditionally assumed. Some scholars have suggested that a regime approaches consolidation when its institutions are routinized and internalized, when all politically significant groups accept the institutions of the state as the only legitimate framework for contestation and dispute resolution.[19] Yet it is clear that in three of the four case studies, the performance of the judiciary is not taken for granted as a formal institution, at least not in a positive sense. The consistently poor performance of the courts and the fraying of the rule of law have given rise to incomplete citizenship:

> For large sections of the population, basic liberal freedoms are denied or recurrently trampled. The rights of battered women to sue their husbands and of peasants to obtain a fair trial against their landlords, the inviolability of domiciles in poor neighborhoods, and in general the right of the poor and various minorities to decent treatment and fair access to public agencies and courts are often denied. The effectiveness of the whole ensemble of rights, democratic and liberal, make for full civic and political citizenship. In many of the new polyarchies, individuals are only citizens in relation to the one institution that functions in a manner close to what its formal rules prescribe—elections. As for full citizenship, only the members of a privileged minority enjoy it.[20]

The void created by weak, inefficient, and inaccessible courts has been filled by a combination of mob action, vigilante justice, and law-and-order politicians tapping public frustration and exposing some of the more base impulses of society. Throughout the region, polls show a growing dissatisfaction with the judiciary: various polls indicate that between 60 and 85 percent of the public in Bolivia, Colombia, Mexico, and Peru express little or no confidence in the courts.[21] Even in some of the region's more stable democracies, public disenchantment is growing. More than 90 percent of the Venezuelan public express dissatisfaction with the court system—a rate which even government officials conceded was one of the highest in the world—and mainstream parties, frustrated by the judiciary's frequent high-profile corruption scandals, have pushed legislation that would force all sitting judges to undergo psychological testing to prove their competence.[22]

This sentiment, in turn, has contributed to the notion that it is increasingly acceptable to take the law into one's own hands, giving rise to the "privatization of justice," such as death squads and extermination groups.[23] Observers in Ecuador note that the performance of the judicial sector has been so abysmal that "the lack of faith of both the average Ecuadorian and the elite in the judicial process is nearly total. One consequence is that mob lynching of criminal suspects do not shock the Ecuadorian press nor society."[24] In Colombia, the widespread perception that the courts do not punish criminals has led to public support for death squads and extermination groups promising to clean up the streets and impart justice where the courts have allegedly failed.[25] Even in the region's ostensibly consolidated democracies, civil society has become responsible for a shocking level of human rights abuses that were once the preserve of the most authoritarian government institutions.[26] While few observers in Latin America express desire for the armed forces to return to power, the gap between what the democracies are expected to provide and what they actually deliver is increasingly obvious, creating a vacuum that risks being filled by populist, quasi-authoritarian leaders. According to Larry Diamond:

> Regimes that cannot rein in systemic criminal and terrorist violence and subject the police and the military to accountability before the law are unlikely to garner the legitimacy that is the hallmark of consolidation. . . . The crucial intervening variable here is regime legitimacy: the more shallow, exclusive, abusive, and ineffective the regime, the greater the probability of broad popular disillusionment with it over time, and thus the lower the costs will become for either an elected president or the military (or as in Peru, the two institutions collaborating) to overthrow the system.[27]

Unless and until reformers make greater progress on building independent, efficient, and accessible judiciaries, the future in Latin America is less likely to represent the "end of history" and more likely to resemble a <u>degenerate repetition of it.</u> Indeed, in the 1990s alone, President Carlos Menem in Argentina (1989–99), Fernando Collor in Brazil (1990–92), Alberto Fujimori in Peru (1990–present), Abdalá Bucarám in Ecuador (1996–97), Jorge Serrano in Guatemala (1992–93), and Hugo Chavez in Venezuela (1998–present) all have claimed, at one time or another and to varying degrees, the right to govern without political parties, above politics, or through a personal bond with the masses—and without the constraints imposed by allegedly discredited institutions, and there is no reason to believe that they were either atypical or the last of their kind. Successful judicial reform, as the Chilean example demonstrates, can contribute significantly to the cause of democratic consolidation. But the failure of judicial reform—as the studies on El Salvador, Argentina, and Brazil make clear—can contribute just as mightily to the process of democratic decay. In that case, the future of Latin America may look remarkably similar to the past.

NOTES

1. Edgardo Buscaglia and Pilar Domingo, "Impediments to Judicial Reform in Latin America," Paper presented at the Latin American Studies Association, XIX International Congress, 28–30 September 1995, p. 14.

2. On El Salvador, see Jack Spence and George Vickers, *A Negotiated Revolution?* (Cambridge, Mass.: Hemisphere Initiatives, 1994): 7.

3. Laura Zommer, "Un grupo de jueces pidió que se levante el secreto de su patrimonio," *La Nación*, 26 August 1997, p. 13.

4. "Novo Presidente do STF compara efeito vinculante ao AI-5," *O Globo*, 29 May 1997, 3.

5. For a full discussion of the domestic reaction to reform efforts, see the outstanding study by Louis Bickford, "Democracy, Stakeholdership, and Public Policymaking in Chile,

1990–1997: The Case of Judicial Reform," Paper presented at the XXII Congress of the Latin American Studies Association, 24–26 September 1998.

6. On Paraguay's nascent reform efforts, see "Idoniedad preocupa más que integración de ternas," *ABC Color*, 9 May 1995, 9; "Ministros serán designados en sesión pública," *ABC Color*, 31 March 1995, 13; and "Harán estricta selección de jueces," *ABC Color*, 6 April 1995. On Nicaragua, see Michael B. Wise, "Nicaragua: Judicial Independence in a Time of Transition," *Williamette Law Review* 30 (Summer 1994): 519–79.

7. Angel Paez, "The Dreadful Court," *La República*, 9 October 1994, 8–10, in FBIS-LAT, 29 November 1994; Edward G. Robinson, "Law vs. Power," *Los Angeles Daily Journal*, 2 March 1994, 6; and Jimmy Torres, "Demolición," *Caretas*, 13 June 1996, 11–14, 72. A similar approach has been pursued in Honduras, although it is too early to gauge the results. The project is described in Gary Hansen, William Millsap, Ralph Smith, and Mary Staples Said, *A Strategic Assessment of Legal Systems Development in Honduras* (Washington, D.C.: Agency for International Development, 1993).

8. Juanita Darling, "Colombians Happy to Tell It to the Judge," *Los Angeles Times*, 22 December 1996, A39.

9. Sergio Torres, "Imagem é pior do que em Sao Paulo," *Folha de São Paulo*, 14 January 1996, 3. Good overviews of the quality of police performance in Brazil can be found in *Police Brutality in Urban Brazil* (New York: Human Rights Watch/Americas, 1997), and Alexandre Secco, "A polícia bandida," *Veja*, 4 August 1999, 84–97. Secco notes that public accusations of theft, extortion, murder, and human rights abuses committed by policemen have increased 400 percent since 1994.

10. One report indicates that nearly 80 percent of all homicides in Buenos Aires province involved members of the federal police. See *Argentina: Human Rights Practices, 1997* (Washington, D.C.: Department of State, 1997).

11. See Paul Chevigny, *Edge of the Knife* (New York: The New Press, 1995): Chapter Eight. On the growing perception of narcotics-related corruption in the Mexican police, see "Mexicans Continue to Seek Solutions to Narcotrafficking Problem" (Washington, D.C.: United States Information Agency, 1996).

12. Edgardo Buscaglia and Pilar Domingo Villegas, "Impediments to Judicial Reform in Latin America, " p. 7.

13. There are practical reasons to be dubious, as well. One recent study found that there is no automatic correlation between higher wages for public servants in the developing world and reduced levels of corruption. See Caroline Van Rijckegham and Beatrice Weder, *Corruption and the Rate of Temptation: Do Low Wages in the Civil Service Produce Corruption?* (Washington, D.C.: International Monetary Fund, 1997).

14. Jean Grugel, "Transitions from Authoritarian Rule: Lessons from Latin America," *Political Studies* 39 (June 1991): 364.

15. The term is taken from Felipe Agüero and Jeffrey Stark, "Conclusion," in *Fault Lines of Democracy in Post-Transition Latin America*, eds. Felipe Agüero and Jeffrey Stark (Miami, Fla.: North-South Center Press, 1998).

16. The global shift from a labor-based industrial model to a knowledge-based economic system places a premium on protecting and rewarding innovation and intellectual property, a key variable in promoting economic growth. Shahid Javed Burki, "Economic Development and Judicial Reform," in Malcolm Rowat, Waleed H. Malik, and Maria Dakolias, eds. *Judicial Reform in Latin America and the Caribbean* (Washington, D.C.: The World Bank, 1995): 11–12. For example, a series of World Bank projects found that foreign investors were reluctant to invest in Mexico—despite world-class intellectual property rights legislation—because of fear that

the judiciary was too inefficient to rule on technical issues such as IPR cases with a reliable degree of competence and objectivity. See Edwin Mansfield, *Intellectual Property Rights, Foreign Direct Investment, and Technology Transfer* (Washington, D.C.: The World Bank, 1994).

17. Maria Dakolias, *Judicial Reform: Elements of Reform in Latin America and the Caribbean* (Washington, D.C.: The World Bank, 1996): 1–8. Edgardo Buscaglia and Pilar Domingo make a similar case, arguing, "The shift of most economic transactions toward the market domain and away from the public administrative sphere has created an unprecedented increase in the private sector demand for an improved definition of rights and obligations." See their "Impediments to Judicial Reform in Latin America," p. 1.

18. Dakolias, *Elements of Judicial Reform in Latin America and the Caribbean*, pp. 1–6. Some of the practical, transnational legal issues associated with trade integration can be found in "Broader security issues ahead of Mercosur," *Gazeta Mercantil*, 20 October 1997, 17.

19. Richard Gunther, P. Nikiforos Diamondouros, and Hans-Jürgen-Puhle, "O'Donnell's 'Illusions': A Rejoinder," *Journal of Democracy* 7 (October 1996): 152.

20. Guillermo O'Donnell, "Illusions About Consolidation," *Journal of Democracy* 7 (April 1996): 45.

21. See "Latin Americans Favor Democracy, but Democratic Institutions Poorly Rated," United States Information Agency, 9 November 1994. Asked how they viewed their country's judicial system, those expressing little or no confidence totaled 61 percent in Peru, 57 percent in Colombia, and 56 percent in Mexico, according to a 1994 poll. Those expressing little or no confidence in the Supreme Court reached 82 percent in Peru, 72 percent in Mexico, and 73 percent in Colombia. In Bolivia, a 1994 survey of lawyers, judges, and prosecutors found that 84 percent of all respondents believed the process of obtaining justice was too slow, while 74 percent thought the judicial process was politicized. A separate 1996 study reported that only 22 percent of the public expressed "much" or "some" confidence in the judiciary. See "Slow judicial reform," *Latin America Weekly Report*, 22 April 1997, 5–6.

22. "Jueces itinerantes piden integrarse a la reforma," *El Universal* (Caracas), 26 February 1997, sección especial; and Luisa Alejandra Garcia, "Justice Minister Comments on Judiciary's Weakness," *El Globo* (Caracas), 23 September 1994, 4, in FBIS, 25 September 1994.

23. James Holston and Teresa P. R. Caldeira, "Democracy, Law, and Violence: Disjunctions of Brazilian Citizenship," in *Fault Lines of Democracy in Post-Transition Latin America*, p. 277.

24. "Post to Sponsor Administration of Justice Seminar for Journalists in Quito, October 26–27, 1995," U.S. Department of State, unclassified telegram Quito 05257, 19 August 1995.

25. *Reforma de la Administración de Justicia* (Bogota: Instituto SER, 1987): Chapter Three.

26. Tim Johnson, "Mob justice revives death penalty debate," *Miami Herald*, 16 November 1996, A1.

27. Larry Diamond, "Democracy in Latin America," in *Beyond Sovereignty*, ed. Tom Farer (Baltimore, Md.: Johns Hopkins University Press, 1996): 74–75.

Bibliography

NEWSPAPERS AND MAGAZINES

ABC Color (Asunción)

Boletín de Prensa (San Salvador)

Buenos Aires Herald

Centre for the Independence of Judges and Lawyers Bulletin (Geneva)

Chicago Daily Law Bulletin

Chicago Tribune

Christian Science Monitor (Boston)

Clarín (Buenos Aires)

El Comercio (Lima)

Correio Brasiliense (Brasilia)

Crónica (Guatemala City)

Dallas Morning News

The Economist (London)

La Época (Santiago)

Ercilla (Santiago)

O Estado de São Paulo (São Paulo)

Estrategia (Santiago)

Expreso (Lima)

Financial Times (London)

Folha de São Paulo (São Paulo)

Gazeta Mercantil (São Paulo)

El Globo (Caracas)

O Globo (Rio de Janeiro)

Hoy (Santiago)

Insight (Washington)

International Commission of Jurists Newsletter (Geneva)

IstoÉ (São Paulo)

La Jornada (Mexico City)

Jornal da Tarde (Salvador da Bahia)

Jornal de Brasilia (Brasília)

Jornal do Brasil (Rio de Janeiro)

Latinamerica Press (London)

Latin America Weekly Report (London)

Los Angeles Times

Manchete (Rio de Janeiro)

El Mercurio (Santiago)

Miami Herald

Montreal Gazette

La Nación (Buenos Aires)

La Nación (Santiago)

El Nacional (Caracas)

New York Law Journal

New York Times

Noticias (Buenos Aires)

Noticias (Santiago)

La Prensa Gráfica (San Salvador)

Presencia (La Paz)

Proceso (San Salvador)

Qué Pasa (Santiago)

La República (Lima)

Revista de Estudios Centroamericanos (San Salvador)

Los Tiempos (Cochabamba)

United Nations Chronicle (New York)

El Universal (Caracas)

Veja (São Paulo)

The Wall Street Journal (New York)

Washington Post

Washington Times

BOOKS AND JOURNAL ARTICLES

Abraham, Henry. *The Judicial Process*, 6th ed. New York: Oxford University Press, 1993.

Ackerman, Bruce. *We the People: Foundations*. Cambridge, Mass.: Harvard University Press, 1991.

Agency for International Development. *El Salvador: Revision of Laws Governing International Trade and Investment*. Washington, D.C.: Nathan Associations/USAID, 1990.

———. *Final Report: Judicial Reform Project I*. Washington, D.C.: USAID/Checchi and Company, 1994.

———. *Peru: Administration of Justice*. Washington, D.C.: USAID, 1987.

———. *Strengthening Democratic Institutions in Uruguay and Argentina*. Washington, D.C.: USAID, 1994.

———. *USAID Argentina and Uruguay Closeout Report*. Washington, D.C.: USAID, 1995.

Agüero, Felipe, and Jeffrey Stark, eds. *Fault Lines of Democracy in Post-Transition Latin America*. Miami, Fla.: North-South Center Press, 1998.

Aizcorbe, Roberto. *La Crisis Argentina*. Buenos Aires: Occitania, 1984.

Alaminos, Antonio. *Chile: transición política y sociedad*. Madrid: Siglo XXI, 1991.

Alfonsín, Raúl Ricardo. "The Function of the Judicial Power During the Transition." In *Transition to Democracy in Latin America: The Role of the Judiciary*, ed. Irwin P. Stozky. Boulder, Colo.: Westview Press, 1994: 41-54.

———. "Never Again in Argentina." *Journal of Democracy* 4 (January 1993): 15-19.

Alvarez, Gladys Stella. "Alternative Dispute Resolution Mechanisms: Lessons of the Argentine Experience." In *Judicial Reform in Latin America and the Caribbean*, eds. Malcolm Rowat, Waleed H. Malik, and Maria Dakolias. Washington, D.C.: The World Bank, 1995: 78-91.

Amadeo, Santos. *Argentine Constitutional Law*. New York: Columbia University Press, 1943.

Americas Watch. *El Salvador's Decade of Terror*. New Haven, Conn.: Yale University Press, 1991.

Anderson, Charles W. "Toward a Theory of Latin American Politics." In *Politics and Social Change in Latin America: The Distinct Tradition*, ed. Howard J. Wiarda. Amherst: University of Massachusetts Press, 1982.

Anderson, James, David Brady, and Charles Bullock III. *Public Policy and Politics in America*. North Scituate, Mass.: Duxbury Press, 1978.

Angell, Alan, and Susan Carstairs. "The exile question in Chilean politics." *Third World Quarterly* 9 (January 1987): 148-67.

Armstrong, Janet, and Robert Shenk. *El Salvador: The Face of Revolution*. Boston: South End Press, 1982.

Arriagada, Germán Hermosilla. "Training and Continuing Education for Judges." In *Justice and Development in Latin America and the Caribbean*. Washington, D.C.: InterAmerican Development Bank, 1993.

Asociação de Magistrados Brasileiros. *Justiça: Promessa e Realidade*. Rio de Janeiro: Editora Nova Fronteira, 1995.

Baaklini, Abdo. *The Brazilian Legislature and the Political System*. Westport, Conn.: Greenwood Press, 1992.

Baloyra, Enrique. *Confronting Revolution*. Chapel Hill: University of North Carolina Press, 1982.

Barreto, Drausio. *Justiça para todos*. São Paulo: Editora Angelotti, 1994.

Beer, Samuel H. *To Make a Nation*. Cambridge, Mass.: Harvard University Press, 1993.

Benavides, Maria-Victoria, and Rosa-Maria Fischer Ferriera. "Popular Responses and Urban Violence: Lynching in Brazil." In *Vigilantism and the State in Modern Brazil*, ed. Martha K. Huggins. New York: Praeger, 1991: 21-32.

Bersier, Roland. "Legal Instruments of Repression in Chile." *Review of the International Commission of Jurists* 34. June 1985: 54-60.

Bickford, Louis. "Democracy, Stakeholdership, and Public Policymaking in Chile, 1990-1997: The Case of Judicial Reform." Paper Presented to the XXII International Congress of the Latin American Studies Association. 22-26 September 1998.

Bielsa, Rafael, and Eduardo Grana. *Justicia y Estado*. Buenos Aires: Ediciones Ciudad Argentina, 1996.

Bielsa, Rafael, and Marcelo Perazolo. "Alrededor de la informática, al eficiencia y la reforma del servicio de justicia." *Jurismatica* 5/6 (Fall 1994): 43-67.

Biles, Robert E. "The Position of the Judiciary in the Political Systems of Argentina and Mexico." *Lawyer of the Americas* 8 (Summer 1976): 287-318.

Bin, Rachel Marie. "Drug Lords and the Colombian Judiciary: A Story of Threats, Bribes, and Bullets." *UCLA Pacific Law Journal* 5 (Spring-Fall 1986): 178-82.

Binder, Alberto. *Reform of the Penal System in Latin America*. Arlington, Va.: National Center of State Courts, 1991.

Blair, Harry. *A Strategic Assessment of Legal Systems Development in Uruguay and Argentina*. Washington, D.C.: U.S. Agency for International Development, 1994.

Borge, Tomás. *Los primeros pasos: la revolución popular sandinista*. Mexico: Siglo Veinteuno, 1981.

Bouchey, L. Francis, Roger Fontaine, David C. Jordan, and Gordon Sumner. *Santa Fe II: A Strategy for Latin America in the Nineties*. Washington, D.C.: Council for InterAmerican Security, 1990.

Branes, Raúl. "Access to Justice in Chile." In *Access to Justice: A Worldwide Survey*, vol. 1, ed. Mauro Cappelletti and Bryant Garth. Milan: Pott A. Giuffre Editore, 1978: 345-70.

Burki, Shahid Javed. "Economic Development and Judicial Reform." In *Judicial Reform in Latin America and the Caribbean*, ed. Malcolm Rowat, Waleed H. Malik, and Maria Dakolias. Washington, D.C.: The World Bank, 1995.

Buscaglia, Edgardo. "Legal and Economic Development: The Missing Links." *Journal of Inter-American Studies and World Affairs* 35 (Winter 1993-94): 153-69.

Buscaglia, Edgardo, and Maria Dakolias. *Judicial Reform in Latin America*. Washington, D.C.: The World Bank, 1996.

——. *Judicial Reform in Latin America: Economic Efficiency vs. Institutional Inertia*. Washington, D.C.: Georgetown University School of Business Administration, 1995.

Buscaglia, Edgardo, Maria Dakolias, and William Ratliff. *Judicial Reform in Latin America: A Framework for National Development*. Stanford, Calif.: Hoover Institution, 1995.

Buscaglia, Edgardo, and Pilar Domingo. "The Impediments to Judicial Reform in Latin America." Paper Presented at the XIX International Congress of the Latin American Studies Association. 28-30 September 1995.

Buscaglia, Edgardo, and José Luis Guerrero-Cosumano. *Quality Control Approach to the Understanding of Court Delays*. Washington, D.C.: Georgetown University School of Business Administration, 1995.

Buscaglia, Edgardo, and Thomas Ulen. "A Quantitative Analysis of the Judicial Sectors in Latin America." Paper Presented at the Annual Meeting of the American Law and Economics Association. 11-13 May 1995.

Calderón, Raúl Angel. "La realidad del órgano judicial." *Presencia* 1 (April-June 1988): 161-62.

Cannon, Lou. *President Reagan: The Role of a Lifetime*. New York: Simon and Schuster, 1991.

Cappelletti, Mauro. "Alternative Dispute Resolution Processes within the Framework of the Worldwide Access-to-Justice Movement." *Modern Law Review* 56 (May 1993): 282–85.

———. *The Judicial Process in Comparative Perspective.* Oxford: Clarendon Press, 1989.

———. "Who Watches the Watchmen? A Comparative Study on Judicial Responsibility." *American Journal of Comparative Law* 31 (Winter 1983): 17–63.

Carballo de Cilley, Marita. *¿Que pensamos los argentinos?* Buenos Aires: El Cronista América, 1987.

Cardoso, Fernando Henrique. *Mãos A Obra, Brasil: Proposta de Governo.* Brasilia: N.p., 1994.

Cardozo, Benjamin. *The Nature of the Judicial Process.* New Haven, Conn.: Yale University Press, 1921.

Carjuzaa, Cristina M.L. "Desarrollo y proyectos del sistema de jurisprudencia de la Corte Suprema de Justicia de la Nación." *Jurismatica* 3 (April 1993): 25–34.

Carl, Beverley May. "Erosion of Constitutional Rights in Brazil." *The Virginia Journal of International Law* 12 (March 1972): 157–91.

Carr, Barry, and Steve Ellner, eds. *The Latin American Left.* Boulder, Colo.: Westview Press, 1993.

Carrio, Alejandro. *La Corte Suprema y su independencia.* Buenos Aires: Abeledo Perrot, 1993.

Carvajal A., Santiago. "Descripción y análisis de la situación de los derechos humanos en las zonas rurales indígenas de Chile." In *Derechos humanos y servicios legales en el campo,* ed. Diego Garcia-Sayan. Lima: Comisión de Juristas Andinas, 1987: 181–200.

Casanova, Pablo González. *La democracia en Mexico.* Mexico: Ediciones Era, 1974.

Castañeda, Jorge. *Utopia Unarmed.* New York: Vintage Books, 1993.

Catterberg, Edgardo. *Los argentinos frente a la política.* Buenos Aires: Grupo Editorial Planeta, 1985.

Cavalcanti, Amaro. "The Federal Judiciary in Brazil and the United States of America." *University of Pennsylvania Law Review and American Law Register* (October 1911): 103–22.

Cavallo, Domingo. *El peso de la verdad.* Buenos Aires: Planeta Espejo de la Argentina, 1997.

Cavarozzi, Marcelo, and Maria Gross. "Argentine Politics Under Alfonsín: From Democratic Reinvention to Political Decline and Hyperinflation." *The New Argentine Democracy,* ed. Edward C. Epstein. Westport, Conn.: Praeger Publishers, 1992.

Cea, José Luis. "Chile's Difficult Return to Constitutional Democracy." *Political Science* 20 (Summer 1987): 665–73.

Ceaser, James W. *Liberal Democracy and Political Science.* Baltimore, Md.: Johns Hopkins University Press, 1990.

Centro de Estudios Públicos. *Estudio social y de opinión pública en la población de Santiago.* Santiago: Centro de Estudios Públicos, 1987.

———. *Proposiciones para la reforma judicial,* ed. Eugenio Valenzuela S. Santiago: Centro de Estudios Públicos, 1991.

Cerda, Carlos. *Duración del procedimiento sumario en los juzgados de Santiago.* Santiago: FONDEYCT, 1993.

Chalmers, Douglas A., Maria do Carmen Campello de Souza, and Atilio Boron, eds. *The Right and Democracy in Latin America.* Westport, Conn.: Praeger, 1992.

Checchi and Company. *Analyses and Recommendations for Components One and Two for USAID Judicial Reform II in El Salvador.* Washington, D.C.: Checchi and Company, 1992.

———. *Final Report: Evaluation of the Harvard Law School Program: Guatemala.* Washington, D.C.: Checchi and Company, 1989.

Chinchilla, Laura, and David Stodt. *The Administration of Justice in Ecuador.* Miami: Florida International University, 1993.

Clagett, Helen. *The Administration of Justice in Latin America.* New York: Oceana Publications, 1952.

Cohen, Bernard. "The Salvadoran Criminal Justice System." *International Journal of Comparative and Applied Criminal Justice* 14 (Winter 1990): 1–17.

Cohen, Jerome. "The Chinese Communist Party and Judicial Independence." *Harvard Law Review* 82 (1969): 960–82.

Corporación de Asistencia Judicial de la Región Metropolitana. *Corporación de Asistencia Judicial de la Región Metropolitana, 1995.* Santiago: Corporación de Asistencia Judicial de la Región Metropolitana, 1996.

Corporación de Promoción Universitaria. *Seminario: Justicia y Marginalidad Rural.* Santiago: Corporación de Promoción Universitaria, 1994.

Correa Sutil, Jorge. "The Judiciary and the Political System in Chile." In *Transition to Democracy in Latin America: The Role of the Judiciary,* ed. Irwin P. Stotzky. Boulder, Colo.: Westview Press, 1993.

———. *Justicia y Marginalidad: Percepciones de los Pobres.* Santiago: Corporación de Promoción Universitaria, 1993.

Dakolias, Maria. *Judicial Reform: Elements of Reform in Latin America and the Caribbean.* Washington, D.C.: The World Bank, 1996.

Dalla Via, Alberto Ricardo. *Transformación Económica y Seguridad Jurídica.* Buenos Aires: Libreria Editora Platense SRL, 1994.

Dealy, Glenn C. *The Public Man: An Interpretation of Latin America and Other Catholic Countries.* Amherst: University of Massachusetts Press, 1977.

Delgado, Maurico Godinho. *Democracia e justiça.* São Paulo: Editora Ltr., 1993.

De Madariagada, Salvador. *The Fall of the Spanish American Empire.* New York: The Macmillan Company, 1948.

De Soto, Hernando. "La protección del derecho de propriedad y la sociedad civil." In *La economia política de la reforma judicial,* ed. Edmundo Jarquín and Fernando Carrillo. Washington, D.C.: Banco Interamericano de Desarrollo, 1997.

———. *The Other Path.* New York: Harper and Row, 1989.

De Tocqueville, Alexis. *Democracy in America,* ed. J. P. Mayer. New York: Harper and Row, 1966.

DeWind, Adrian W., and Stephen L. Kass. "Justice in El Salvador: A Report of a Mission of Inquiry of the Association of the Bar of the City of New York." *The Record of the Association of the Bar of the City of New York* 38 (March 1983): 110–43.

Diamond, Larry. "Democracy in Latin America." In *Beyond Sovereignty,* ed. Tom Farer. Baltimore, Md.: Johns Hopkins University Press, 1996.

Dimenstein, Gilberto. *O Cômplo que Elegeu Tancredo.* Rio de Janeiro: JB, 1985.

Diskin, Martin, and Kenneth Sharpe. "El Salvador." In *Confronting Revolution,* ed. Morris Blachman, William Leogrande, and Kenneth Sharpe. New York: Pantheon Press, 1986: 51–87.

Dollinger, Jacob. "The Influence of American Constitutional Law on the Brazilian Legal System." *The American Journal of Comparative Law* 38 (Fall 1990): 803–37.

Duarte, José Napoleón. *My Story.* New York: Putnam and Sons, 1986.

Dulles, John W. F. *President Castello Branco: Brazilian Reformer.* Austin: University of Texas Press, 1980.

Ebener, Patricia. *Court Efforts to Reduce Pretrial Delays in the Los Angeles Superior Court.* Santa Monica, Calif.: Rand Corporation/Institute for Civil Justice, 1981.

Eder, Phanor J. "Judicial Review in Latin America." *Ohio State Law Journal* 21 (Fall 1960): 561–84.

Ely, John Hart. *Democracy and Distrust: A Theory of Judicial Reform*. Cambridge, Mass.: Harvard University Press, 1980.

Ensalaco, Mark, "In with the New, Out with the Old? The Democratising Impact of Constitutional Reform in Chile." *Journal of Latin American Studies* 26 (May 1994): 402–29.

Evans, Peter. *Embedded Autonomy*. Princeton, N.J.: Princeton University Press, 1995.

Fairbanks, Michael, and Stace Lindsay. *Ploughing the Sea*. Cambridge, Mass.: Harvard Business School Press, 1996.

Faoro, Raimundo. "Constituente: a verdade e o sofismo." In *Constituente e Democracia no Brazil Hoje*, ed. Emir Sader. São Paulo: Brasiliense, 1986.

Faro de Castro, Marcus. "Política e economía no judiciário: as açoes direitas de inconstituicionalidade dos partidos politicos." *Caderno de Ciência Política* 7 (May 1993): 1–26.

Figueiredo, Odail. "Verdades e mitos sobre a cultura brasileira." In *Ouvindo O Brasil*, ed. Bolívar Lamounier. São Paulo: Editora Sumare, 1992.

Fiss, Owen. "The Right Degree of Independence." In *Transition to Democracy in Latin America: The Role of the Judiciary*, ed. Irwin P. Stotzky. Boulder, Colo.: Westview Press, 1994.

Fitch, J. Samuel. *The Armed Forces and Democracy in Latin America*. Baltimore, Md.: Johns Hopkins University Press, 1998.

Fitzgibbon, Russell, and Julio Fernandez. *Latin America: Political Culture and Development*. Englewood Cliffs, N.J.: Prentice-Hall 1981.

Flanders, Steven. "Court administration in Colombia: an American visitor's perspective." *Judicature* 71 (June–July 1987): 36–39.

Fox, Jonathan. "The Difficult Transition from Clientelism to Citizenship." *World Politics* 46 (February 1994): 170–97.

———. "Latin America's Emerging Local Politics." *Journal of Democracy* 5 (Fall 1994): 105–16.

Fricker, Richard L. "A Judiciary Under Fire." *ABA Journal* (February 1990): 54–59.

Fruhling, Hügo. *Derechos humanos y democracia: la contribución de las organizaciones no gobermentales*. Santiago: Instituto Inter-Americano de Derechos Humanos, 1991.

———. "Repressive Policies and Legal Dissent in Authoritarian Regimes: Chile, 1973–81." *International Journal of Sociology and Law*. Fall 1984: 338–61.

Galleguidos, Nibaldo. "Checks and Balances in New Democracies: The Role of the Judiciaries in the Chilean and Mexican Transitions: A Comparative Analysis." Paper Presented at the XXI Meeting of the Latin American Studies Association. 17–19 April 1997.

Galleher, Watson. "State Repression's Façade of Legality: The Military Courts in Chile." *Temple International and Comparative Law Journal* 2 (Fall 1988): 183–98.

Geddes, Barbara. *Politician's Dilemma*. Berkeley: University of California Press, 1994.

Golbert, Albert, and Yenny Nun. *Latin American Laws and Institutions*. New York: Praeger, 1982.

Goldstein, Joseph. "The Opinion-Writing Function of the Judiciary in Latin American Governments in Transitions to Democracy: Martinez v. Provincia de Mendoza." In *Transition to Democracy in Latin America: The Role of the Juciciary*, ed. Irwin P. Stotzky. Boulder, Colo.: Westview Press, 1994.

González, Carlos Peña. "Los abogados y la administración de justicia." In *Proposiciones para la reforma judicial*, ed. Eugenio Valenzuela S. Santiago: Centro de Estudios Públicos, 1990.

Gonzalez, Mirtha Ulloa, and Macarena Vargas Pavez. "Políticas públicas y necesidades de justicia de los sectores pobres." *Estudios Sociales* 83 (1995): 51–97.

Grindle, Merilee S. *Bureaucrats, Politicians, and Peasants in Mexico: A Case Study in Public Policy.* Berkeley: University of California Press, 1977.

———. *Politics and Policy Implementation in the Third World.* Princeton, N.J.: Princeton University Press, 1988.

Groviner, Ada Pelligrini. "Deformalising Procedure in Brazil." *Civil Justice Quarterly* 7 (1988): 234–52.

Grugel, Jean. "Transitions from Authoritarian Rule: Lessons from Latin America." *Political Studies* 39 (June 1991): 361–73.

Gunther, Richard P., Nikiforos Diamondouros, and Hans-Jürgen-Puhle. "O'Donnell's 'Illusions': A Rejoinder." *Journal of Democracy* 7 (October 1996): 144–56.

Gutierrez Castro, Mauricio. *La Independencia Judicial.* San Salvador: Talleres Gráficos, 1992.

Guzmán Vial, José. "La modernización del sistema judicial." *Mensaje* 400 (July 1991): 240–42.

———. "Reflexiones sobre el poder estatal y el poder judicial." *Estudios Sociales* 50 (1986): 71–88.

Haggard, Stephen, and Robert Kaufman. "Economic Adjustment and the Prospects for Democracy." In *The Politics of Economic Adjustment,* ed. Stephen Haggard and Robert Kaufman. Princeton, N.J.: Princeton University Press, 1992.

Hagopian, Frances. "Democracy and Political Representation in Latin America in the 1990s: Pause, Reorganization, or Decline?" In *Fault Lines of Democracy in Post-Transition Latin America,* ed. Felipe Agüero and Jeffrey Stark. Miami, Fla.: North-South Center Press, 1998.

———. "Democracy By Undemocratic Means." *Comparative Political Studies* 23 (July 1990): 147–70.

Hamilton, William. "Computer-Induced Improvements in the Administration of Justice. *Computer/Law Journal* 4 (Summer 1983): 55–76.

Hammergren, Linn A. "Corporatism in Latin American Politics: A Reexamination of the 'Unique' Tradition." *Comparative Politics* 9 (July 1977): 441–64.

———. *The Politics of Justice and Justice Sector Reform in Latin America.* Boulder, Colo.: Westview Press, 1998.

Hand, Learned. *The Bill of Rights.* Cambridge, Mass.: Harvard University Press, 1958.

Hansen, Gary, William Millsap, Ralph Smith, and Mary Staples Said. *A Strategic Assessment of Legal System Development in Honduras.* Washington, D.C.: Agency for International Development, 1993.

Hayes, Michael T. *Incrementalism and Public Policy.* New York: Longman Publishing Group, 1992.

Hilbink, Lisa. "What is the Role of the Judiciary in a Democracy? The Judicial Reform Debate in Chile and Proposals for Future Research." Paper Presented to the XIX International Congress of the Latin American Studies Association. 28–30 September 1995.

Hojmon, Eugenio. *Memorial de la dictadura.* Santiago: Emisión, 1989.

Holston, James, and Teresa P. R. Caldeira, "Democracy, Law, and Violence: Disjunctions of Brazilian Citizenship." In *Fault Lines of Democracy in Post-Transition Latin America,* ed. Felipe Agüero and Jeffrey Stark. Miami, Fla.: North-South Center Press, 1998.

Holzer, Marc, and Kathe Callah. *Government at Work.* Thousand Oaks, Calif.: Sage Publishers, 1998.

Howell, Katrina. "Politicized Justice? Judicial Review in Democratizing Brazil." Paper Presented to the XIX International Congress of the Latin American Studies Association. 28–30 September 1995.

Hughes, Steven W., and Kenneth Mijelski. *Politics and Public Policy in Latin America*. Boulder, Colo.: Westview Press, 1988.

Human Rights Watch. *Chile: Unsettled Business: Human Rights at the Start of the Frei Presidency*. New York: Human Rights Watch/Americas Watch, 1994.

———. *Paraguay: An Encouraging Victory in the Search for Truth and Justice*. New York: Human Rights Watch/Americas Watch, 1992.

———. *Police Brutality in Urban Brazil*. New York: Human Rights Watch/Americas Watch, 1997.

Hunter, Wendy. *Eroding Military Influence in Brazil: Politicians Against Soldiers*. Chapel Hill: University of North Carolina Press, 1997.

Huntington, Samuel P. "The Goals of Development." In *Understanding Political Development*, ed. Samuel P. Huntington and Myron Weiner. Boston: Little, Brown, and Co., 1987: 1–32.

Illanes Benitez, Osvaldo. "The Supreme Court of Justice in Chile." *Journal of the International Commission of Jurists* 2 (Winter 1966): 269–77.

Instituto Gallup. *Estudio de Opinión Acerca de la Administración de Justicia*. Buenos Aires: CEJURA, 1994.

Instituto SER. *Reforma de la administracion de justicia*. Bogota: Instituto SER, 1987.

International Commission of Jurists. *Chile: A Time of Reckoning*. Geneva: International Commission of Jurists, 1992.

Irizarry y Puente, J. "The Nature and Powers of a De Facto Government in Latin America." *Tulane Law Review* 30 (December 1955): 25–72.

Jackson, Donald, and J. Michael Dodson. "Protegiendo los derechos humanos: la legitimidad de las reformas del Sistema Judicial en El Salvador." *Revista de Estudios Centroamericanos* 606 (April 1999): 319–35.

Jackson, Donald, and C. Neal Tate, eds. *Comparative Judicial Review and Public Policy*. Westport, Conn.: Greenwood Press, 1992.

Jara, Eduardo. "Discurso de Clausura." In *Asistencia Legal en América Latina*, ed. Marco A. Lillo de la Cruz. Santiago: Centro de Desarrollo Jurídico, 1996: 143–47.

Jara, Umberto. "El Poder Judicial." *Debate* XVI (December 1993–January 1994): 43–45.

Jordan, David C. "Argentina's Bureaucratic Oligarchies." *Current History* (February 1972): 70–75.

———. "Argentina's Military Commonwealth." *Current History* (February 1977): 66–69.

Kakalik, James, Molly Selvin, and Nicholas Pace. *Strategies for Reducing Civil Delay in the Los Angeles Superior Court*. Santa Monica, Calif.: Rand Corporation, 1990.

Karl, Terry Lynn. "Negotiations or Total War?" *World Policy Journal* 6 (Spring 1989): 321–52.

Katz, Saul M. "A System Approach to Development Administration." In *Frontiers of Development*, ed. Fred W. Riggs. Durham, N.C.: Duke University Press, 1970: 109–38.

Keck, Margaret, and Kathryn Sikkink. *Activist Beyond Borders: Advocacy Networks in International Politics*. Ithaca, N.Y.: Cornell University Press, 1998.

Kinzo, Maria D'Avila G. *Legal Opposition Politics Under Authoritarian Rule in Brazil*. New York: St. Martin's Press, 1988.

Lacefield, Patrick. "The Generals Don't Repent." *Commonweal* 3 (January 1989): 583–84.

Larkins, Christopher. "The Judiciary and Delegative Democracy in Latin America." *Comparative Politics* 30 (April 1998): 423–41.

Lavados, Ivan, and Juan Enrique Vargas. "La Gestión Judicial." *Estudios Sociales* 78 (1993): 203–25.

Laver, Ross. "Beginning anew in Brazil." *Maclean's* 21 (January 1985): 24–26.

Lawyers Committee for International Human Rights. *From the Ashes: A Report on Justice in El Salvador.* New York: Lawyers Committee for Human Rights, 1987.
——. *The Jesuit Case A Year Later: An Interim Report.* New York: Lawyers Committee for International Human Rights, 1990.
——. *Justice Denied.* New York: Lawyers Committee for Human Rights, 1985.
Layton, Robert. "Changing Attitudes Toward Dispute Resolution in Latin America." *Journal of International Arbitration* 10 (January 1993): 123–41.
Leonhard, Alan T. "Constitutionalism and the Argentine Judiciary." *InterAmerican Law Review* 8 (January–December 1966): 245–56.
Lewis, Paul H. *The Crisis of Argentine Capitalism.* Chapel Hill: University of North Carolina Press, 1988.
——. *Paraguay Under Stroessner.* Chapel Hill: University of North Carolina Press, 1980.
Lindblom, Charles E. *The Intelligence of Democracy: Decision-making Through Mutual Adjustment.* New York: Free Press, 1965.
——. *The Policy-making Process,* 2nd ed. Englewood Cliffs, N.J.: Prentice-Hall, 1980.
——. "The Science of Muddling Through." *Public Administration Review* 19 (Spring 1959): 79–88.
Linz, Juan. "Legitimacy of democracy and the socioeconomic system." In *Comparing Pluralist Democracies,* ed. Mattei Dogan. Boulder, Colo.: Westview Press, 1988.
Loveman, Brian. "¿Misión Cumplida? Civil-Military Relations and the Chilean Political Transition." *Journal of InterAmerican Studies and World Affairs* 33 (Fall 1991): 35–63.
Lowenstein, Steven. *Lawyers, Legal Education, and Development: An Examination of the Process of Reform in Chile.* New York: International Legal Center, 1970.
Luna, Felix. *Argentina: de Perón a Lanusse.* Buenos Aires: Sudamericana/Planeta, 1984.
Lynch, John. "Lawyers in Colombia: Perspectives on the Organization and the Allocation of Legal Services." *Texas International Law Journal* (Fall 1978): 190–210.
Maclean, Roberto. "Efectos de la administración de justicia en la propriedad." In *La economía política de la reforma judicial,* ed. Edmundo Jarquín and Fernando Carrillo. Washington, D.C.: Banco Interamericano de Desarrollo, 1997.
Madison, James, Alexander Hamilton, and John Jay. *The Federalist Papers.* New York: NAL Penguin, 1961.
Maher, James P. "How to Integrate a Criminal Justice System." *LAW/Technology* 23 (1990): 1–18.
Mainwaring, Scott. "Brazilian Party Underdevelopment in Comparative Perspective." *Political Science Quarterly* 107 (Winter 1992–93): 677–707.
——. "Political Parties and Democratization in Brazil and the Southern Cone." *Comparative Politics* 21 (October 1988): 91–119.
——. "Presidentialism, Multipartism, and Democracy." *Comparative Political Studies* 26 (1993): 196–228.
Mainwaring, Scott, and Timothy R. Scully, eds. *Building Democratic Institutions: Party Systems in Latin America.* Stanford, Calif.: Stanford University Press, 1997.
Mainwaring, Scott, and Matthew Soberg Shugart. *Presidentialism and Democracy in Latin America.* Cambridge, Mass.: Cambridge University Press, 1997.
Malamud-Goti, Jaime. *Game Without End: State Terror and the Politics of Justice.* Norman: University of Oklahoma Press, 1996.
——. "Human Rights Abuses in Fledgling Democracies: The Role of Discretion." In *Transition to Democracy in Latin America: The Role of the Juciciary,* ed. Irwin P. Stotzky. Boulder, Colo.: Westview Press, 1994: 221–47.

Mansfield, Edward. *Intellectual Property Rights, Foreign Direct Investment, and Technology Transfer.* Washington, D.C.: The World Bank, 1994.

Martin-Baró, Ignacio, and Arely Hernández. *La opinión pública Salvadoreña, 1987–88.* San Salvador: UCA Editores, 1989.

Martinez-Lara, Javier. *Building Democracy in Brazil.* London: Macmillan Press, 1996.

Mason, Paul E. "The Benefits of Arbitration and Mediation for North-South Business Transactions." *Latin American Law and Business Report* 5 (May 1996): 1–3.

Mendes, João Batista Peteren. *A CPI do PC e Os Crimes do Poder.* Rio de Janeiro: Foglia Editora, 1992.

Menges, Constantine C. *Inside the National Security Council.* New York: Touchstone/Simon and Schuster, 1988.

Ministério de Justicia. *Acceso a la Justicia: Programa de Asistencia Jurídica.* Santiago: Ministério de Justicia, 1997.

Miranda, Roger, and William Ratliff. *The Civil War in Nicaragua.* New Brunswick, N.J.: Transaction Publishers, 1993.

Moñiz de Aragão, E. D. "The Brazilian Judicial Organization." *Revista Jurídica Interamericana* 6 (July–December 1964): 251–79.

Montgomery, Tommie Sue. *Revolution in El Salvador,* 2nd ed. Boulder Colo.: Westview Press, 1995.

———. "The United Nations and Peacemaking in El Salvador." *North-South Issues* 4 (1995): 1–5.

Montoro Filho, Andres Franco. "O federalismo e reforma fiscal." *Revista de Economía Política* 14 (July–September 1994): 20–30.

Mooney, Joseph P. "Was It a WORSENING of Economic and Social Conditions That Brought Violence and Civil War to El Salvador?" *InterAmerican Economic Affairs* 38 (Autumn 1984): 61–69.

Moreira Leite, Paulo. "Entrevista com Alberto Fujimori: O Poder Sou Eu." *Veja,* 23 June 1993.

Mosse, Robert, and Leigh Ellen Sontheimer. *Performance Monitoring Indicators Handbook.* Washington, D.C.: The World Bank, 1996.

Mudge, Arthur, Robert Ewigleben, and Robert Page. *Project Evaluation of the Administration of Justice Project in Peru.* Washington, D.C.: Checchi and Co./U.S. Agency for International Development, 1990.

Mudge, Arthur, Steve Flanders, Miguel Sanchez, Adolfo Saenz, and Gilberto Trujillo. *Evaluation of the Judicial Reform Project.* Washington, D.C.: U.S. Agency for International Development, 1988.

Munck, Gerardo. "Democratic Stability and Its Limits: Analysis of Chile's 1993 Elections." *Journal of Interamerican Studies and World Affairs* 36 (Summer 1994): 1–35.

Nagel, Robert. *Constitutional Cultures: The Mentality and Consequences of Judicial Review.* Berkeley: University of California Press, 1989.

Needler, Martin. *Political Development in Latin America.* New York: Random House, 1968.

Nelson, Laura Sue. "The Defense of Honor: Is It Still Honored in Brazil?" *Wisconsin Journal of International Law* 11 (Spring 1993): 531–56.

Neri da Silveira, José. "Aspectos institucionais e estructurais do Poder Judiciário brasileiro." In *O Judiciário e a Constituição,* ed. Salvio de Figueiredo. São Paulo: Editora Saraiva, 1992: 1–22.

Nikken, Pedro. "Human Rights Accountability and Reform of the Police, Military, and Judiciary." In *El Salvador: Sustaining Peace, Nourishing Democracy,* ed. Gary Bland. Washington, D.C.: The Woodrow Wilson Center, 1993.

Niño, Carlos S. "On the Exercise of Judicial Review in Argentina." In *Transition to Democracy in Latin America*, ed. Irwin P. Stotzky. Boulder, Colo.: Westview Press, 1994.

Nogueira A., Humberto. *El poder judicial chileno: su crisis actual y vías alternativas de solución*. Santiago: Instituto Chileno de Estudios Humanos, 1987.

North, Douglass, and Robert Paul Thomas. *The Rise of the Western World*. London: Cambridge Press, 1973.

Novoa, Eduardo. "¿Justicia de clases?" *Mensaje* 187 (March–April 1970): 121–27.

O'Brien, David M., and Yasuo Ohkoshi. "Stifling Judicial Independence from Within: The Japanese Judiciary." Paper Presented at the 1996 Interim Meeting of the Research Committee on Comparative Judicial Studies of the International Political Science Association. 1–4 July 1996.

O'Donnell, Guillermo. "Delegative Democracy." *Journal of Democracy* 5 (January 1994): 55–69.

———. "Do Economists Know Best?" *Journal of Democracy* 6 (January 1995): 24–31.

———. "Illusions About Consolidation." *Journal of Democracy* 7 (April 1996): 36–44.

———. *On the State, Democratization, and Some Conceptual Problems: A Latin American View with Glances at Some Post-Communist Countries*. Notre Dame, Ind.: Helen Kellogg Institute for International Studies, 1993.

———. "Transitions, Continuities, and Paradoxes." In *Issues in Democratic Consolidation*, ed. Scott Mainwaring, Guillermo O'Donnell, and J. Samuel Valenzuela. Notre Dame, Ind.: University of Notre Dame Press, 1992.

O'Keefe, Thomas Andrew. "The Use of the Military Justice System to Try Civilians in Chile." *New York State Bar Journal* 61 (November 1989): 43–47.

Olivera, Raúl Israel, and Manuel J. Israel Olivera. *Corrupción en el Poder Judicial y el Ministério Público*. Lima: Editorial San Marcos, 1985.

O'Malley, Anthony Holland. "Chile's Constitution, Chile's Congress: Prospects for Judicial, Legal, and Constitutional Reform." *Canadian Journal of Latin American and Caribbean Studies* 15 (1990): 85–111.

O'Reilly, Gregory W. "Opening Up Argentina's Courts." *Judicature* 80 (March–April 1997): 237–41.

Osiel, Mark J. "Dialogue with Dictators: Judicial Resistance in Argentina and Brazil." *Law and Social Inquiry* 20 (Spring 1995): 521–63.

Oteiza, Eduardo. *La Corte Suprema: Entre la justicia sin política y la política sin justicia*. La Plata: Libreria Editora Platense, 1994.

Pahl, Michael. "Concealing Justices or Concealing Injustices?: Colombia's Secret Courts." *Denver Journal of International Law and Policy* 21. (Winter 1993): 421–43.

———. "Wanted: Criminal Justice—Colombia's Adoption of a Prosecutorial System of Criminal Procedure." *Fordham International Law Journal* 16 (1992–93).

Pang, Eul-Soo. "The Darker Side of Brazilian Democracy." *Current History* 87 (January 1988): 21–24.

Panish, Neil. "Chile Under Allende: The Decline of the Judiciary and the Rise of A State of Necessity." *Loyola of Los Angeles International and Comparative Law Journal* 9 (Summer 1987): 693–709.

Pásara, Luis. *Jueces, justicia, y poder en Peru*. Lima: CEDYS, 1980.

Perdomo, Rogelio Perez. "Justice in Times of Globalization: Challenges and Perspectives for Change in the Administration of Justice in Latin America." In *Justice and Development in Latin America and the Caribbean*. Washington, D.C.: InterAmerican Development Bank, 1993.

Pereira, Fernando. "Decompression in Brazil?" *Foreign Affairs* 53 (April 1975): 498–512.

Pereznieto Castro, Leonel. "La reforma judicial." *Examen* (January 1995): 13-19.

Philipsborn, John. "After the election: Nicaragua discusses reform of its judicial system." *Judicature* 74 (August–September 1990): 102-4.

———. "Nicaragua: a legal system developing in difficult times." *Judicature* 71 (December–January 1988): 43-47.

Popkin, Margaret. *El Salvador's Negotiated Revolution: Prospects for Legal Reform*. New York: Lawyers Committee for Human Rights, 1993.

———. "Judicial Reform in El Salvador: Missed Opportunities." Paper Presented at the XXIV Latin American Studies Association. 28-30 September 1995.

Popkin, Margaret, Jack Spence, and George Vickers. *Justice Delayed: The Slow Pace of Judicial Reform in El Salvador*. Washington, D.C.: Washington Office on Latin America, 1994.

Posner, Michael, and R. Scott Bankhead. "Justice in El Salvador: A Report by the Lawyers Committee for International Human Rights on the Investigation Into the Killing of Four U.S. Churchwomen." *Columbia Human Rights Law Review* 14 (Fall–Winter 1982-83): 182-203.

Power, Timothy J. "The Pen is Mightier than the Congress: Presidential Decree Power in Brazil." Paper Presented to the XVIII Congress of the Latin American Studies Association. 10-12 March 1994.

———. "Politicized Democracy: Competition, Institutions, and Civic Fatigue in Brazil." *Journal of InterAmerican Studies and World Affairs* 33 (Fall 1991): 75-112.

Prada, Ricardo Hernandez. "La agonia de la justicia." In *Síntesis 95: Anuario Social, Político, y Económico de Colombia*, ed. Luis Alberto Restrepo Moreno. Bogota: Editores TM, 1995.

Prosterman, Roy. "Land Reform in Latin America: How to Have a Revolution without a Revolution." *Washington Law Review* 42 (Fall 1966): 189-211.

———. "The Unmaking of Land Reform." *The New Republic* 9 (August 1982): 21-25.

Prosterman, Roy, Jeffrey M. Reidinger, and Mary N. Temple. "Land Reform in El Salvador: The Democratic Alternative." *World Affairs* 144 (Summer 1981): 36-64.

Przeworski, Adam. *Democracy and the Market: Political and Economic Reforms in Eastern Europe and Latin America*. Cambridge: Cambridge University Press, 1991.

Quinn, Robert J. "Will the Rule of Law End? Challenging Grants of Amnesty for the Human Rights Violations of a Prior Regime: Chile's New Model." *Fordham Law Review* 62 (February 1994): 905-60.

Rabkin, Rhoda. "Redemocratization, Electoral Engineering, and Party Strategies in Chile, 1989-1995." *Comparative Political Studies* 29 (June 1996): 335-56.

Ramseyer, Mark. "The Puzzling (In)dependence of Courts: A Comparative Approach." *Journal of Legal Studies* 23 (June 1994): 721-47.

Rangel, Carlos. *El tercermundismo*. Caracas: Monte Avila Editores, 1982.

Resende Chaves, Maria Isabel de Sa Earp, Katia Maria de Souza Fialho, and Cecelia Maria Martins Antunes. "Juizado de pequenas causas: estudo comparativo entre Brasil, Inglaterra, Australia, EUA, e Canada." *Revista de Ciência Política* 33 (May–June 1990): 54-78.

Reyes, Luis Manrique. "Modernization of Judicial Systems in Developing Countries: The Case of Chile." In *Judicial Reform in Latin America and the Caribbean*, ed. Malcolm Rowat, Waleed H. Malik, and Maria Dakolias. Washington, D.C.: The World Bank, 1995: 195-200.

Ribeiro Bastos, Celso. "A Constituição de 1988." In *As Constituições Brasileiras: Análise Histórica e Propostas de Mudança*. São Paulo: Editor Brasiliense, 1993.

Roett, Riordan. *Brazil: Politics in a Patrimonial Society*. New York: Praeger, 1984.

———. "Brazil's Transition to Democracy." *Current History* 88 (March 1989): 117–20.

Rogers, William. *La Corte Suprema de la Justicia y la Segúridad Jurídica.* Buenos Aires: Abeledo-Perrot, 1994.

Rosenn, Keith. "The Brazilian Constitution After Seven Years." Paper Presented to the XXXII Conference of the Inter-American Bar Association. 12–17 November 1995.

———. "Brazil's Legal Culture: The Jeito Revisited." *Florida International Law Journal* 1 (Fall 1984): 1–23.

———. "Brazil's New Constitution: An Exercise in Transient Constitutionalism for a Transitional Society." *The American Journal of Comparative Law* 38 (Fall 1990).

———. "Civil Procedure in Brazil." *The American Journal of Comparative Law* 34 (1986): 487–524.

———. "A Comparison of the Protection of Individual Rights in the New Constitutions of Colombia and Brazil." *University of Miami Inter-American Law Review* 23 (Spring–Summer 1992).

Rosett, Claudia. "Economic Paralysis in El Salvador." *Policy Review* 30 (Fall 1984): 44–47.

Rubio, Maurio. "Crimen y crecimiento en Colombia." In *Hacia un enfoque del desarrollo: ética, violencia, y segúridad ciudadana, encuentro y reflexión.* Washington, D.C.: Banco Interamericano de Desarrollo, 1996.

Rudolph, James D. "Government and Politics." In *Brazil: A Country Study,* ed. Richard Nyrop. Washington, D.C.: The American University, 1983.

Ruiz Tagle, Pablo. "Análisis comparado de la función judicial." *Estudios Públicos* 39 (1990): 131–62.

Saba, Roberto Pablo, and Luigi Manzetti. "Privatization in Argentina: The implications for corruption." *Crime, Law, and Social Change* 25 (1997): 342–67.

Sadek, Maria Tereza. "A crise do judiciário vista pelos juízes: resultados da pesquisa quantitativa." In *Uma Introdução ao Estudo da Justiça,* ed. Maria Tereza Sadek. São Paulo: Editora Sumare/IDESP, 1995.

———. "A organização do poder judiciário no Brasil." In *Uma Introdução ao Estudo da Justiça,* ed. Maria Tereza Sadek. São Paulo: Editora Sumare/IDESP, 1995.

Salas, Luis, and José Maria Rico. *Independencia Judicial: Replantamiento de un tema tradicional.* San José: Centro para la Administración de Justicia, 1990.

———. *La justicia penal en Honduras.* San José: Editorial Universitaria Centroamericana, 1990.

Salinas Rivera, Alejandro. "Two Examples of Battling Impunity in Chile." *Review of the International Commission of Jurists* 53 (December 1994): 13–18.

Samway, Michael. "Access to Justice: A Study of Legal Assistance: Programs for the Poor in Santiago, Chile." *Duke Journal of Comparative and International Law* 6 (Summer 1996): 347–69.

Sancinetti, Marcelo. *Assessment of the Performance of CORELESAL.* Washington, D.C.: U.S. Agency for International Development, 1990.

Sarmientos Sosa, Carmen J. "Judicial Corruption and the Administration of Justice: A Comparative International Perspective." Paper Presented to the XXXIII Conference of the InterAmerican Bar Association. 9 August 1995.

Schmitter, Philippe. *Interest Conflict and Political Change in Brazil.* Stanford, Calif.: Stanford University Press, 1971.

Schneider, Ben Ross. *Politics within the State: Elite Bureaucrats and Industrial Policy in Authoritarian Brazil.* Pittsburgh, Pa.: University of Pittsburgh Press, 1991.

Schneider, Ronald. "Brazil's Political Future." In *Political Liberalization in Brazil,* ed. Wayne Selcher. Boulder, Colo.: Westview Press, 1986.

——. *Order and Progress: A Political History of Brazil.* Boulder, Colo.: Westview Press, 1991.

Sherwood, Robert, Geoffrey Shepherd, and Celso Marcos de Souza. "Judicial Systems and Economic Performance." *Quarterly Review of Economics and Finance* 34 (Summer 1994): 101–16.

Shetreet, Shimon. "Judicial Independence: New Conceptual Dimensions and Contemporary Challenges." In *Judicial Independence: The Contemporary Debate*, ed. Shimon Shetreet. Boston: Dorderecht, 1985.

Shirley, Robert. "A Brief Survey of Law in Brazil." *Canadian Journal of Latin American and Caribbean Studies* 23 (1987): 1–14.

Sieder, Rachel, and Patrick Costello. "Judicial Reform in Central America: Prospects for the Rule of Law." In *Central America: Fragile Transition*, ed. Rachel Sieder. New York: St. Martin's Press, Inc./University of London, 1996.

Sigmund, Paul. *The Overthrow of Allende and the Politics of Chile, 1970–76.* Pittsburgh, Pa.: University of Pittsburgh Press, 1977.

Sikkink, Kathryn. "Nongovernment Organizations, Democracy, and Human Rights in Latin America. In *Beyond Sovereignty*, ed. Tom Farer. Baltimore, Md.: Johns Hopkins University, 150–68.

Silva, Patricio. "Technocrats and Politics in Chile: From the Chicago Boys to the CIEPLAN Monks." *Journal of Latin American Studies* 23 (May 1991): 383–421.

Skidmore, Thomas. *The Politics of Military Rule in Brazil, 1964–85.* New York: Oxford University Press, 1988.

Sloan, John. *Public Policy in Latin America.* Pittsburgh, Pa.: University of Pittsburgh Press, 1984.

Smith, B. C. *Understanding Third World Politics.* Bloomington: Indiana University Press, 1996.

Smith, Ralph G. *Washington and El Salvador's Views on CORELESAL Priorities.* Washington, D.C.: Checchi and Company, 1990.

Snyder, Frederick, "State of Siege and Rule of Law in Argentina: The Politics and Rhetoric of Vindication." *Lawyer of the Americas* 15 (Winter 1984): 503–20.

Solis, Luis G., and Richard J. Wilson. *Political Transition and the Administration of Justice in Nicaragua.* Miami: Florida International University, 1991.

Somerset, Douglas. "The Myths of Reducing Delay." *Judges Journal* 26 (Fall 1987): 26–29.

Spell, Jefferson Rea. *Rousseau in the Spanish World Before 1833.* Austin: University of Texas Press, 1938.

Spence, Jack. "Institutionalizing Neighborhood Courts: Two Chilean Experiences." *Law and Society* 13 (Fall 1978): 139–82.

——. "Strong Language Versus Political Realities: Implementing the Peace Accords in El Salvador." Paper Presented at the XXIV Latin American Studies Association. 28–30 September 1995.

Spence, Jack, and George Vickers. *A Negotiated Revolution?* Cambridge, Mass.: Hemisphere Initiatives, 1994.

Sponzo, Maurice J. "Independence vs. Accountability." *Judges' Journal* 26 (Spring 1987): 13–16, 42–43.

Steiner, Henry J. "Legal Education and Socioeconomic Change: Brazilian Perspectives." *The American Journal of Comparative Law* 18 (Fall 1971): 39–90.

Stepan, Alfred. *Rethinking Military Politics: Brazil and the Southern Cone.* Princeton, N.J.: Princeton University Press, 1988.

Storing, Herbert J. *The Complete Anti-Federalist*, vol 2. Chicago, Ill.: University of Chicago Press, 1981.

Tate, C. Neal, and Torbjorn Vallinder, eds. *The Global Expansion of Judicial Power*. New York: New York University Press, 1995.

Tunc, Andre. "The Quest for Justice." In *Access to Justice and the Welfare State*, ed. Mauro Cappalletti. Le Monnier: Firenze, 1981.

United Nations. *De la locura a la esperanza: la guerra de 12 años en El Salvador*. San Salvador: Naciones Unidas, 1992-93.

United States Department of State. *The Administration of Justice in El Salvador*. Washington, D.C.: Department of State/AID/DOJ, 1992.

——. "The State of Human Rights." In *The Continuing Crisis*, ed. Mark Falcoff and Robert Royal. Lanham, Md.: University Press of America/Ethics and Public Policy Forum, 1987: 267-88.

United States Government Accounting Office. *Colombia: Promising Approach to Judicial Reform*. Washington, D.C.: U.S. GAO, 1992.

——. *Efforts to Improve the Judicial System in El Salvador*. Washington, D.C.: U.S. GAO, 1990.

United States Information Agency. "Latin Americans Favor Democracy, but Democratic Institutions Rated Poorly," November 1994.

——. "Latin Americans See Need for Civic Education." Washington, D.C.: USIA, 1996.

——. "Mexicans Continue to Seek Solutions to Narcotrafficking Problem." Washington, D.C.: USIA, 1996.

——. "Second Thoughts on Democracy in Brazil." Washington, D.C.: USIA, 1994.

Valenzuela, Arturo. "Origins, Consolidation, and Breakdown of a Democratic Regime." In *Democracy in Developing Countries: Latin America*, ed. Larry Diamond, Juan Linz, and Seymour Martin Lipset. Boulder, Colo.: Lynne Reinner Publishers, 1989.

Valenzuela, Arturo, and Pamela Constable. *A Nation of Enemies*. New York: W. W. Norton and Co., 1991.

Valenzuela, Arturo, and Juan J. Linz. *Presidential Democracy*. Baltimore, Md.: Johns Hopkins University Press, 1994.

Valenzuela, Eugenio. "Proposiciones para una reforma al poder judicial." *Mensaje* 400 (July 1991): 241-43.

Vallinder, Torbjorn. "When the Courts Go Marching In." In *The Global Expansion of Judicial Power*, ed. C. Neal Tate and Torbjorn Vallinder. New York: New York University Press, 1995.

Vanderbilt, Arthur T. *The Challenge of Law Reform*. Princeton, N.J.: Princeton University Press, 1955.

Van Rijckegham, Caroline, and Beatrice Weder. *Corruption and the Rate of Temptation: Do Low Wages in the Civil Service Product Corruption?* Washington, D.C.: International Monetary Fund, 1997.

Vargas Viancos, Juan Enrique, and Jorge Correa Sutil. *Diagnóstico del sistema judicial chileno*. Santiago: Corporación de Promoción Universitaria, 1995.

Vaughn, Robert. "Proposals for Judicial Reform in Chile." *Fordham International Law Journal* 16 (1992-93): 564-97.

Velloso, Carlos Mario da Silva, "O Contrôle Externo do Poder Judiciário." *Revista Brasileira de Estudos Políticos* 80 (January 1995): 53-76.

——. "Seminario Ibero-americano." In *Justiça: Promessa e realidad*. Rio de Janeiro: Editora Nova Fronteira, 1996: 13-32.

Verbitsky, Horacio. *Robo para la corona*. Buenos Aires: Planeta Espejo de la Argentina, 1993.

Verucci, Floriza, et al. "O Judiciário e o Acesso a Justica." In *O Judiciário em Debate*. São Paulo: IDESP/Editora Sumare, 1994: 9-30.

Viera, José Ribas. "O Poder Judiciário e A República: A Democratização Adiada." *Revista de Ciência Política* 33 (February/April 1990): 83-109.

Viera-Gallo, Jose Antonio. "Law and Socialism in Chile." *Review of the International Commission of Jurists* 7 (December 1971): 44-47.

Voegelin, Eric. *The New Science of Politics*. Chicago, Ill.: University of Chicago Press, 1952.

Von Muhlenbrock, Gisela. "Discretion and corruption: the Chilean Judiciary." *Crime, Law, and Social Change* 25 (1997): 335-51.

Walker, Laurens, et al. "The Relations Between Procedural Justice and Distributive Justice." *Virginia Law Review* 65 (December 1979): 1401-20.

Warren, Charles. *The Supreme Court in United States History*. Boston: Little, Brown, and Co., 1937.

Washington Office on Latin America. *The Administration of Injustice: Military Accountability in Guatemala*. Washington, D.C.: WOLA, 1989.

Weber, Max. *The Theory of Economic and Social Organization*, trans. Talcott Parsons. London:William Hodge, 1947.

Weiner, Robert. *A Decade of Failed Promises: The Investigation of Archbishop Romero's Murder*. New York: The Lawyers Committee for Human Rights, 1990.

Wesson, Robert, and David Fleischer. *Brazil in Transition*. New York: Praeger Publishers, 1983.

Williams, Jaime. "Reformas de la administración de justicia." In *Conferencia Iberoamericana sobre reforma de la justicia penal*. San Salvador: Ministério de Justicia, 1991.

Wilson, Richard J. *Proyecto de capacitación, política, y gestión judicial*. Washington, D.C.: Checchi and Co./U.S. Agency for International Development, 1991.

Wise, Michael. "Nicaragua: Judicial Independence in a Time of Transition." *Williamette Law Review* 30 (Summer 1994): 519-79.

Wood, Gordon. *The Creation of the American Republic, 1776-1787*. New York: W. W. Norton and Co., 1969.

World Bank. *Bolivia: Judicial Reform Project*. Washington, D.C.: The World Bank, 1994.

———. *Crime and Violence as Development Issues in Latin America and the Caribbean*. Washington, D.C./Rio de Janeiro: The World Bank, 1997.

———. *Ecuador: Judicial Sector Assessment*. Washington, D.C.: The World Bank, 1994.

———. *Peru: Judicial Sector Assessment*. Washington, D.C.: The World Bank, 1994.

———. *Venezuela: Judicial Sector Assessment*. Washington, D.C.: The World Bank, 1994.

———. *World Development Report. 1997: The State in a Changing World*. Washington, D.C.: The World Bank, 1997.

Wyler, Marcus. "The Development of the Brazilian Constitution, 1891-1946." *The Journal of Comparative Legislation and International Law* 31 (November 1949): 53-60.

Wynia, Gary. "Campaigning for President in Argentina." *Current History* 88 (March 1989): 133-36.

———. "Democracy in Argentina." *Current History* 84 (February 1984): 53-56.

———. "Readjusting to Democracy in Argentina." *Current History* 86 (January 1987): 5-8.

Yañez, José H. "Servicios solicitados y prestados por la administración de justicia en Chile." In *Proyecto de capacitación, formación, perfeccionamiento, y política judicial*. Santiago: Corporación de Promoción Universitaria, 1991.

Zabel, William, Diane Orenlichter, and David Nachman. "Human Rights and the Adminis-
    tration of Justice in Chile: Report of a Delegation of the Association of the Bar of the
    City of New York and of the International Bar Association." *The Record of the Associa-
    tion of the Bar of the City of New York* 42 (May 1987): 431–84.
Zagorski, Paul. *Democracy vs. National Security*. Boulder, Colo.: Lynne Reinner Publishers,
    1992.

Index

About the Author

WILLIAM C. PRILLAMAN currently serves as a senior Latin American analyst with the U.S. government. Dr. Prillaman has served or traveled in more than a dozen countries in Latin America, where he conducted field research for this study.

ISBN 0-275-96849-9

HARDCOVER BAR CODE